KU-114-003

More Delectable Desserts

ROBERT CARRIER'S KITCHEN

More
Delectable
Desserts

Marshall Cavendish   London Sydney & New York

Editor	Roz Fishel
Editorial Staff	Caroline Macy
	Penny Smith
	Anne Wiltsher
Designer	Alan White
Series Editor	Pepita Aris
Production Executive	Robert Paulley
Production Controller	Steve Roberts

Photography
Tom Belshaw: 13
Paul Bussell: 11, 17, 30, 52, 59, 68, 105
Chris Crofton: 53
Laurie Evans: 2, 9, 28, 43, 44, 105
Robert Golden: 69
Edmund Goldspink: 102
Melvin Grey: 92
Peter Howard-Smith: 42
James Jackson: 19, 74, 76, 91
Chris Knaggs: 16, 24, 40, 45, 75, 86
Don Last: 41, 77
David Levin: 72
Peter Myers: 10, 25, 49, 50, 74, 81, 97
Paul Williams: 31, 93, 104
Cover picture: **Laurie Evans**

Weights and measures
Both metric and imperial measurements are given. As these are not exact equivalents, please work from one set of figures or the other. Use graded measuring spoons levelled across.

Time symbols
The time needed to prepare the dish is given on each recipe. The symbols are as follows:

 simple to prepare and cook

 straightforward but requires more skill or attention

 time-consuming to prepare or requires extra skill

 must be started 1 day or more ahead

On the cover: Chocolate meringue pie, page 99

This edition published 1986
© Marshall Cavendish Limited 1986

Printed in Italy by
L.E.G.O. S.p.a. Vicenza

Typeset by Quadraset Limited, Midsomer Norton, Bath, Avon

Published by Marshall Cavendish House
58 Old Compton Street London W1V 5PA
ISBN 0 86307 264 X (series)
ISBN 0 86307 413 8 (this volume)

All rights reserved. No part of this book may be reproduced or utilized in any form or by any means electronic or mechanical, including photocopying, recording, or by information storage and retrieval system, without permission from the copyright holders. Some of the material in this title has previously appeared in the publication **Robert Carrier's Kitchen.**

Contents

Everyone who has collected my first book about desserts in this series will be thrilled to see that I have now brought out another book on the same subject — *More Delectable Desserts*. This colourful book contains more recipes to satisfy every sweet-tooth and occasion.

The book begins with a section of light and luscious desserts ranging from a selection of classic recipes — Blancmange, Coeurs à la crème, Lemon soufflé — to a host of unusual recipes which use easily obtainable ingredients — Moulded lime cream, Tangy orange dessert, Plums Vouvray and Italian pears. The variety is enormous, but the results are always the same — delicious desserts and contented guests.

For occasions that warrant substantial desserts, *More Delectable Desserts* includes recipes for the ever-popular cheesecakes, gateaux, cakes, pies and tarts. My section on cheesecakes gives a comprehensive guide to the best types of cheese to use, hints on making bases, and tips on cooking and serving. When you browse through my pages of gateaux and cakes, you will be spoilt for choice — Savarins, Croquembouche and Profiteroles being found among the chocolate gateaux and Swiss rolls. Further on you'll find good, old family favourites — Old fashioned apple pie and Old English Bakewell tart.

For cool and sophisticated desserts, look at my sections on Mousses, Party ice creams and Sorbets & water-ices. My mousses — lovely, chilled, fluffy sweets — are easy to make, and are best prepared the day before the meal so that they have a chance to set completely, and to save you last minute preparation. My section on Party ice creams gives a guide to making bombes, with suggestions on the best equipment to use, and how to use it — together with information on and recipes for other delicious ice-cream dishes. Alternatively, serve one of my sorbets, an ideal ending for a substantial and filling meal.

Of course, even the most tasty and bright dishes benefit from the lift that decoration gives them, so I have included a chapter showing you how to complement a dish with the appropriate decoration — whipped cream, fruit, chocolate, nuts. It also includes a selection of biscuits to serve with light desserts. In this section, too, are recipes which use meringue as a base or a topping, for example, my French meringue cake. Finally, look through my selection of 'tipsy' desserts where you'll find, among others, recipes for trifles, flambéed fruit and wine jellies — dishes with a flavour of luxury that all your guests will enjoy.

Happy cooking and bon appétit!

Robert Carrier

Light & Luscious

MOULDED DESSERTS

Smooth and creamy, rich and decorative, these beautiful dishes are a favourite on every dinner table. They need a little patience to make, but on the plus side, they can always be prepared a day ahead.

In this chapter I concentrate on moulded desserts — cold desserts made with milk and cream, and rice or eggs or gelatine.

The simplest of my moulded desserts is the blancmange. To many people nowadays the word blancmange (from the French *blanc*, meaning white, and *manger*, meaning eat) evokes a milk pudding thickened with cornflour and set in a mould — it has been a favourite nursery pudding for generations. The original blancmange was quite different, a subtle, creamy concoction delicately flavoured with pounded almonds. My recipe is very close to the classic French version.

Another classic is the bavarois or Bavarian cream. Many of the recipes in this chapter are a variation on this, the desserts having a custard base, subtly flavoured and enriched with thick cream. To make these you first need to master the technique of making custard. This is easy to do if you use a double boiler, which enables you to cook the custard over the steady heat of simmering water with no danger of curdling.

Making a custard
First heat the milk to boiling point, then remove it from the heat and set it aside. Whisk together egg yolks and sugar to a thick mousse — the mixture should leave a thick, ribbon-like trail when the beaters are lifted. Add the hot milk to the mousse in a thin stream, whisking constantly as you do so, then pour the mixture into the top pan of a double boiler. Place the pan over simmering water and cook the custard, stirring it constantly with a wooden spoon, until it thickens. (The custard is ready when it thickly coats the back of the wooden spoon.) As you stir, be sure that the spoon covers the whole of the area of the pan and gets right into the curves of the base, so that none of the mixture can become lumpy and burn. When the custard is thickened, strain it through a sieve into a bowl and leave it to cool, beating it occasionally to prevent a skin forming.

Adding the gelatine
Meanwhile, prepare the gelatine: soften it in a little liquid and then stand it over a pan of hot water and allow it to dissolve. When it has dissolved, leave it to cool a little — the gelatine and custard are ready to mix together when they are both at the same temperature, preferably tepid. (Beware of recipes that appear to save you time and tell you to cook the gelatine in the custard — this method produces an unpleasant after-taste.)

Place the bowl of custard in a larger bowl of ice and stir until the gelatine just starts to set the custard.

Completing the method
Fold the flavourings into the custard and whip the cream very softly — until it is the same consistency as the thickened custard.

Lightly fold them together, using a large metal spoon, until there are no streaks of cream left in the mixture.

As for simple jellies, it helps to wet the mould before you pour in the mixture. Alternatively, if you are using sponge to line the mould, cling film put in first will help you to turn it out easily. To use cling film, oil the mould lightly, line it with cling film and then oil the film lightly.

Once you have poured the mixture into the mould, leave it in the refrigerator to set. It will usually take at least 12 hours before the dessert is firm enough to turn out. To turn out the moulded dessert, dip the mould very briefly in hot water. Invert a wetted plate over the mould, then invert the plate and the mould together and shake the dessert firmly once or twice. The mould should now come away easily.

Decorate the dessert with whipped cream, fruits, nuts, biscuit crumbs or sauce as appropriate, and leave it to stand at room temperature for about 30 minutes before serving it. This restores its full flavour and soft texture. However, do not leave these delicate mixtures for too long at room temperature as they start to collapse, ruining the effect.

Blancmange

🕐 🍴 30 minutes, plus cooling, then at least 12 hours setting

Serves 4
275 g /10 oz blanched almonds
600 ml /1 pt milk
10 ml /2 tsp powdered gelatine
50 g /2 oz sugar
30 ml /2 tbls kirsch
4 sugared almonds, to decorate

1 Place the blanched almonds and the milk in an electric blender, set it to a slow speed and blend for 2 minutes. (You may find it necessary to blend in 2 batches.) Alternatively, pound the almonds to a paste in a mortar, adding the milk gradually.
2 Strain the almond mixture through a muslin-lined sieve into a saucepan. Squeeze the muslin with your hands to extract as much of the almond milk as possible. Over a low heat, bring the milk just to the boil, stirring it constantly. Strain it through a fine sieve and leave it to cool.
3 In a small bowl, sprinkle the gelatine over 30 ml /2 tbls cold water and leave it until the liquid is absorbed. Place the bowl in a saucepan of hot water until the gelatine has dissolved and the liquid is clear; leave it to cool a little.
4 When the 2 are roughly at the same temperature, add the dissolved gelatine to the almond milk and stir in the sugar and the kirsch. Set the mixture over a bowl of ice,

stirring regularly, until the blancmange is on the point of setting.
5 Rinse a 425 ml /15 fl oz decorative mould with cold water. Pour in the almond mixture and chill it until it is firmly set — this will take at least 12 hours.
6 About 30 minutes before serving, turn out the blancmange onto a serving dish and decorate it with the sugared almonds.

Blackcurrant bavarois

🕐 🍴 1½ hours, plus cooling, then at least 12 hours setting

Serves 4
225 g /8 oz blackcurrants, topped and tailed
75 g /3 oz caster sugar
125 ml /4 fl oz milk
1 egg yolk
5 ml /1 tsp powdered gelatine
5–10 ml /1–2 tsp lemon juice
125 ml /4 fl oz thick cream
mint sprigs, to decorate

1 In a saucepan, combine the prepared blackcurrants with 50 ml /2 fl oz water and 15–30 ml /1–2 tbls of the sugar. Simmer gently for 10 minutes, or until the blackcurrants are cooked but still whole. Remove them from the heat.
2 In the top pan of a double boiler, combine the milk and 25 g /1 oz of the sugar and bring it to the boil over direct heat. Remove it from the heat and set aside.
3 In a bowl, whisk the egg yolk with the remaining sugar until the mixture leaves a trail on the surface when the beaters are lifted. Gradually pour in the hot milk in a thin stream, whisking constantly, and return the mixture to the double boiler. Cook it over simmering water, stirring constantly, until the mixture is thick enough to coat the back of the spoon. Strain it into a bowl.
4 Strain the blackcurrants and reserve the juice. Purée half the blackcurrants in an electric blender and sieve the purée to remove the skins and seeds. Measure the purée and make it up to 50 ml /2 fl oz with the reserved juice. Reserve the remaining blackcurrants. Add the purée to the custard and stir them to blend well. Allow the custard to cool, beating it occasionally to prevent a skin forming.
5 In a small bowl, sprinkle the gelatine over 15 ml /1 tbls cold water and leave it to absorb the liquid. Put the bowl in a saucepan of hot water until the gelatine has dissolved. Remove it from the heat and leave it to cool slightly, then stir the gelatine mixture into the custard. Add lemon juice to taste.
6 Lightly whip the thick cream. Set the bowl of custard in a larger bowl of ice and stir it until it is on the point of setting, then fold in the whipped cream.
7 Rinse four 75 ml /3 fl oz ring moulds with cold water and then fill them with the blackcurrant cream. Leave them in the refrigerator to set.
8 About 30 minutes before serving, turn out the blackcurrant rings onto individual serving plates and place a quarter of the

remaining blackcurrants and a small sprig of mint in the centre of each ring.

Orange ring

🕐 ⚬||| 1¾ hours, then at least 12 hours setting

Serves 8–10
275 g /10 oz sugar
3–4 large oranges, peeled
1 × Fatless sponge (see page 30) baked in a
* 16 cm /6½ in square cake tin*
For the bavarois
3 egg yolks
175 g /6 oz caster sugar
175 ml /6 fl oz orange juice (approximately
* 3 oranges)*
juice of 1 lemon
150 g /5 oz butter, diced
10 ml /2 tsp gelatine
400 ml /14 fl oz thick cream
For the decoration
150 ml /5 fl oz thick cream, whipped
3 orange segments, to garnish

1 Combine the sugar with 300 ml /10 fl oz water in a heavy-based saucepan. Stir it over a low heat until the sugar has completely dissolved, then bring the liquid to the boil and boil it for 5 minutes.

2 Cut the oranges into thin slices and remove any pips. Add the orange slices to the pan and poach them slowly in the sugar syrup for 30 minutes, or until they are tender but still firm. Remove them from the syrup using a slotted spoon and leave them to drain on a wire rack.

3 When the orange slices have drained, carefully line a 1.4 L /2½ pt ring mould with the slices, overlapping them attractively, then set the mould aside in the refrigerator until it is needed.

4 Make a bavarois: combine the egg yolks with the sugar, the orange juice and the lemon juice in the top pan of a double boiler. Place it over simmering water and whisk until the mixture leaves a trail on the surface when the beaters are lifted. Remove the pan from the heat and whisk in the diced butter, a little at a time.

5 In a small bowl, sprinkle the gelatine over 30 ml /2 tbls cold water and leave it to absorb the liquid. Place the bowl in the saucepan of hot water until the gelatine has completely dissolved. Remove the bowl from the hot water and then allow the dissolved gelatine to cool a little.

6 Add the dissolved gelatine to the egg yolk mixture. Place the bowl in another bowl containing ice and stir the mixture until it is on the point of setting.

7 In a bowl, whip the thick cream until soft peaks form and then fold it into the bavarois mixture. Pour the mixture into the prepared ring mould.

8 Slice the sponge in 3 horizontally. Cut pieces of sponge to fit the mould and place the pieces on top of the bavarois mixture. Place the mould in the refrigerator to set for at least 12 hours.

9 About 30 minutes before serving, unmould the bavarois onto a flat serving plate and fill the centre with whipped thick cream and arrange the 3 orange segments attractively on top of the cream.

Orange ring

9

Cherry and almond blancmange

⏲ 1 hour,
plus setting

Serves 6
500 g /1 lb almonds, blanched
20 g /¾ oz gelatine
100 g /4 oz caster sugar
60 ml /4 tbls cherry brandy
250 g /8 oz fresh red cherries, stoned

1 Pound the almonds, a few at a time, to a smooth paste, using a pestle and mortar. Put the paste into a bowl and mix in 600 ml / 1 pt tepid water. Leave it for 20 minutes.
2 Put a sieve lined with muslin over a bowl and pour in the almond mixture. Squeeze the muslin until you have extracted 600 ml /1 pt almond milk.
3 Put the gelatine in 60 ml /4 tbls of the almond milk and allow it to soften for a few minutes. Now stand the bowl over a pan of gently simmering water and allow the gelatine to dissolve completely.
4 Pour the rest of the milk into a saucepan and stir in the sugar. Set the pan over a low heat and stir until the sugar has dissolved.
5 Stir the dissolved gelatine into the almond milk and mix until it is thoroughly blended. Cool the almond milk a little, then stir in the cherry brandy.
6 Lightly oil a 600 ml /1 pt jelly mould and pour in the contents of the saucepan. Let the blancmange become cold and then put it into the refrigerator for 2 hours, or until it is set firm enough to hold its own shape.
7 Carefully turn out the cherry and almond blancmange onto a serving plate, and serve it with the fresh, stoned cherries.

Creamy rice and fruit pudding

⏲ 45 minutes,
plus at least 1 hour chilling

Serves 4–6
250 g /9 oz short-grain rice
1.4 L /2½ pt milk
90 g /3½ oz sugar
5 ml /1 tsp vanilla sugar (see note below)
300–400 g /11–14 oz soft or canned fruit
  (see note below)
10 ml /2 tsp maraschino
250 ml /9 fl oz thick cream
To decorate
strawberries or other fruit (see note below)
a few non-toxic leaves
150 ml /5 fl oz thick cream, whipped

1 Wash and drain the rice and set it aside. Pour the milk into a large saucepan, add the sugars and bring to the boil. Add the rice, lower the heat and simmer until it is soft, 20–30 minutes. Leave it to get cold.
2 Meanwhile, prepare the fruit, stoning the cherries or cutting any large fruit, such as peaches and apricots, into raspberry-size pieces. Put the fruit in a bowl, add the maraschino, and stir well.
3 When the rice is cold, whisk the cream until it is stiff. Fold the whipped cream into the rice. Drain the fruit, then fold the drained fruit into the rice mixture.
4 Rinse a 1.7 L /3 pt jelly mould with cold water and spoon in the rice mixture. Chill well, for at least 1 hour, before serving. Turn out the pudding onto a serving dish and decorate with strawberries and a few leaves, or other fruit, and piped whipped cream.

● To make vanilla sugar, bury a vanilla pod in a jar of caster sugar for at least two weeks — it will impregnate the sugar with a mild vanilla flavour.
● Fresh soft fruit such as strawberries, raspberries and/or cherries are suitable for this dish, but canned fruit, especially peaches and apricots, may be used provided they have been well drained. Use non-toxic green leaves to decorate the pudding.

Raspberry charlotte

⏲ 1¼ hours,
plus at least 6 hours chilling

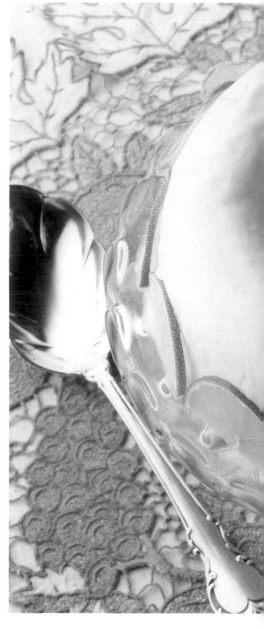

Serves 6–8
750 g /1 lb 10 oz raspberries, defrosted if frozen
250 g /9 oz icing sugar, plus extra for
  garnishing
15 ml /1 tbls gelatine
600 ml /1 pt thick cream
butter, for greasing
36 sponge fingers (3 packets of boudoir biscuits)
extra raspberries, to garnish

1 Put 250 g /9 oz raspberries with 30 ml / 2 tbls sugar and 45 ml /3 tbls water in a small saucepan and cook them over a low heat for 5 minutes. Press the mixture through a sieve, sprinkle the gelatine on top of the warm purée, whisk it, then allow it to stand.
2 Whip the cream until it is thick but not dry. Reserve 30 ml /2 tbls in a piping bag fitted with a rosette nozzle, for decorating. Gradually incorporate first the remaining sugar and then the cooled gelatine mixture into the cream. Fold in the rest of the raspberries.
3 Butter a 1 L /1¾ pt charlotte mould and line the bottom and sides with the sponge

Creamy rice and fruit pudding

mould with melted butter and then sprinkle it with caster sugar. Tip out any excess sugar. Spoon in the lime/lemon mixture and chill it in the refrigerator for 12 hours.

7 When ready to serve, unmould the jelly onto a flat serving dish. To do this, wrap a hot towel around the bottom of the mould. Invert a rinsed serving dish over the mould and then turn out the pudding onto the dish. Garnish with the lime slices and serve.

Caramel bavarois

45 minutes,
plus cooling and setting

Serves 4
oil, for greasing
275 g /10 oz caster sugar
275 ml /10 fl oz milk
3 medium-sized egg yolks
15 ml /1 tbls gelatine
150 ml /5 fl oz thick cream

1 Lightly oil a 600 ml /1 pt mould. Put 100 g /4 oz of water in a medium-sized saucepan. Place it over a low heat and dissolve the sugar. Now turn up the heat and boil it steadily to form a dark brown caramel.

2 Pour 50 ml /2 fl oz water into the saucepan and stir with a wooden spoon until well mixed. Add the milk and bring it to boiling point, then remove the pan from the heat.

3 In a heatproof bowl, beat the egg yolks with 40 g /1½ oz of the sugar until the mixture becomes light-coloured, then pour the caramel milk onto this mixture. Stir and return to the saucepan. Place the pan over a low heat and stir, without boiling, until the custard is thick. Strain the custard into a bowl and allow it to cool.

4 Put the gelatine in a cup and add 75 ml / 5 tbls water. Allow it to soak for a few minutes, then stand the cup in a pan of gently simmering water and dissolve the gelatine over a low heat. Whip the cream until it is thick and then set it aside.

5 Gradually add the dissolved gelatine, in a stream, to the custard. Place the bowl in a larger bowl filled with ice and stir until the custard has thickened, then quickly fold in 30 ml /2 tbls of the whipped cream. Pour the mixture into the prepared mould and leave it to set for about 1½ hours.

6 To make the caramel chips, put the rest of the caster sugar with 45 ml /3 tbls water in a small, heavy-based saucepan over a low heat. Dissolve the sugar, stirring, then boil it until the sugar turns to a golden-brown caramel — 170C /325F on a sugar thermometer.

7 Line a baking tray with foil and grease it well. Pour the caramel onto the baking tray and allow it to become completely cold. Remove the foil from the tray and break the caramel in half. Remove one half, and fold the foil over the remaining caramel. Beat the foil-covered caramel with a rolling pin to break it into chips. Repeat the procedure with the other piece of caramel.

8 Turn the mould onto a serving dish and decorate it with the remaining cream and the caramel chips.

fingers, sugar side out. Spoon the fruit and cream mixture into the centre of the lined charlotte mould.

4 Cover the top with the remaining sponge fingers, cut in half lengthways, and chill for at least 6 hours. Unmould the charlotte and decorate the centre with a rosette of cream and extra raspberries. Dust it with a little icing sugar before serving.

Moulded lime cream

50 minutes,
plus 12 hours chilling

Serves 8–10
200 g /7 oz sugar, plus extra for dusting
2 medium-sized eggs
150 g /5 oz butter, melted, plus extra for greasing
125 ml /4 fl oz lime juice
125 ml /4 fl oz lemon juice
10 ml /2 tsp powdered gelatine
lime slices, to garnish
For the crème chantilly
275 ml /10 fl oz thick cream
25 g /1 oz caster sugar

1 Start the day ahead to make this creamy moulded pudding. Whisk the sugar and the eggs in the top of a double boiler, over warm water, until the mixture is a pale lemon colour, and leaves a thin trail when the beaters are lifted.

2 Remove the top of the saucepan from the heat and whisk in the melted butter. Now whisk in the lime and lemon juices.

3 Replace the top of the double boiler and cook the mixture over simmering water, stirring continuously until the mixture is thick enough to coat the back of the spoon. Meanwhile, place the gelatine in a cup with 30 ml /2 tbls water and leave it to soften for 5 minutes. Stand the cup in a pan of gently simmering water and stir until the gelatine is completely dissolved, then stir it into the lemon/lime curd. Refrigerate until the jelly is on the point of setting.

4 Meanwhile, make the crème chantilly. Whisk the thick cream until soft peaks form. Add the caster sugar and beat until the mixture is stiff. Add 30 ml /2 tbls iced water and beat until smooth.

5 When the lemon/lime curd is almost set, fold it into the crème chantilly.

6 Brush a 1.4 L /2½ pt non-metal ring

Rice à la royale

🕐🍴 1 hour 20 minutes, plus cooling, then at least 12 hours setting

Serves 8
175 g /6 oz short-grain rice
90 ml /6 tbls sugar
1.3 L /2¼ pt milk
45 ml /3 tbls cornflour
6 egg yolks
105 ml /7 tbls caster sugar
22.5 ml /1½ tbls gelatine
5–7.5 ml /1–1½ tsp vanilla essence
90 ml /6 tbls thick cream
45–60 ml /3–4 tbls kirsch
For the decoration
2 small dessert pears, poached (see note)
30 ml /2 tbls raspberry jam
10 ml /2 tsp kirsch

1 Put the rice in a heavy-based, medium-sized saucepan. Cover with cold water to come 5 cm /2 in above the top of the rice. Bring it to the boil and then simmer it for 5 minutes, stirring occasionally.
2 Drain the rice thoroughly in a colander. Return it to the pan and add the sugar and half the milk. Bring it to simmering point, stirring frequently, and simmer, uncovered, until the rice is soft and most of the milk is absorbed — this should take about 20 minutes. Remove the pan from the heat, cover it and allow the rice mixture to cool.
3 Blend the cornflour to a thin, smooth paste with a little of the remaining milk. Next, combine the cornflour mixture with all the remaining milk in the top pan of a double boiler. Bring the liquid to the boil over a direct heat and simmer gently for 5 minutes, stirring constantly. Remove it from the heat.
4 Combine the egg yolks and the sugar in a bowl, and whisk until light and fluffy. Add the cornflour and milk mixture in a thin stream, whisking constantly. Return the mixture to the top pan of a double boiler.
5 Cook over gently simmering water, stirring frequently, for about 20 minutes or until the custard is thick enough to coat the back of a spoon. Remove the custard from the heat, strain it through a fine sieve into a bowl and allow it to cool, beating occasionally to prevent a skin forming on the top.
6 In a small bowl, sprinkle the gelatine over 60 ml /4 tbls cold water and leave it until the liquid is absorbed. Place the bowl in a pan of hot water until the gelatine dissolves. Allow the mixture to cool.
7 Beat the gelatine into the cooled custard and flavour it to taste with vanilla essence.
8 Stir the custard over a bowl or ice until it is on the point of setting. Combine the custard with the cooked rice mixture and blend in the cream and kirsch to taste. Pour the mixture into a deep, round 1.7 L /3 pt mould and chill it in the refrigerator until firmly set.
9 About 30 minutes before serving, carefully unmould the rice onto a large serving dish. Slice the poached pears thinly, drain them on absorbent paper and place them, overlapping, in a circle on top of the dessert.
10 Put the jam and the kirsch in a small saucepan and melt them over a low heat. Stir

and then strain the mixture through a fine sieve, brush it over pears and then serve.

● Make a syrup with 60 g /2 oz sugar, 275 ml /½ pt water and a piece of vanilla pod; bring to the boil; remove from the heat. Peel, halve, core, then brush the pears with lemon juice; poach them in the syrup until tender, about 5 minutes. Remove from the heat and cool the pears in the syrup.

Macaroon bavarois with peaches

🕐🍴 1 hour, plus cooling, then at least 12 hours setting

Serves 6–8
225 ml /8 fl oz milk
125 g /4 oz caster sugar
3 egg yolks
15 g /½ oz powdered gelatine
5 ml /1 tsp vanilla essence
425 ml /15 fl oz thick cream
85 g /3½ oz almond macaroons, crumbled
400 g /14 oz canned peaches, drained and roughly chopped
45 ml /3 tbls kirsch
500 g /1 lb jar of brandied peaches, sliced, to decorate (see note below)

1 In the top part of a double boiler, over direct heat, bring the milk and 25 g /1 oz sugar to the boil.
2 In a bowl, whisk the egg yolks with the remaining sugar until the mixture leaves a ribbon trail when the beaters are lifted. Gradually pour in the hot milk, in a thin stream, whisking constantly, and return the custard to the double boiler. Cook it over simmering water, stirring constantly, until it is thick enough to coat the back of a spoon. Strain it through a fine sieve into a bowl and leave it to cool, beating occasionally.
3 Meanwhile, in a small bowl, sprinkle the gelatine over 45 ml /3 tbls cold water and leave until the liquid is absorbed. Place the bowl in a saucepan of hot water until the gelatine has dissolved. Leave to cool a little.
4 Stir the dissolved gelatine and the vanilla essence into the cooled custard. Set it over a bowl of ice and stir until it is on the point of setting. Whip the cream to soft peaks.
5 Fold the whipped cream into the custard. Next, fold in the macaroons, peaches and the kirsch. Rinse a 1.1 L /2 pt mould with cold water and pour in the custard. Leave overnight in the refrigerator to set.
6 About 30 minutes before serving, unmould the bavarois onto a serving dish and decorate it with sliced brandied peaches.

● To prepare brandied peaches at home, blanch, skin and halve 1 kg /2 lb peaches. Make a sugar syrup by dissolving 225 g /8 oz sugar in 600 ml /1 pt water and boil it for 2 minutes. Poach the peaches in the syrup for 5 minutes, then allow them to cool. Spoon the peaches into a large, sterilized, warmed jar. Add 150 ml /5 fl oz brandy to the syrup and pour it over the peaches. Cover them and keep them in the refrigerator for 2 weeks to mature before using.

Chocolate and cognac charlotte

🕐🍴 making the sponge, 1½ hours, then at least 12 hours setting

Serves 8
1 × Fatless sponge (page 30) cooked in a 16 cm / 6½ in square cake tin
oil, for greasing
350 ml /12 fl oz milk
175 g /6 oz sugar
3 egg yolks
15 g /½ oz powdered gelatine
75 g /3 oz unsweetened chocolate
75 ml /3 fl oz cognac
425 ml /15 fl oz thick cream
150 ml /5 fl oz thick cream, whipped, to decorate

1 Slice the fatless sponge-cake into 3 pieces horizontally. Brush a 1.4 L /2½ pt charlotte mould with the oil, line the mould with cling film and brush it again with more oil. Cut a circle of sponge and cover the base of the mould. Line the mould with the remaining sponge cut into strips.
2 In a large saucepan, heat the milk and 75 g /3 oz of the sugar, stirring until the sugar is dissolved. Bring to just below boiling point and set aside.
3 In a large mixing bowl, whisk the egg yolks with the remaining sugar until the mixture is light and fluffy and leaves a trail on the surface when the beaters are lifted. Gradually pour in the scalded milk in a thin stream, whisking constantly, and then transfer the mixture to the top pan of a double boiler.
4 Cook it over gently simmering water, stirring constantly, until the custard is thick enough to coat the back of a spoon. Strain the custard through a fine sieve into a bowl and leave it to cool, beating it occasionally to prevent a skin forming.
5 In a small bowl, sprinkle the gelatine over 45 ml /3 tbls cold water and leave it to absorb the liquid. Put the bowl in a pan of hot water and leave it until the gelatine is dissolved. Allow the mixture to cool a little, and then stir the dissolved gelatine into the custard, until it is thoroughly blended.
6 In the top pan of a double boiler over hot water, melt the chocolate in the cognac. Beat it until the mixture is smooth and then leave it to cool but not harden. Now fold it into the custard mixture. Place the bowl in a larger bowl containing ice, and stir until the custard is on the point of setting.
7 Whip the thick cream until soft peaks form, and then fold it into the custard. Pour the mixture into the prepared charlotte mould and chill it in the refrigerator for at least 12 hours, or overnight.
8 About 30 minutes before serving, unmould the charlotte: trim the sponge level with the filling, then dip the mould in hot water for 2–3 minutes. Carefully turn it out onto a serving dish. Remove the cling film and then pipe whipped cream around the base in a decorative pattern.

Chocolate and cognac charlotte

Hazelnut bavarois

Serves 4
100 g /4 oz caster sugar
4 egg yolks
275 ml /10 fl oz milk
15 ml /1 tbls lemon juice
5 ml /1 tsp vanilla essence
30 ml /2 tbls powdered gelatine
275 ml /10 fl oz thick cream
175 g /6 oz hazelnuts, ground
For the decoration
15 g /½ oz plain chocolate
8 whole hazelnuts
150 ml /5 fl oz thick cream

1 In a large bowl, whisk the sugar and egg yolks until the mixture becomes pale and light. Bring the milk to just below boiling point, then pour it, in a thin stream, onto the egg yolk mixture, whisking constantly.
2 Pour the mixture into the top half of a double boiler and then cook it over gently simmering water until the custard is thick enough to coat the back of a wooden spoon — do not allow the custard to boil, or the eggs will curdle. Place the pan over a bowl of cracked ice. Stir in the lemon juice and the vanilla essence. Leave the mixture to cool slightly, stirring occasionally.
3 Meanwhile, in a small bowl, sprinkle the gelatine over 75 ml / 5 tbls cold water and leave it to soften. Place the bowl in a saucepan of simmering water and leave it until the gelatine has completely dissolved. Leave the mixture to cool slightly, then pour the dissolved gelatine into the custard in a thin stream, stirring constantly until the custard is on the point of setting.
4 In another bowl, whip the cream to soft peaks. Quickly fold the whipped cream into the custard, then add the ground hazelnuts. Pour it into a 1.1 L /2 pt soufflé dish and leave it in the refrigerator to set.
5 For the decoration, break the chocolate into a bowl and melt it over simmering water. Dip each reserved hazelnut into the melted chocolate and then leave them to dry on waxed paper. Whip the cream to soft peaks.
6 Just before serving, dip the dish in hot water for a few seconds, then invert it onto a dampened serving plate and remove the dish. Using a piping bag fitted with a star-shaped nozzle, pipe 8 rosettes of whipped cream around the top edge. Place a chocolate hazelnut on the centre of each and serve as soon as possible.

 1½ hours, plus setting

Charlotte russe

Serves 6
7.5 ml /1½ tsp gelatine
16 or more sponge fingers, split in half lengthways
4 medium-sized egg yolks, well beaten
100 g /4 oz sugar
250 ml /9 fl oz milk
5 cm /2 in piece of vanilla pod, split to allow the seeds to escape during cooking
300 ml /11 fl oz soured cream
300 ml /11 fl oz thick cream
thick cream, whipped, to decorate
For the purée
225 g /8 oz fresh or frozen raspberries, puréed
caster sugar
cherry liqueur

1 Soak the gelatine in 15 ml /1 tbls cold water for 10 minutes to soften it. Cut a piece of greaseproof paper to fit the bottom of a 1 L / 1¾ pt charlotte mould. Lay the paper on the table, then trim some of the halved sponge fingers so that they cover the circle completely, coming out from the centre like the spokes of a wheel.
2 Place the greaseproof paper in the bottom of the mould and arrange the trimmed sponge fingers, uncut side down, on the paper. Line the sides of the mould with a layer of split sponge fingers, uncut side outwards.
3 Beat the egg yolks and sugar until they are pale yellow and frothy. Pour the milk into a saucepan, add the split vanilla pod and place over a medium heat until bubbles begin to appear around the edges.
4 Remove the vanilla pod and pour the milk over the egg yolk and sugar mixture, beating it over a low heat until it is thick enough to coat the back of a spoon. Do not boil the mixture or it will curdle.
5 Remove the pan from the heat and stir in the softened gelatine. When it has dissolved, sieve the custard into a bowl.
6 Whip the soured cream with the double cream until stiff. Set the bowl of custard in a bowl of cracked ice and stir it for 5 minutes, or until it is completely cold and just beginning to thicken.
7 Gently fold the whipped cream into the custard. Pour the mixture into the lined charlotte mould, smooth the top and cover it with plastic film. Refrigerate for at least 6 hours or until it is firm.
8 Unmould the charlotte onto a serving plate, decorate the top of it with whipped cream and serve with raspberry purée, sweetened with caster sugar, and cherry liqueur.

 1½ hours, plus 6 hours chilling

Tangy orange dessert

Serves 4
butter, for greasing
3 eggs, separated
175 g /6 oz caster sugar
grated zest of 1 orange
125 ml /4 fl oz fresh orange juice
30 ml /2 tbls lemon juice
250 ml /8 fl oz thick cream, whipped
120 ml /8 tbls crumbs from chocolate-coated digestive biscuits

1 Cut a circle of greaseproof paper to fit the base of a 1.7 L /3 pt
charlotte mould. Butter the paper and line the base of the mould with
it. Turn the freezer compartment of the refrigerator to low, (the
highest setting).
2 In a bowl, whisk the egg yolks until they are smooth. Gradually
whisk in the caster sugar and continue to whisk until the mixture is
light and fluffy.
3 Stir the grated orange zest and the fresh orange and lemon juice
into the egg and sugar mixture. Fold in the whipped thick cream.
4 In a clean bowl, whisk the egg whites until they are stiff. With a
large metal spoon, fold them into the orange mixture until they are
blended. Pour the mixture into the prepared charlotte mould and
freeze until it has set to a depth of 25 mm /1 in around the edge.
Beat the dessert with a fork until it is smooth, then freeze it for a
further 2 hours or until the top of the orange mixture is hard.
5 Reserve 30 ml /2 tbls of the biscuit crumbs and sprinkle the rest
over the top of the orange mixture, pressing them lightly into the
surface. Freeze for a further 4 hours, or until it is completely set.
6 When you are ready to serve, dip the charlotte mould into hot
water for a few seconds. Run a knife around the edge and quickly
turn the dessert onto a serving plate, so that the biscuit crumb base
does not have a chance to fall out of place. Remove the greaseproof
paper. If the surface of the dessert has melted too much, return the
dessert to the freezer for a couple of minutes to harden it again.
7 Carefully sprinkle the reserved chocolate biscuit crumbs around
the top edge of the dessert in a fine line. Serve immediately.

● An easy way to make the biscuit crumbs is to put the chocolate-
coated digestive biscuits in a strong polythene bag, chill them in the
refrigerator, and then crush them with a rolling pin.

 30 minutes,
plus freezing

Frangipane rice pudding with apricot sauce

Serves 4–6
425 ml /15 fl oz milk
45 ml /3 tbls sugar
5 cm /2 in piece of vanilla pod
75 g /3 oz long-grain rice
15 g /½ oz butter
3 egg yolks
butter, for greasing
For the frangipane cream
30 ml /2 tbls flour

50 g /2 oz ground almonds
30 ml /2 tbls sugar
2 eggs
a few drops of almond essence
300 ml /10 fl oz milk
For the apricot sauce
425 g /15 oz canned apricots,
  drained, with a little juice
  reserved

1 Heat the oven to 190C /375F /gas 5.
2 In a saucepan, combine the milk, the sugar and the vanilla pod.
Bring to just below boiling point and then dribble in the rice. Stir in
the butter, then cover and simmer gently, stirring occasionally, for 30
minutes or until the rice is tender and most of the milk has been
absorbed.
3 Meanwhile, make the frangipane cream. In a bowl, combine the
flour, the ground almonds, the sugar, the eggs and the almond
essence. Stir with a wooden spoon until the mixture is well blended.
In the top pan of a double boiler, bring the milk to scalding point,
over direct heat. Pour the scalded milk onto the frangipane mixture,
stirring well to blend.
4 Return the mixture to the pan. Stir over simmering water for
about 2 minutes, or until the mixture is thick enough to coat the back
of a wooden spoon.
5 Stir the egg yolks into the rice mixture, blend well, then stir in the
frangipane cream.
6 Cut a circle of greaseproof paper to fit the bottom of a 850 ml /
1½ pt pudding basin. Butter the dish and the circle of greaseproof
paper, and spoon the rice mixture into the dish. Place it in a roasting
tin, pour in hot water to come halfway up the sides of the dish, and
then cook the pudding in the oven for 20 minutes, or until set.
7 Meanwhile, purée the apricots in a blender with a little of the
reserved juice. Pour the purée into a saucepan and heat it through.
8 Leave the cooked rice pudding to cool for a few minutes, then run
a knife around the edge of the dish and turn out the frangipane
pudding onto a heated serving platter. Swirl a little apricot sauce over
the top of the pudding, and serve the remaining sauce separately.

 1 hour

CREAMY DESSERTS

These rich confections, served either in tall, elegant champagne glasses or pretty glass bowls, make a luxurious end to a meal. Here are some classic recipes. Try them and spoil yourself!

The versatility of cream is well illustrated in this chapter: set it with gelatine, enrich it with egg yolks or mix it with fluffy egg whites to make these delicious desserts. It can be flavoured with fruit of all kinds, such as apples, blackberries, plums, pears, strawberries and gooseberries, as well as with liqueurs or wine, nuts or chocolate.

Poires Véfour, pears served on a bed of crème pâtissière and garnished with macaroons, is a traditional French dessert. It originates from the Grand Véfour in Paris, one of France's most famous restaurants and it is simple to make, provided you take it step by step. Coeurs à la crème is another delectable French summer sweet, this time made with white cheese moulded in charming heart-shaped dishes of porcelain or metal and served with colourful, fresh strawberries. Cold sabayon cream, flavoured with brandy and Marsala, or light and airy Ginger custard petits pots are other treats to try. All provide a light, and luscious gastronomic finale to a special meal.

Mixed fruit fool

🍴 40 minutes,
plus chilling

Serves 4
450 g /1 lb cooking apples
225 g /8 oz blackberries
25–50 g /1–2 oz caster sugar
5–10 ml /1–2 tsp lemon juice
150 ml /5 fl oz thick cream, whipped
For the crème pâtissière
150 ml /5 fl oz milk
2 egg yolks
30 ml /2 tbls caster sugar
15 ml /1 tbls flour
15 ml /1 tbls cornflour
For the garnish
20 ml /4 tsp crème de cassis (blackcurrant liqueur) or crème de myrtilles (blueberry liqueur)
75–150 ml /3–5 fl oz whipped cream
4 blackberries

1   Peel, core and slice the apples. Wash the blackberries and cook the fruit with the sugar in 30 ml /2 tbls water, covered, for 10 minutes or until the fruit is thoroughly softened.
2   Remove the pan from the heat and sieve the fruit.
3   To prepare the crème pâtissière, pour the milk into a medium-sized pan and bring it to boiling point. In a bowl, whisk the egg yolks with the sugar until they are thick and light. Gradually whisk in the flours. Carefully pour the milk onto the egg yolk mixture, beating with the whisk until it is well blended. Pour the mixture back into the pan. Bring it to the boil over a medium heat, stirring constantly, then simmer for 3 minutes, beating vigorously with a wooden spoon to disperse any lumps. Remove the pan from the heat and then add it immediately to the apple and blackberry purée.
4   Add the lemon juice to taste, and fold in the whipped cream. Spoon the fool into individual serving glasses and chill them until ready to serve.
5   Just before serving, spoon 5 ml /1 tsp of the blackcurrant liqueur or blueberry liqueur over each fool. Pipe a large rosette of whipped cream onto each dessert and then top it with a blackberry.

Grape crème brûlée

This deliciously rich dessert combines the velvety texture of a thick cream custard with a crunchy caramel topping.

🕐🍴 30 minutes, plus chilling,
10 minutes grilling, plus chilling

Serves 4
600 ml /1 pt thick cream
1 vanilla pod
4 egg yolks
75 ml /5 tbls caster sugar
12 grapes

1   Heat the oven to 170C /325F /gas 3. Put the cream and vanilla pod in the top pan of a double boiler or in a bowl over a pan of boiling water (it should not touch the water) and bring it almost to boiling point.
2   Meanwhile, whisk the egg yolks and 15 ml /1 tbls of the sugar in a separate bowl, until they are light and creamy.
3   Remove the vanilla pod from the cream and pour the hot cream onto the egg yolk mixture, stirring continuously. Return the mixture to the pan or bowl over the boiling water and stir with a wooden spoon until the custard thickens enough to coat the back of the spoon.
4   Strain the custard into a shallow, ovenproof dish and put it in the oven for 5 minutes, until a skin has formed on top. Leave it until cold, then chill it overnight in the refrigerator.
5   Heat the grill to very hot. Pour boiling water over the grapes, then skin them, halve them and remove the seeds. Arrange the grape halves on the surface of the cream custard and sprinkle the remaining 60 ml /

Mixed fruit fool

Plums Vouvray

4 tbls caster sugar over the top of them.
6 Place the dish under the hot grill and allow the sugar to melt and caramelize. Remember, however, to watch it constantly, turning the dish if necessary to ensure that the surface browns evenly. Leave it to cool, then chill it in the refrigerator for about 2 hours before serving.

● You can tap the caramel surface with the back of a knife to crack it before serving.

Plums Vouvray

marinating, then 30 minutes, plus cooling

Serves 4–6

900 g /2 lb plums
105 ml /7 tbls sugar
275 ml /10 fl oz Vouvray or dry white wine
100 g /4 oz cream cheese
275 ml /10 fl oz thick cream
90 ml /6 tbls icing sugar, sifted
2 egg whites

1 Wipe the plums with a damp cloth. In a bowl, stir the sugar with the dry white wine until the sugar is dissolved. Add the plums and leave them to marinate for 24 hours.
2 Put the plums and their marinade in a stainless steel or enamelled saucepan and bring to the boil. Simmer over a medium heat for 5–15 minutes, depending on ripeness, until the plums are tender. Strain them and leave until cool enough to handle.

3 Cut the cooled plums in half and remove the stones, being careful not to break up the plums. Reserve the marinade syrup.
4 In a bowl, beat the cream cheese with a little of the thick cream to form a smooth paste. Gradually beat in the remaining cream and the sifted icing sugar.
5 In a clean dry bowl, whisk the egg whites to stiff peaks. With a large metal spoon, fold them into the cream cheese mixture.
6 Divide the stoned plums among 4–6 individual serving dishes, or long-stemmed glasses. Pour a little reserved marinade syrup over the plums. Now spoon the cream over the entire dish. Serve immediateiy.

● Do not cook the plums in an aluminium pan — the metal will taint the flavour.
● Try using prunes instead of plums.

17

Poires Véfour

🔪 1 hour,
plus cooling and chilling

Serves 6
175 g /6 oz sugar
1 vanilla pod, split
6 large, firm, dessert pears
15–30 ml /1–2 tbls lemon juice
For the crème pâtissière
425 ml /15 fl oz milk
5 cm /2 in piece of vanilla pod, split
5 egg yolks
100 g /4 oz caster sugar
30 ml /2 tbls flour
15 ml /1 tbls cornflour
25 g /1 oz butter
45–60 ml /3–4 tbls Grand Marnier
150 ml /5 fl oz thick cream, whipped
For the decoration
18 small ratafias, or 6 large macaroons
425 ml /15 fl oz thick cream
15 ml /1 tbls caster sugar
12–18 crystallized violets

1 Place the sugar in a wide saucepan with the split vanilla pod and 800 ml–1 L /1½–2 pt water. (The syrup must cover the pears when they are added to the pan.) Stir it over a gentle heat until the sugar has completely dissolved, then bring the syrup to the boil. Remove the pan from the heat.
2 Peel the pears, halve them lengthways and scoop out the cores with a teaspoon. Liberally brush each pear half with lemon juice as soon as it is prepared, to prevent discoloration.
3 Lower the pear halves into the syrup. Bring the syrup to the boil, cover the surface with a piece of greaseproof paper and poach the pears very gently for 5–10 minutes, until they are just tender. Do not overcook them or let any part of them become mushy.
4 Remove the saucepan from the heat. Leave the pears to cool in the syrup.
5 Next, make the crème pâtissière. Pour the milk into a medium-sized saucepan and add the piece of split vanilla pod. Stand the pan over a low heat, bring the milk to the boil and then remove the pan from the heat. Cover the milk with a tightly fitting lid and leave it until it is needed.
6 Place the egg yolks and sugar in a bowl and whisk them until thick and light. Gradually whisk the flour and cornflour into the mixture.
7 Remove the piece of vanilla pod from the milk. Gradually pour the milk onto the egg yolk mixture, whisking continuously, then continue to whisk until well blended.
8 Pour the mixture back into the pan. Bring it to the boil over a medium heat, stirring constantly with a wooden spoon. Simmer the mixture for 3 minutes, beating vigorously so that it thickens slowly.
9 Remove the pan from the heat, beat in the butter and continue to beat for 1–2 minutes, until the mixture has cooled slightly. Stir in the Grand Marnier.
10 Pour the crème pâtissière into a bowl, passing it through a sieve if it is not absolutely smooth. Cover the mixture with a sheet of lightly buttered greaseproof paper,

buttered side down, to prevent a skin forming. Leave it until it is cold.
11 When the crème pâtissière is cold, fold in the whipped thick cream.
12 Select 6 tall, deep glass bowls, each large enough to take a pear standing up. Spread 45 ml /3 tbls of the crème pâtissière in the base of each bowl, smoothing it out evenly with a spatula.
13 Cut the macaroons in half, then scatter them, and the resulting crumbs, evenly over the crème pâtissière. Cover the macaroons with the rest of the crème pâtissière. Drain the cool, poached pear halves.
14 Place 2 pear halves, re-assembled to form a pear, standing upright, in each dish. Whisk the thick cream with the caster sugar until it just holds its shape. Top the pears with the whipped cream, dot the cream with the crystallized violets and chill the dessert lightly before serving.

Strawberry and cheese delight

🔪 15 minutes,
plus chilling

Serves 4
350 g /12 oz cream cheese or cottage cheese
30–45 ml /2–3 tbls icing sugar, plus extra for dusting
1 medium-sized egg yolk
225 g /8 oz strawberries, hulled
juice of ¾–1 small lemon

1 If using cottage cheese, press it through a sieve to get a smooth consistency. Stir 30–45 ml /2–3 tbls icing sugar into the cream cheese or sieved cheese, add the egg yolk and blend well.
2 Select two-thirds of the best looking strawberries, put them in a bowl, dust them with icing sugar to taste, add the lemon juice and reserve. Press the rest of the berries through a sieve.
3 Mix the sieved strawberries with the cheese and put the mixture into a deep platter. Cover it with the reserved strawberries and any juice that has collected. Chill for 2 hours before serving.

● Serve this dessert with sweet biscuits, such as German pepper cookies (see page 88) or Almond butter biscuits (see page 89).

Cold sabayon cream

🔪 45 minutes,
plus chilling and decorating

Serves 4
6 egg yolks
60 ml /4 tbls sugar
90 ml /6 tbls Marsala
7.5 ml /1½ tsp gelatine
45 ml /3 tbls brandy
2.5 ml /½ tsp orange zest, finely grated
150 ml /5 fl oz thick cream, whipped
For the decoration
150 ml /5 fl oz thick cream, whipped
1 orange

1 In the top pan of a double boiler, combine the egg yolks, sugar and Marsala. Whisk the mixture over hot, but not boiling, water for about 10–15 minutes, until the mixture thickens and increases in volume. Remove the top pan from the heat.
2 Put 22 ml /1½ tbls cold water in a small bowl and sprinkle the gelatine over it. Leave it for 1–2 minutes to soften. Place the bowl in a small saucepan of hot water until the gelatine has completely dissolved. Remove the bowl from the saucepan and allow the gelatine to cool slightly.
3 Stir the dissolved gelatine into the egg yolk mixture.
4 Stand the top pan of the double boiler in a bowl of ice cubes and stir the sabayon continuously until it begins to set. Remove the pan from the ice.
5 With a large metal spoon, fold the brandy, finely grated orange zest and whipped thick cream into the sabayon. Pour it into champagne glasses and chill.
6 Pipe a rosette of whipped cream in the centre of each sabayon. Cut across the orange to make 4 thin slices, then cut from the centre to the side, twist the slices and place them on the rosettes.

● Substitute lemon rind for the orange zest if preferred and use lemon slices instead of orange slices to garnish.

Gooseberry fool

🔪 1¼ hours,
plus chilling

Serves 6
1.1 kg /2½ lb canned gooseberries
275 ml /10 fl oz milk
10 ml /2 tsp cornflour
60 ml /4 tbls caster sugar
4 medium-sized egg yolks
125 ml /4 fl oz thick cream
30 ml /2 tbls lemon juice
grated zest of 1 orange
To garnish
125 ml /4 fl oz thick cream, whipped

1 Drain the gooseberries and reserve 9 for the decoration. Purée the remaining gooseberries in a blender until smooth. Now press the pulp through a sieve into a bowl.
2 In a pan bring the milk to just below boiling point.
3 Combine the cornflour, caster sugar and egg yolks in the top of a double saucepan and whisk them until light and fluffy. Add the scalded milk and whisk vigorously. Cook it over simmering water for 15–20 minutes, or until it has thickened, stirring constantly. Remove it from the heat and leave to cool.
4 Stir in the gooseberry purée, the thick cream, the lemon juice and grated orange zest. Pour the mixture into 6 individual glasses and chill it.
5 Just before serving, pipe a rosette of the whipped cream on top of each gooseberry fool. Cut the reserved gooseberries in half and arrange 3 halves on the rosettes of cream, pip side outwards.

Cold sabayon cream

Orange apricot chantilly

Serves 4–6
1 orange
500 g /1 lb dried apricots
100 g /4 oz sugar
30–60 ml /2–4 tbls Cointreau
300 ml /10 fl oz thick cream, whipped
30 ml /2 tbls blanched almonds, slivered

1 Peel the zest from the orange with a potato peeler and put it in a pan. Remove and discard the white pith from the orange. Cut the orange between the membranes into segments, again discarding any pith, and add the segments to the pan.
2 Rinse the dried apricots well and add them to the pan, with just enough water to cover. Simmer gently, uncovered, for 15 minutes. Stir in all of the sugar with a wooden spoon and continue to cook over a very low heat until most of the liquid is absorbed and the apricots are cooked through, adding more water if necessary. Allow the apricot mixture to cool.
3 Purée the apricot mixture in a blender, or rub it through a fine sieve. Add the Cointreau to taste, and stir in three-quarters of the whipped cream. Spoon the chantilly into individual champagne glasses, soufflé dishes or custard dishes and chill them in the refrigerator. When ready to serve, spoon the remaining cream into a piping bag fitted with a star nozzle and pipe a swirl of cream onto each dessert. Sprinkle them with the blanched slivered almonds.

20 minutes,
plus chilling

Rhubarb fool

Serves 8
700 g /1½ lb rhubarb
225 g /8 oz sugar
60 ml /4 tbls lemon juice
25 g /1 oz butter
425 ml /15 fl oz thick cream, whipped
non-toxic shiny leaves, to garnish

1 Wash and trim the rhubarb stalks, then cut them into 25 mm /1 in pieces.
2 In a heavy-based saucepan, combine the rhubarb, sugar, 30 ml /2 tbls lemon juice and butter. Bring the ingredients gently to the boil, stirring continuously with a wooden spoon.
3 Lower the heat and simmer the rhubarb gently for 5–8 minutes, stirring all the time, until it is soft but not mushy.
4 Purée the rhubarb mixture in a blender until it is smooth or press it through a fine sieve into a bowl, using the back of the wooden spoon.
5 Allow it to cool, then chill the cooled purée in the refrigerator until ready to use.
6 Just before serving, fold the whipped cream into the purée with a large metal spoon, reserving 120 ml /8 tbls cream to decorate. Flavour the purée to taste with the remaining lemon juice. Spoon it into individual glass dishes and decorate each dish with a dollop of cream and a sprig of non-toxic shiny leaves. Serve immediately.

40 minutes,
plus chilling

Coeurs à la crème

Serves 4
Recipe 1
175 g /6 oz cream cheese
30 ml /2 tbls icing sugar, sifted
  (see note below)
1.5 ml /¼ tsp vanilla essence
175 ml /6 fl oz thick cream,
  whipped
Recipe 2
350 g /12 oz curd cheese
45 ml /3 tbls icing sugar, sifted

1.5 ml /¼ tsp vanilla essence
90 ml /6 tbls soured cream
Recipe 3
250 g /9 oz cream cheese
15 ml /1 tbls icing sugar
1.5 ml /¼ tsp vanilla essence
150 ml /5 fl oz soured cream
To serve
fresh strawberries, raspberries or
  blueberries, prepared
caster sugar

1 Line 4 coeur à la crème moulds with damp, double-thickness squares of cheesecloth, large enough to fold over the moulds when filled.
2 Beat the cheese in a bowl until light and fluffy. Add the sugar and vanilla essence, and beat again.
3 With a spatula, fold in the whipped thick cream or soured cream.
4 Fill the lined moulds with the cheese mixture, piling it in a dome, and fold the cheesecloth over the top.
5 Place the moulds on a tray and leave them to drain in the refrigerator overnight. If the whey does not seem to be draining off, press the top of the mould gently with the flat of your hand.
6 To serve, unmould each little heart onto a flat dessert plate and carefully remove the cheesecloth, then decorate with 2 strawberry slices. Rinse and dry the empty moulds. Fill them with fresh berries (strawberries, raspberries or blueberries, etc) and place one mould on each plate beside the cheese. Serve with caster sugar.

● In every case the flavour of these desserts is more delicate if you use Vanilla sugar (see page 10) and omit the vanilla essence.
● This delectable French summer sweet, made with white cheese, is moulded in special heart-shaped dishes of porcelain or metal, hence the name. The dishes have holes punched in the bottom to allow the whey to drain away. I love this dessert so much that I have a selection of three different recipes. The first tastes like a very light, soft, uncooked cheesecake; the second has a more pronounced cheese flavour; and the third is the smoothest of all.

 35 minutes,
then draining overnight

Raspberry cheese

Serves 8
650 g /1¼ lb cream cheese
125 g /4 oz caster sugar
250 ml /9 fl oz thick cream
juice of 1 lemon
550 g /1¼ lb raspberries

1 Beat the cream cheese in a bowl with a wooden spoon for 2 minutes until soft.
2 Add the caster sugar and beat until it is well blended. Add the cream and lemon juice and mix well.
3 Reserve 125 g /4 oz of the raspberries for decorating and fold the remainder into the cream cheese mixture. Cover it and chill it overnight in the refrigerator.
4 To serve, divide the cheese mixture among 8 glass dessert dishes or champagne glasses, and decorate them with the reserved raspberries.

10 minutes,
then chilling

Elisabeth Moxon's lemon posset

Serves 4–6
zest of 2 lemons, finely grated
600 ml /1 pt thick cream
150 ml /5 fl oz dry white wine
juice of 2 lemons
15 ml /1 tbls sugar
3 egg whites
For the garnish
lemon slices

1   In a large bowl, add the grated lemon zest to the thick cream and whisk until it is stiff. Stir in the dry white wine and then whisk in the lemon juice, little by little. Add sugar to taste — posset should not be over sweet.
2   Whisk the egg whites until they form stiff peaks and fold them into the thick cream mixture. Chill.
3   When ready to serve, whisk the posset one more time and pile it into individual glasses or a glass serving dish. Garnish it with attractively cut lemon slices.

●   Elisabeth Moxon was an 18th century English cookery writer.
●   You can use candied violets, or when in season, fresh raspberries or strawberries to garnish this posset.

Strawberry fool

Serves 6
500 g /1 lb fresh strawberries
30 ml /2 tbls lemon juice
275 ml /10 fl oz thick cream
150 ml /5 fl oz dry white wine
60–90 ml /4–6 tbls caster sugar
red food colouring (optional)
To decorate
6 strawberries, halved

1   To remove the seeds, press the strawberries through a sieve into a bowl, using the back of a wooden spoon. Stir in the lemon juice.
2   In a large bowl, whisk together until stiff the thick cream, white wine and caster sugar to taste. Fold in the strawberry purée and a few drops of red food colouring, if wished.
3   Carefully pour the mixture into 6 glass dishes. Chill for at least 2 hours.
4   To serve, decorate each strawberry fool with 2 strawberry halves.

●   If fresh strawberries are not available, use 500 g /1 lb frozen strawberries, defrosted and drained, and decorate the servings with candied violets and angelica leaves.

Orange bowl with rum-flavoured sabayon

Serves 4
2–3 medium-sized oranges
60 ml /4 tbls soft brown sugar
4 eggs, separated
90 ml /6 tbls rum
2.5 ml /½ tsp grated nutmeg
150 ml /5 fl oz thick cream, stiffly beaten
50 g /2 oz dessert chocolate, chopped
chocolate caraque, to garnish (see page 87)

1 Finely grate a little zest from one of the oranges and reserve it for garnishing. Peel and slice into rings enough oranges to line an 850 ml / 1½ pt glass bowl. Line the bowl with orange slices. Chill.
2 In a medium-sized saucepan, dissolve the brown sugar in 30 ml / 2 tbls water over a low heat, stirring constantly with a wooden spoon. Increase the heat to medium and boil the syrup for 2 minutes. Set it aside to cool, but do not allow the syrup to set.
3 In a small mixing bowl, beat the egg yolks, rum and grated nutmeg with a wire whisk or rotary beater until the yolks are thick and pale. Fill a medium-sized saucepan one-third full of boiling water. Place the bowl containing the egg yolk mixture in the pan and place the pan over a medium heat. Do not let the bowl touch the water, or the mixture will curdle. Continue beating the egg yolk mixture until it stiffens and rises slightly. Remove the saucepan from the heat, and continue to beat the mixture until it is cool.
4 In a large bowl, beat the egg whites with a wire whisk or a rotary beater until they form stiff peaks. Pour the cooled syrup onto the egg whites and fold it in with a large metal spoon.
5 Pour the cooked egg yolk mixture onto the stiffly beaten thick cream. Fold in the chopped chocolate with a metal spoon and then fold in the egg white and syrup mixture.
6 Fill the orange-lined bowl with the rum-flavoured sabayon cream and chill it in the refrigerator.
7 Decorate the sabayon with the chocolate caraque and the reserved orange zest.

 1 hour,
plus chilling

Ginger custard petits pots

Serves 6
3 eggs, separated
50 g /2 oz caster sugar
finely grated zest of 1 orange
175 ml /6 fl oz thick cream
2 pieces preserved ginger, finely chopped
For the decoration
12 slices preserved ginger
60 ml /4 tbls ginger syrup

1 Bring to the boil the water in the bottom pan of a double boiler, then reduce the heat to a gentle simmer.
2 In the top pan, combine the egg yolks and caster sugar. Set it over the lightly simmering water. (The base of the pan should not touch the water.) Using a wire whisk, whisk the egg yolks and sugar mixture for 5 minutes, or until they are thick and creamy.
3 Remove the top pan from the water. Whisk in the finely grated orange zest and leave the mixture to cool.
4 In a bowl, whisk the cream until it just holds its shape. In a clean, dry bowl, and using a clean whisk, beat the egg whites until they are stiff but not dry.
5 Using a large metal spoon or spatula, fold the whipped cream into the cooled egg mixture, with the finely chopped preserved ginger. Then gently but thoroughly fold in the beaten egg whites, working as lightly and swiftly as possible.
6 Spoon the mixture into six 125 ml /4 fl oz individual soufflé dishes and chill for 2–3 hours.
7 To serve, overlap two pieces of sliced ginger in the centre of each petit pot and pour 10 ml /2 tsp ginger syrup over each one. Serve immediately.

● Do not leave the petits pots overnight in the refrigerator, as the mixture will separate.

 1 hour,
plus chilling

COLD, SWEET SOUFFLES

A light and frothy chilled soufflé flavoured with fruit, nuts or chocolate is often the ideal dessert to follow a rich main course. Cold, sweet soufflés can look as spectacular as they taste.

Cold soufflés are usually set with gelatine and chilled until firm. My selection here is very tempting; they all look so pretty and taste delicious! Sharp, refreshing Lemon soufflé and Chilled chocolate soufflé, made with best-quality, dark chocolate, are classics which are bound to please your guests. But why not try cool, green Chilled lime soufflés or an exotic Mango soufflé as well?

The Striped soufflé glacé needs time allowed for freezing when preparing it, but the layers of cream, egg yolk and sugar mixed alternately with apricot purée, pistachio nuts and ground almonds, topped with apricot sauce, make an unusual and attractive-looking dessert. Gooseberry and elderflower soufflés have a definite taste of muscat grapes which, surprisingly, comes from the elder-flower heads (you can buy these in any good health food store). These last two recipes are a good choice for those people who prefer something less sweet.

My Rose petal soufflé has a pale, delicate, romantic look, decorated as it is with rose petals dipped in egg white and then sugar.

Lemon soufflé

50 minutes,
plus 2 hours chilling

Serves 6
oil, for greasing
20 ml /4 tsp gelatine
4 eggs, separated
150 g /5 oz caster sugar
strained juice and grated zest of 4 lemons
300 ml /10 fl oz thick cream
To garnish
150 g /5 oz almonds, blanched and split
300 ml /10 fl oz thick cream, whipped

1   Pin a double thickness of oiled grease-proof paper around the edge of an 850 ml / 1½ pt soufflé dish so that the collar stands at least 5 cm /2 in above the rim.
2   Put 60 ml /4 tbls warm water in a small bowl, sprinkle on and stir in the gelatine. Leave it to stand for a few minutes.
3   Put the egg yolks and sugar in a large bowl, mix them well and place it over a pan of boiling water, making sure the base of the bowl does not touch the water. Beat the mixture until it is smooth and pale yellow and beginning to thicken. Remove it from the heat and continue whisking the mixture until it cools, then whisk in the lemon juice and zest.
4   Put the bowl containing the gelatine over a small pan of hot water and stir until the gelatine has dissolved completely. Do not let the gelatine mixture boil. Stir it into the lemon mixture. Chill the lemon mixture in the refrigerator until it is on the point of setting — watch it carefully, it sets quickly.

5   Whip the cream. Whisk the egg whites until stiff peaks form.
6   Remove the lemon mixture from the refrigerator and fold in the cream, then the egg whites. Pour the mixture carefully into the prepared soufflé dish and refrigerate it for at least 2 hours or until it is set.
7   Meanwhile, dry-fry the almonds in an ungreased frying-pan, stirring frequently until they turn pale brown.
8   When the soufflé has set, run a knife dipped in hot water around the inside of the greaseproof paper band to loosen it, and discard the paper. Chop the almonds and gently pat most of them around the sides of the soufflé above the rim of the dish. Garnish it with whipped cream and the remaining chopped almonds.

Gooseberry and elderflower soufflés

1½ hours, plus 3½ hours
chilling and resting

Serves 4
225 g /8 oz gooseberries
8 elderflower heads
25 g /1 oz sugar
15 g /½ oz gelatine
150 ml /5 fl oz thick cream
5 medium-sized egg whites
whipped cream and sprigs of mint, to decorate

1   Put the gooseberries into a large pan and add 40 ml /2½ tbls water. Tie the elder-flowers in muslin and bury them among the gooseberries. Bring them to the boil and simmer them gently for 20 minutes or until the gooseberries are soft, then let them cool, leaving them in the pan.
2   Remove the elderflower bouquet and discard it. Push the gooseberries through a sieve and sweeten the purée with sugar.
3   Pour 45 ml /3 tbls water into a cup, add the gelatine and put the cup in a pan of barely simmering water until the gelatine dissolves. Remove it from the heat and allow it to cool, then stir it into the purée and leave it until it is almost set.
4   Meanwhile, pin a double thickness of greaseproof paper around each of 4 ramekin dishes to stand 5 cm /2 in above the rims.
5   Whip the cream until it forms soft peaks, then mix it into the purée.
6   Whisk the egg whites until they form soft peaks, fold them into the gooseberry mixture and pour it into the ramekins. Refrigerate for at least 3 hours.
7   Remove the ramekins from the refrigerator 30 minutes before serving. Remove the pins from the paper. Dip a knife into hot water and, holding it with the back of the blade against the paper, carefully ease away

the paper. Let the soufflés rest at room temperature before serving. Decorate each soufflé with a swirl of whipped cream and a sprig of mint.

● You can buy elderflower heads at a health food store.

Chilled chocolate soufflé

45–50 minutes, plus
at least 2 hours chilling

Serves 6
175 g /6 oz best-quality, dark chocolate
30 ml /2 tbls made, strong black coffee
10 ml /2 tsp powdered gelatine
4 eggs at room temperature, separated
80 g /3¼ oz sugar
250 ml /9 fl oz thick cream
a generous pinch of salt
icing sugar or chocolate shavings, to decorate

1   Break up the chocolate into a small heat-proof pot or jug and pour the coffee over it. Dissolve the gelatine in 50 ml /2 fl oz water in a similar heatproof container and stand both in a saucepan of hot water over a very low heat. Whisk the egg yolks lightly in a large bowl and reserve.
2   Dissolve the sugar in 50 ml /2 fl oz water

Gooseberry and elderflower soufflés

in a small, heavy-based saucepan. Boil it over a medium-high heat until it reaches 118C / 240F on a sugar thermometer or forms a soft ball when it is tested in cold water.

3 Immediately remove the saucepan from the heat and pour the syrup into the egg yolks in a thin stream, whisking continuously until the mixture is quite cool. Whisk in the tepid gelatine mixture.

4 Check that the pieces of chocolate are quite soft by prodding them with the tip of a sharp knife (if not, raise the heat briefly). Stir the chocolate until it is smooth, then whisk it into the egg mixture.

5 Whip the cream until it holds peaks and then stir it into the chocolate mixture.

6 Beat the egg whites with the salt until they are stiff. Carefully fold the whites into the chocolate mixture using a metal spoon.

7 Tie a strip of greaseproof paper or foil around the outside of a 800 ml /1½ pt soufflé dish so that it sticks up about 25 mm /1 in above the rim. Pour the mixture into the dish and refrigerate it for at least 2 hours. Remove the paper and sprinkle the top with icing sugar or chocolate shavings before serving.

Striped soufflé glacé

1½ hours,
plus freezing the soufflé layers

Serves 6–8
350 g /12 oz dried apricots
100 g /4 oz shelled pistachio nuts, blanched and skinned
9 egg yolks
250 g /8 oz caster sugar
750 ml /1¼ pt thick cream
3 drops each of orange and green food colouring
100 g /4 oz ground almonds
8–16 langues de chat biscuits

1 Simmer the apricots with enough water to cover them for 25 minutes. Drain them, reserving the cooking liquid. Purée the fruit with 75 ml /3 fl oz of the liquid. Measure 275 ml /10 fl oz purée into a jug and add 75 ml /3 fl oz cooking liquid. Stir, then set aside for the sauce. Reserve the remaining thick purée for the apricot layers of the dessert.

2 Reserve 9 pistachio nuts for decorating and blend the rest to a coarse paste. Cut the reserved nuts in half.

3 Wrap a collar of double-thickness grease-proof paper around a 12.5 cm /5 in soufflé dish, so that the collar extends 10 cm /4 in above the rim. Secure it with an elastic band.

4 In a large bowl set over a pan of simmering water, whisk the yolks and sugar until the mixture is pale and thick and doubled in bulk — this takes about 10 minutes. Stand the bowl in a larger bowl containing crushed ice and continue to whisk until it is cold.

5 Whip the cream to soft peaks, then fold it into the yolk and sugar mixture. Divide the mixture equally among 3 bowls. Stir the thick apricot purée and orange food colouring into one of the bowls. Stir the pistachio paste and green food colouring into the second, and the ground almonds into the third.

6 Put half the apricot mixture in the soufflé dish and transfer it to the freezer; put the bowls in the refrigerator to chill. When the apricot layer has set (about 45 minutes), add a second layer using half of the almond mixture; freeze until set. Add a third layer using half of the pistachio mixture; freeze again. Continue in this way until the 6 layers are complete, making sure that the top 3 layers stand above the rim of the soufflé dish. Freeze for 4 hours or until firm.

7 Transfer the soufflé glacé to the refrigerator 30 minutes before serving. Just before serving, slip a knife between the paper and the soufflé all round, then peel away the paper collar. Decorate the top with the reserved pistachio nuts. To serve, cut the top trio of layers into quarters, then cut horizontally across the soufflé. Cut the second trio of layers into quarters and serve, accompanied by the apricot sauce and biscuits.

Rose petal soufflé

1 hour, plus
2 hours chilling

Serves 4
15 ml /1 tbls gelatine
3 medium-sized eggs, separated
100 g /4 oz rose petal sugar (see note below)
15 ml /1 tbls rose-flavoured water (see note below)
a few drops of pink food colouring (optional)
300 ml /10 fl oz thick cream, whipped

For the decoration
10–12 rose petals, washed and dried
1 medium-sized egg white, lightly whisked
15 ml /1 tbls caster sugar

1 Sprinkle the gelatine over 45 ml /3 tbls cold water in a small bowl. Leave it to soften, then dissolve, standing the bowl in hot water.

2 In a bowl, whisk together the egg yolks and rose petal sugar until the mixture is thick and creamy. Pour in the dissolved gelatine, beating all the time. Stir in the rose-flavoured water, and colouring if wished. Now fold in the whipped cream.

3 Leave the mixture in a cool place. When the mixture begins to run syrupy, whisk the egg whites until they are stiff. Gently fold them into the mixture.

4 Turn the mixture into a serving dish and leave it in the refrigerator to set for 2 hours.

5 To make the decoration, dip the rose petals in egg white, shake off the excess and dip them in sugar. Leave them on kitchen foil in a dry place for 2 hours.

6 Decorate the soufflé with the sugar-coated petals before serving.

● To make rose petal sugar, wash and dry at least 2 cups of rose petals, toss them with twice the quantity of caster sugar, then spread them on a baking tray. Dry them in a low oven, stirring occasionally for 1½–2 hours. Cool, then store in a covered container, away from the light.

● Rose-flavoured water can be bought from some supermarkets or a good chemist.

Striped soufflé glacé

Chilled lime soufflés

Serves 6
25 ml /1½ tbls gelatine
8 limes
6 eggs, separated
175 g /6 oz caster sugar
a few drops of green food colouring (optional)
250 ml /9 fl oz thick cream, whipped
For the garnish
150 ml /5 fl oz thick cream, whipped
12 slivers crystallized citrus peel

1 Tie collars of double thickness greaseproof paper around 6 individual 150 ml /5 fl oz ramekins or small soufflé dishes: the collars should stand 4 cm /1½ in above the rims.
2 In a small bowl, sprinkle the gelatine over 60 ml /4 tbls cold water. Leave it to soften for a few minutes. Meanwhile, grate the zest of 5 limes and squeeze the juice out of all the limes into a small bowl.
3 Fill the bottom pan of a double boiler with 25 mm /1 in simmering water and stand the bowl of softened gelatine in it. Heat until the gelatine has dissolved. Stir once and remove the bowl.
4 Put the egg yolks, caster sugar, lime juice and zest in the top pan of the double boiler. Put the pan over the gently simmering water and whisk, preferably with a hand-held electric beater, until the mixture becomes thick and mousse-like, and increases in volume. This will take about 10 minutes. Remove the mousse from the heat and whisk in a few drops of food colouring to make the mixture a very pale green, if wished.
5 Stir the dissolved gelatine into the mousse mixture and place it over a bowl of crushed ice. Stir continuously until the mousse is on the point of setting. Remove the pan from the ice. Fold in the whipped cream, using a large metal spoon.
6 In a clean bowl, whisk the egg whites until they form stiff peaks. Using a large metal spoon, fold them carefully into the lime mousse. Pour the mixture immediately into the prepared soufflé dishes and leave them to set in the refrigerator for at least 2 hours.
7 To serve, carefully ease the collars from the soufflé dishes with a sharp knife. Fit a piping bag with a 15 mm /½ in star nozzle, spoon in the whipped cream and pipe a rosette on each lime soufflé. Decorate each soufflé with 2 pieces of crystallized citrus peel.

 50 minutes,
plus 2 hours chilling

Cold praline soufflé

Serves 4
10 ml /2 tsp gelatine
5 ml /1 tsp instant coffee
* granules*
3 eggs, separated
60 ml /4 tbls caster sugar
300 ml /10 fl oz thick cream,
* lightly whipped*

For the praline
oil, for greasing
50 g /2 oz whole almonds
60 ml /4 tbls sugar
For the decoration
150 ml /5 fl oz thick cream,
* whipped*

1 To prepare the praline, grease a heavy metal tray with oil. In a small, heavy-based saucepan, combine the whole almonds and sugar and cook over a moderate heat for 7 minutes, or until a deep caramel forms and the almonds are browned, shaking the pan very carefully to ensure even cooking.
2 Pour the praline immediately onto the greased tray and leave it to cool. When the praline is cold, break it up and grind it coarsely using a mortar and pestle.
3 Tie a double thickness of greaseproof paper around a 600 ml /1 pt soufflé dish to project 8 cm /3 in above the rim.
4 Put 15 ml /1 tbls cold water in a small bowl and sprinkle the gelatine over it. Leave it to soften. Now put the bowl in a saucepan of water over a low heat for a few minutes to dissolve the gelatine. Dissolve the coffee granules in 15 ml /1 tbls hot water.
5 In the top pan of a double boiler, over simmering water, combine the egg yolks, sugar and dissolved coffee. Whisk for about 10 minutes until the mixture is light and fluffy and the beaters leave a trail when lifted. Stir in the dissolved gelatine. Place the pan over a bowl of crushed ice and stir constantly until it is on the point of setting.
6 Remove the pan from the ice and, with a large metal spoon, fold in the lightly whipped cream and the ground praline, reserving 30 ml /2 tbls praline for a decoration.
7 Whisk the egg whites until they form soft peaks. Carefully fold them into the soufflé mixture, using a large metal spoon. Pour the mixture immediately into the prepared soufflé dish and put it into the refrigerator to set for at least 1 hour.
8 To serve, carefully remove the greaseproof paper, slowly easing it away with a palette knife. Spread the top of the soufflé with a little whipped cream, smoothing it with a palette knife. Fit a piping bag with a 15 m /½ in star nozzle, spoon in the remaining cream and pipe rosettes. Sprinkle each rosette with a little reserved praline and pat the remainder around the edge of the soufflé. Serve it immediately.

 1¾ hours, 2 hours chilling,
then decorating

Amaretti soufflés glacés

Serves 6
6 eggs, separated
75 g /3 oz caster sugar
45 ml /3 tbls dry white wine
15 ml /1 tbls gelatine
275 ml /10 fl oz thick cream
45–60 ml /3–4 tbls Amaretto di Saronno
6 amaretti (small Italian macaroons), crushed

1 Prepare six 150 ml /5 fl oz individual soufflé dishes with collars of double thickness greaseproof paper, to stand about 5 cm /2 in above the rims.
2 Combine the egg yolks, sugar and white wine in the top pan of a double boiler. Whisk vigorously over simmering water until the mixture is thick and the whisk leaves a trail when lifted. Remove from the heat and whisk until cool.
3 Meanwhile, in a small bowl, sprinkle the gelatine over 45 ml /3 tbls cold water and leave until it has softened. Place the bowl in lightly simmering water and leave the gelatine to dissolve.
4 Stir the dissolved gelatine into the cooled egg mixture and place over a bowl of cracked ice. Stir until the mixture is on the point of setting.
5 In a bowl, whisk the thick cream until soft peaks form. Whisk in the Amaretto, them fold it into the yolk mixture.
6 In a clean, dry bowl, whisk the egg whites until they are stiff and then fold them into the mixture with a large metal spoon, working quickly and lightly.
7 Ladle the soufflé mixture into the prepared dishes and leave them to set in the refrigerator.
8 To serve, sprinkle the top of each chilled soufflé with finely crushed amaretti, patting the crumbs in lightly to make them stick. Carefully peel away the paper collars and serve them immediately.

● Amaretto di Saronno is a sweet almond-flavoured Italian liqueur.

40 minutes,
plus 2 hours or more chilling

Mango soufflé

Serves 6
oil, for greasing
700 g /1½ lb fresh mangoes (about 3)
15 ml /1 tbls gelatine
126 ml /4 fl oz orange juice
25 ml /1 fl oz lemon juice
275 ml /10 fl oz thick cream
2 egg whites
25 g /1 oz caster sugar
50–75 g /2–3 oz desiccated coconut, toasted in a low oven
2 very thin slices fresh orange

1 Tie a collar of lightly oiled greaseproof paper tightly around an 850 ml /1½ pt soufflé dish so that it extends 5–7.5 cm /2–3 in above the rim.
2 To prepare the mangoes, peel them with a knife and cut and scrape the flesh away from the stone. Place the flesh in a blender, purée and then sieve the mango flesh to make it absolutely smooth.
3 Place the gelatine in a small bowl and add 45 ml /3 tbls water, stand the bowl in a saucepan of gently simmering water and stir until the gelatine is dissolved. In a bowl, combine the mango pulp and the orange and lemon juice. Strain the gelatine into the mango mixture, stirring constantly. Chill the mixture for 30–45 minutes or until it is slightly thick.
4 In a bowl, whip 150 ml /5 fl oz of the thick cream until it forms soft peaks. In another bowl, beat the egg whites until they are stiff but not dry and gradually whisk in the sugar until the mixture is thick and glossy.
5 Fold first the whipped cream and then the beaten egg whites into the mango mixture and pour the mixture into the prepared soufflé dish. Level the surface of the soufflé and chill it for about 3 hours or until it is firmly set.
6 When the soufflé is set, untie and carefully remove the collar. Press the toasted coconut evenly onto the sides of the soufflé which project above the rim.
7 Whip the remaining cream until it holds its shape and spoon it into a piping bag fitted with a 20 mm /¾ in star nozzle. Pipe 8 rosettes around the edges of the soufflé. Quarter the orange slices and spike each rosette of cream with one of these.

30 minutes,
plus 3¾ hours chilling

FRESH & FRUITY

It takes quite a lot to beat a simple, but delicious, dessert of fresh fruit and cream. However, here I give you ideas using strawberries, oranges, melons, peaches, pears and pineapples which add up to an extravaganza of dishes.

Browse through the next few pages and see how desserts using fresh fruit from different countries feature. From Russia comes Pineapple Romanoff; from Italy come Peach amaretti and Italian pears; from France comes Normandy baked apples; from England comes English spring pudding, a rhubarb pudding with custard, and from a combination of countries comes the Exotic fruit and berry salad.

Several recipes only take 10 or 20 minutes to prepare (Strawberries in orange juice, Orange slices ambrosia, Fresh fruit compote) while others take longer (Special orange trifle, Glazed fruit bande, Stuffed melon). Often the recipes need some time allowed for soaking or chilling the fruit or dessert before serving.

This chapter has many suggestions for using apples ranging from Little green apples to Florentine apples which are cooked with almonds, brown sugar and lemon zest. A marvellous selection of ideas for you to try.

Summer fruit in a blanket

Vary this deliciously simple sweet to your heart's content by using other combinations of fresh fruit in season, and flavouring them with a suitable liqueur in place of the brandy. Try a mixture of wild strawberries, raspberries and redcurrants, tossed in Grand Marnier or kirsch, for example.

 20 minutes,
plus chilling

Serves 4
4 slices of fresh pineapple (250 g /8 oz in all)
60 ml /4 tbls brandy
2 large, ripe peaches
8–12 large strawberries, hulled and sliced
425 ml /15 fl oz thick cream
50–75 g /2–3 oz Demerara sugar

1 Cut each pineapple slice into 8 pieces. Sprinkle with brandy and leave them to steep while you prepare the peaches.
2 Pour boiling water over the peaches, skin them and cut each peach into quarters, then cut each quarter into 3 slices.
3 Put the peach slices and their juice in a glass serving bowl, add the pineapple pieces and their liquid and toss the fruit together lightly. Add the sliced strawberries.
4 Whip the cream until it holds its shape. Spread the whipped cream thickly over the fruit, smoothing it with the back of a spoon. Chill until ready to serve.
5 Sprinkle the Demerara sugar over the top of the cream just before serving.

Exotic fruit and berry salad

Gingered pears

 1–1¼ hours

Serves 6–8
1 kg /2 lb firm Conference pears
*4 pieces preserved stem ginger, halved and
    thinly sliced*
60 ml /4 tbls syrup from the ginger jar
275 ml /10 fl oz dry white wine
150 ml /5 fl oz soured cream, to serve

1 Heat the oven to 180C /350F /gas 4. Peel the pears, then quarter and core them and cut them into pieces about 3 × 1 cm /1¼ × ⅓ in. Place them in an ovenproof dish.
2 Mix the pieces of ginger in with the pears, spoon the syrup over them and pour in the wine. Bake the pieces of pear, uncovered, for 45–60 minutes, until they are soft.
3 Serve the pears hot, with the soured cream handed round separately in a bowl.

Exotic fruit and berry salad

This unusual combination of berries and foreign fruits will tickle the taste-buds of your guests. Serve it with a dessert wine such as Muscat de Beaumes de Venise.

 20 minutes,
plus chilling

Serves 6
4 passion fruit
2 mangoes, peeled and sliced
225 g /8 oz blueberries
225 g /8 oz loganberries
225 g /8 oz raspberries
30 ml /2 tbls sugar
juice and grated zest of 1 lime
5 ml /1 tsp angostura bitters
5–7 sprigs of fresh mint

1 Cut the passion fruit in half. Using a teaspoon, scoop out the flesh into a sieve placed over a bowl. Push the flesh through the sieve, discarding the seeds.
2 Combine the passion fruit flesh with the mangoes and berries, sprinkle them with sugar, add the lime juice and zest and the bitters; toss well.
3 Reserve a few whole mint sprigs for garnishing. Strip the remaining leaves from their stalks and, with scissors, cut the leaves in thin strips. Scatter the strips over the fruit, toss, put the salad in a serving bowl and chill it for at least 2 hours.
4 Just before you are ready to serve the salad, tuck the reserved whole mint sprigs in amongst the fruit.

Special orange trifle

🕐🍴🍴🍴 preparing the sponge, 40 minutes, plus chilling and decorating

Serves 6–8
60 ml /4 tbls orange marmalade
30 ml /2 tbls brandy
90 ml /6 tbls Grand Marnier
3 oranges
2 lemons
30 ml /2 tbls icing sugar, sifted
450 ml /15 fl oz thick cream
For the fatless sponge
melted butter, for the tins
75 g /3 oz flour, plus extra for dusting
3 eggs
75 g /3 oz caster sugar
a few drops of vanilla essence
For the decoration
150 ml /5 fl oz thick cream, whipped
8 whole strawberries

1 Heat the oven to 180C /350F /gas 4.
2 Brush the bases and sides of two 18 cm / 7 in layer tins with melted butter. Line the base of each tin with a neat circle of grease-proof paper and brush that with melted butter as well. Lightly dust the bases and sides of the tins with flour, knocking the tins to shake off the surplus.
3 Choose a heatproof bowl with a capacity of 1.5 L /2½ pt or more to whisk up the cake, and select a large saucepan over which it will fit firmly. Pour 5 cm /2 in water into the pan and bring it to the boil. Reduce the heat until the water in the pan is barely simmering.
4 Put the eggs, sugar and vanilla essence in the bowl. Set it over the simmering water and whisk continuously until the mixture is very thick, light and lukewarm. This will take 10 minutes if you are using a hand-held electric mixer at high speed. The mixture should increase to about 4 times its original volume.
5 Remove the bowl from the heat. Stand it on a cool surface and continue to whisk the mixture until it leaves a distinct trail on the surface when the beaters are lifted and the mixture has cooled. This will take about 5 minutes if you use an electric mixer at high speed.
6 Sift the flour a little at a time over the egg mixture, folding it in lightly but thoroughly with a large metal spoon.
7 Divide the batter between the prepared layer tins. If necessary, level the tops lightly with a spatula. Place the tins in the hot oven and bake for 20–25 minutes. The cakes are cooked when they shrink away slightly from the sides of the baking tins and spring back into shape when pressed lightly.
8 Remove the cakes from the oven and leave them for 1–2 minutes to settle. Then turn them out onto a clean tea-towel. Peel off the greaseproof paper and invert the cakes onto a wire rack so that they cool resting right side up.
9 In a small bowl, beat the orange marma-lade with the brandy until they are well blended. Spread the mixture evenly over one layer of sponge. Sandwich the 2 layers together and place them in a shallow 20 cm / 8 in glass bowl. It is best to use a bowl which is slightly larger than the sponge layers — the cream mixture poured over the cake at a later stage will then fall down the sides of the cake and soak in well.
10 Sprinkle 60 ml /4 tbls Grand Marnier over the top of the sponge, cover the bowl and leave it to soak for at least 2 hours in a cool place.
11 Grate the zest of 2 of the oranges and 1 of the lemons into a small bowl.
12 Squeeze the juice from the citrus fruit and add it to the grated zests with the sifted icing sugar. Stir together until the sugar has dissolved.
13 In a large bowl, whip the thick cream to soft peaks. Stir in the remaining Grand Marnier and the fruit juice and sugar mixture. Pour the runny cream and juice mixture over the sponge layers. Cover the trifle and then chill it for at least 8 hours — this is to ensure that the flavours are thoroughly blended.
14 About 30 minutes before serving, remove the orange trifle from the refrigerator and bring it to a cool room temperature. Using a piping bag fitted with a 15 mm /½ in star nozzle, pipe 8 rosettes of whipped thick cream between the edge of the glass bowl and the cake. Arrange a whole straw-berry on top of each rosette and then serve the orange trifle immediately.

Little green apples

🍴🍴 soaking the raisins, then 40 minutes, plus chilling

Serves 4–8
60 ml /4 tbls raisins or sultanas
45–60 ml /3–4 tbls crème de menthe
8 green, dessert apples
250 g /8 oz sugar
juice of 2 lemons
1–2 drops of green food colouring
90 ml /6 tbls almonds, blanched and chopped

1 Put the raisins or sultanas in a cup, sprinkle with 10 ml /2 tsp crème de menthe and leave them to soak until needed.
2 Core the apples with an apple corer, leaving them whole, and then peel them.
3 Combine the sugar and lemon juice with 425 ml /15 fl oz water in a heavy pan wide enough to take all the apples in a single layer. Stir over a medium heat until the sugar has dissolved. Next, flavour the syrup with 30–45 ml /2–3 tbls crème de menthe and deepen the colour slightly with 1–2 drops of green food colouring.
4 Poach the apples in the syrup for 5–7 minutes, or until they are tender, turning them once or twice.
5 Using a slotted spoon, transfer the apples to a serving dish.
6 Combine the soaked raisins or sultanas with the chopped almonds and fill the centre of each apple with this mixture. Allow to cool.
7 Boil the poaching liquid until it is reduced to a light syrup. Cool slightly.
8 Spoon some of the syrup over each apple to cover it with a delicate green glaze. Chill.
9 Just before serving, stir 5 ml /1 tsp crème de menthe into the remaining syrup to give added flavour. Spoon the glaze over the apples again to give them a high gloss.

Little green apples

Timbale of fruit

the soft inside of the brioche can be removed easily in one piece.

5 Remove the centre of the brioche, leaving a shell 15 mm /1½ in thick at the sides and 25 mm /1 in thick at the bottom.

6 Warm the apricot jam with the kirsch in a saucepan. Strain the mixture through a nylon sieve into a clean pan, bring quickly to the boil and add the lemon juice. Brush the brioche case generously, inside and out, with the apricot glaze. Reserve the remaining glaze. Combine the mixed peel and the flaked almonds and use them to coat the outside of the brioche case. The glaze and peel and nuts will cover the knife insertions in the side of the brioche.

7 Prepare the fruit filling: in a bowl, combine the diced pear, sliced strawberries, raspberries, grapes and well-drained pineapple chunks and add the reserved apricot glaze.

8 Just before serving, fill the glazed brioche with the mixed fruit. Replace the lid and serve immediately, with the cream.

● Serve the removed inside of the brioche at another time, sliced, with butter and jam.

Cinnamon plum crumble

Here is a favourite pudding with a difference — the addition of cinnamon to the plums and the crumble gives it extra flavour, while the oats add texture to the topping.

1¼ hours

Serves 4
500 g /1 lb cooking plums
50 g /2 oz sugar
2.5 ml /½ tsp cinnamon powder
For the crumble topping
100 g /4 oz flour
100 g /4 oz rolled oats
5 ml /1 tsp cinnamon powder
100 g /4 oz soft margarine
50 g /2 oz sugar
custard, thin cream or ice cream, to serve

1 Heat the oven to 170C /325F /gas 3. Wash, halve and stone the plums; place them in a shallow, ovenproof dish and sprinkle them with the sugar and cinnamon.

2 To make the topping, place the flour, oats and cinnamon in a bowl and rub in the fat with your fingertips until the mixture resembles fine breadcrumbs, then stir in the sugar. Spoon the crumble mixture lightly over the plums and smooth the top.

3 Bake for about 40 minutes, or until the topping is crisp and golden and the plums tender when pierced with the point of a knife. Serve the plum crumble with hot custard, thin cream or vanilla ice cream.

● Damsons are best for this recipe, but Victoria plums can be used.

● As variations, try adding crushed cornflakes or finely chopped nuts or desiccated coconut to your crumble topping.

Fresh fruit compote

40 minutes,
plus 2–3 hours chilling

Serves 4
2 oranges
1 grapefruit
30 ml /2 tbls clear honey
45–60 ml /3–4 tbls lemon juice
2 kiwi fruit
1 banana
125 g /4 oz strawberries, hulled, to decorate
15–25 g /½–1 oz shelled pistachio nuts, chopped, to decorate
sprigs of fresh mint, to decorate

1 Using a sharp knife, peel the oranges and the grapefruit taking care to remove every scrap of bitter white pith. Next, cut between the segments and membranes to remove the segments. Remove any pips with the point of the knife.

2 Mix the honey with the lemon juice in a large bowl, add the fruit segments and stir well. Peel the kiwi fruit and cut the flesh into 3 mm /⅛ in thick slices; add to the bowl and toss well. Cover and chill for 2–3 hours.

3 Just before serving, peel the banana and slice it into the fruit salad. Toss gently.

4 Decorate the salad with whole strawberries, chopped pistachio nuts and sprigs of mint around the edge.

Timbale of fruit

45 minutes

Serves 4
1 large brioche
450 g /1 lb apricot jam
30–60 ml /2–4 tbls kirsch
juice of 1 lemon
25 g /1 oz chopped mixed peel
25–50 g /1–2 oz flaked almonds
1 ripe pear, peeled, cored and diced
250 g /8 oz strawberries, sliced
250 g /8 oz raspberries
125–175 g /4–6 oz seedless white grapes
250 g /8 oz canned pineapple chunks, drained
whipped thick cream, to serve

1 First make the timbale: using a sharp knife, cut a slice from the top of the brioche and reserve it for a 'lid'.

2 Cut around the inside edge of the brioche, leaving a 15 mm /1½ in shell, and cutting to within 25 mm /1 in of the base.

3 Insert the knife in the side of the brioche 25 mm /1 in up from the base. Without making the hole larger than the knife so as not to cut the outside edge of the brioche, move the point of the knife to and fro to loosen the soft inside of the brioche.

4 Remove the knife, turn the brioche a half circle and insert it again. Cut, as before, until

Stuffed melon

Serves 6
1 small, ripe water-melon
500 g /1 lb strawberries
15–30 ml /1–2 tbls brandy
icing sugar, sifted

1   Slice the melon horizontally about one-third of the way down. Scoop out the flesh from both pieces with a large, sharp spoon. Reserve the larger shell. Using a pointed knife, cut the flesh into cubes and remove the seeds from the flesh. Place most or all of the cubes (according to the size of the melon and the number of guests) in a large bowl.
2   If you like, cut the edges of the reserved melon shell into scallops with a sharp knife.
3   Hull the strawberries and add them to the bowl.
4   Add brandy and icing sugar to taste to the bowl and toss. Chill in the refrigerator until very cold. Meanwhile, place the reserved melon shell in a bowl packed with ice.
5   When ready to serve, fill the centre of the chilled melon shell with the prepared fruit. Pour over all the juices left in the bowl so that they seep through to the bottom of the shell. Serve immediately.

● Try adding 500 g /1 lb redcurrants, stripped from their stalks, to the melon cubes and strawberries.
● A Galia or cantaloupe melon could be used instead of the watermelon.
● Frosted redcurrants make an elegant garnish. Lightly beat an egg white until it is foamy but not making peaks. Dip 2 or 3 bunches of redcurrants into it until all the berries are coated and then gently shake off the excess. Next, dip the bunches in caster sugar so that each berry is lightly coated. Set them aside on greaseproof paper to dry for about 1 hour. Use for garnishing just before serving.
● Use any suitable combination of apples, pears, apricots, redcurrants, peaches and oranges instead of the strawberries and substitute white wine for the brandy.

Normandy baked apples

Serves 6
75 g /3 oz sultanas
90 ml /6 tbls soft brown sugar
grated zest of 2 oranges
1.5–2.5 ml /¼–½ tsp ground cinnamon
6 medium-sized cooking apples
210 g /7½ oz frozen puff pastry, defrosted
2 egg yolks, beaten
caster sugar, for dusting

1   Heat the oven to 230C /450F /gas 8. In a bowl, combine the sultanas, soft brown sugar, orange zest and cinnamon.
2   Peel the apples with a vegetable peeler. Core them and fill the hole with the sultana mixture.
3   Roll out the pastry to 3 mm /⅛ in thick and with a sharp knife cut out six 15 cm /6 in squares. Place an apple in the centre of each square. Brush a little beaten egg along the edges of each pastry square and bring the pastry up the sides of the apple, making the four corners meet in the centre to enclose the apple completely. Cut away any excess pastry and seal the edges by gently pressing with the fingertips.
4   Thinly roll out the scraps of pastry and cut circles to fit the tops of the apples like little caps. Brush these caps with a little beaten egg and press down firmly on the apple tops. Cut out leaves from the remaining pastry and arrange them overlapping the sides of the caps.
5   Place the apples on a baking sheet, brush the pastry well with beaten egg, and bake for 10 minutes in the oven. Lower the temperature to 220C /425F /gas 7 and continue to bake for a further 20 minutes, or until the pastry is puffed and a rich golden colour.
6   Serve the apples hot, or warm, dusted with a little caster sugar.

 1 hour,
plus chilling

 1¼ hours

Orange slices ambrosia

Serves 6
6 oranges
60 ml /4 tbls curaçao or Grand Marnier or Cointreau
30 ml /2 tbls lemon juice
For the garnish
100 g /4 oz small strawberries
60–90 ml /4–6 tbls long shredded coconut

1   Peel the skin and pith from the oranges and slice them, removing the pips. Arrange the orange slices in a large, shallow bowl and pour the curaçao or Grand Marnier or Cointreau over them. Add the lemon juice. Chill overnight.
2   When ready to serve, arrange the orange slices on individual serving dishes and pour the steeping juices over them. Hull the strawberries and use them to garnish the dishes. Arrange the long shredded coconut in a clump in the centre of each or sprinkle it over each serving.

Peaches with fresh raspberry sauce

Serves 4–6
225 g /8 oz sugar
1 strip of orange peel
a pinch of cinnamon
5 ml /1 tsp lemon juice
4–6 large, ripe peaches
600 ml /1 pt vanilla ice cream
425 ml /15 fl oz thick cream, whipped, to decorate
slivered toasted almonds, to decorate
Almond butter biscuits, to serve (see page 89)
For the fresh raspberry sauce
500 g /1 lb fresh raspberries
30–45 ml /2–3 tbls lemon juice
30–45 ml /2–3 tbls icing sugar

1   Put the sugar, orange peel and 275 ml /10 fl oz water in a pan. Boil for 2 minutes to make a syrup, then flavour it to taste with cinnamon and lemon juice.
2   Add the peaches and gently poach them, uncovered, until they are tender — about 10–15 minutes.
3   While the peaches are still hot, remove them, one at a time, from the syrup with a slotted spoon. Then, holding each peach in a clean tea-towel so that you do not burn your hands, peel the skin off each peach with a sharp knife or your fingers, taking care not to bruise or crush the flesh.
4   Return the peeled peaches to the syrup to cool, then chill them until ready to serve.
5   To make the fresh raspberry sauce, wash the raspberries if necessary, then drain and purée them until smooth in an electric blender. Pass the purée through a fine sieve. Add the lemon juice and icing sugar, mixing them together well. Chill until needed.
6   When ready to serve, place a portion of the vanilla ice cream in a sorbet cup or sundae glass. Place a poached peach on top of the ice cream and spoon over some fresh raspberry sauce. Decorate with swirls of whipped cream and slivered toasted almonds. Serve accompanied by the remaining cream in a small bowl or jug and Almond butter biscuits.

 10 minutes,
plus overnight chilling

 35 minutes,
plus chilling

Ananas sabayon

Serves 8

1 large pineapple
125 g /4 oz strawberries, halved
30 ml /2 tbls kirsch
For the pineapple sabayon
4 egg yolks

175 ml /6 fl oz dry white wine
75 g /3 oz sugar
30 ml /2 tbls kirsch
225 ml /8 fl oz thick cream,
*   whipped*

1 Cut a thin slice from the base of the pineapple to ensure that it stands up firmly. Place the pineapple on a large, flat dish.
2 With 6 wooden cocktail sticks, mark 6 equidistant points around the circumference of the pineapple, 15 mm /½ in from the top. Tie a piece of string around the pineapple 4 cm /1½ in below the cocktail sticks. Place another cocktail stick opposite one of the sticks in the top row, about 15 mm /½ in below it. Distinguish these two cocktail sticks from the others by bending the ends. Matching up these two will indicate where the lid should be replaced.
3 Use another cocktail stick and the string as a guide to cut 6 'V's: with the cocktail stick, mark a spot on the string line equidistant between two of the top-row cocktail sticks. With a sharp knife, cut from the top cocktail stick down to the one on the string, then back up to the third cocktail stick, forming a 'V'. Repeat this around the pineapple, moving the cocktail stick along the string. Cut deeply towards the centre of the pineapple each time, so that when you have made the 6 'V's the top of the pineapple will lift off completely. Remove the string and all the cocktail sticks except the 2 markers.
4 Using a sawing action, release the flesh by cutting around it, 5 mm /¼ in inside the pineapple skin. Cut from the centres of the 'V's down to within 5 mm /¼ in of the bottom of the pineapple. Remove the flesh without damaging the skin. Reserve the juice and the flesh.
5 Re-form the pineapple skin and tie it back into shape with string.
6 Cut the reserved pineapple flesh into 15 mm /½ in cubes. Place them in a bowl with the strawberries and macerate in the kirsch.
7 To make the sabayon, beat the egg yolks, dry white wine and sugar in a heavy-based saucepan over a low heat until the mixture becomes yellow and frothy. Add the kirsch and pineapple juice; remove the pan from the heat and whisk the mixture until cool. In a bowl, whisk the cream until stiff and fold it into the sabayon mixture. Refrigerate until ready to use.
8 Just before serving, put the macerated fruit into the hollowed-out pineapple, replace the lid, remove the markers and cut the string. At the table, remove the lid so the pineapple skin falls away from the macerated fruit. Serve the pineapple sabayon separately.

 1 hour,
plus chilling

Strawberries in orange juice

Serves 6

700 g /1½ lb small strawberries
juice of 2 oranges, strained
sifted icing sugar
thick cream, to serve

1 Hull the strawberries. Put them in a bowl with the strained orange juice and sifted icing sugar to taste, and toss lightly. Chill them in the refrigerator, covered, for at least 1 hour.
2 Serve the strawberries and juice in individual bowls, with a little thick cream.

● If you are able to get wild strawberries, they are the best type to use for this dish.
● Strawberries are available, at a price, throughout the year. Though plump, mild, summer strawberries may be full of flavour when served on their own or with sugar and cream, out-of-season strawberries often need a little help. Orange juice brings out the flavour of the strawberries marvellously.

10 minutes,
plus chilling

Italian pears

Serves 4
75 g /3 oz sugar
120 ml /8 tbls rum
4 large, firm pears
a few drops of red food colouring
50 g /2 oz ground almonds
50 g /2 oz icing sugar, sifted
2 drops of almond essence
1 egg yolk
50 g /2 oz fine cake crumbs
4 whole cloves

1 In a large saucepan, combine 600 ml /1 pt water, the sugar and 60 ml /4 tbls rum. Bring to the boil and simmer for 5 minutes.
2 Peel the pears, cut them in half and carefully remove the cores with a teaspoon. Put the pear halves into the rum syrup and poach them for 10–15 minutes or until they are tender, turning them carefully with a spatula once during cooking. Remove the pears with a slotted spoon and leave them until cold.
4 Add the remaining rum to the syrup and boil it rapidly for 7–10 minutes or until the liquid is reduced to half the original quantity. Add a few drops of red food colouring to colour it a pastel pink. Leave it to cool.
5 A short while before serving, combine the ground almonds and sifted icing sugar in a small bowl. With a wooden spoon, mix in the almond essence and egg yolk. Beat until smooth. Divide into 4 equal balls and flatten each ball until it is pear-shaped but slightly smaller than the pear itself. Place each ball between 2 cold pear halves and squeeze together gently to form a whole pear.
6 Sprinkle the cake crumbs onto a plate and roll each pear in the crumbs to coat, shaking off the excess. Stud a whole clove into the top of each pear for a 'stalk'.
7 Pour the cold rum syrup onto 4 individual serving plates to cover the base. Stand a pear upright in the centre. Serve immediately.

 25 minutes, plus cooling, then 15 minutes

Rhubarb fritters

Serves 4
700 g /1½ lb small rhubarb stalks
150 g /5 oz soft brown sugar
oil, for deep frying
caster sugar, to serve
For the fritter batter
100 g /4 oz flour
salt
30 ml /2 tbls caster sugar
2 eggs, separated
15 ml /1 tbls olive oil
150 ml /5 fl oz milk

1 Wipe the rhubarb stalks with a damp cloth and slice away any woody ends if necessary. Cut each stalk into 5 cm /2 in lengths.
2 Transfer the sliced rhubarb to a heavy-based saucepan with the brown sugar. Heat gently, until the rhubarb gives off some juice, then simmer it for 4 minutes, shaking the pan constantly. Do not overcook; the rhubarb must remain firm. Leave the rhubarb to get cold in the cooking juices.
3 Meanwhile, prepare the fritter batter. Sift the flour and a pinch of salt into a bowl, then stir in the caster sugar. Make a well in the centre and add the egg yolks, the olive oil and a little of the milk. Using a wooden spoon, gradually work in the flour and beat until the mixture becomes smooth, gradually adding the remaining milk. Leave to stand until the rhubarb is cold.
4 Lift the rhubarb out of its juices with a slotted spoon, then drain it on absorbent paper. Discard the juices or reserve them for use in another recipe (see note below).
5 In a clean, dry bowl, whisk the egg whites with a pinch of salt until they become stiff but not dry. With a large metal spoon, fold them into the batter.
6 Heat the oil in a deep-fat frier to 190C /375F; at this temperature a bread cube browns in 50 seconds.
7 Working in small batches, coat each piece of rhubarb with the batter, allowing the excess to drip back into the bowl.
8 Deep fry for 2–3 minutes, or until puffed and golden brown, turning the fritters over occasionally. Remove them with the slotted spoon and drain them well on absorbent paper. Transfer them to a heated serving dish. Dust generously with caster sugar.

● The rhubarb juices can be used for sweetening natural yoghurt.

about 30 minutes, plus cooling

Glazed fruit bande

Serves 4–6

1 × shortcrust pastry base
  (see page 58)
For the crème pâtissière
100 g /4 oz caster sugar
50 g /2 oz cornflour
575 ml /1 pt milk
6 medium-sized egg yolks
2.5 ml /½ tsp vanilla essence
5 ml /1 tsp kirsch

For the fruit topping
1 small eating apple, thinly sliced
juice of ½ lemon
1 banana
black grapes, halved and seeded
hulled strawberries, raspberries,
  sliced peaches or other soft fruit
For the apricot glaze
45 ml /3 tbls apricot jam, sieved
2.5 ml /½ tsp kirsch

1 Heat the oven to 200C /400F /gas 6. Place a baking sheet in the centre of the oven. Roll out the pastry large enough to line the sides and base of a shallow, 35 × 10 cm /14 × 4 tin or one 23 × 18 cm /9 × 7 in. Now transfer the pastry, rolled around the rolling pin, to the tin. Fit the pastry into the tin. Prick the base with a fork. Refrigerate for 30 minutes.
2 Meanwhile, make the crème pâtissière. Mix the sugar and cornflour in a bowl and blend to a smooth paste with a little cold milk. Warm the remaining milk in a saucepan. Stir this into the cornflour paste and beat vigorously. Return the mixture to the pan and bring to the boil, stirring constantly. Boil for 1 minute.
3 Beat the egg yolks lightly in the top of a double boiler, then beat in a little of the thick white sauce and mix well. Pour in the remaining sauce and cook over hot water, stirring, until the mixture is smooth and thick — this takes about 20 minutes. Strain into a bowl and leave to cool. Flavour with vanilla essence and kirsch. Cover with waxed paper and chill in the refrigerator until quite firm.
4 Line the pastry with foil and beans and bake it for 10 minutes. Lift out the foil and beans, reduce the heat to 180C /350F /gas 4 and bake the pastry until it is crisp — 10–15 minutes more. Remove it from the oven and leave it to cool.
5 When the pastry is cold, spread it with the crème pâtissière, then return it to the refrigerator to chill.
6 Not more than 3 hours before serving, prepare the fruit. Put the apple slices into a bowl of water which has some of the lemon juice added, to prevent the apple slices turning brown. Slice the banana and brush with lemon juice as well.
7 Make the apricot glaze. Melt the sieved jam with 15 ml /1 tbls water over a low heat. Cool slightly, then stir in the kirsch.
8 Arrange the fruit in rows on the pastry spread with the crème pâtissière. Brush the fruit with the apricot glaze. Serve at once.

 1 hour 10 minutes

Florentine apples

Serves 4

4 cooking apples
175 g /6 oz softened butter, plus extra for greasing
225 g /8 oz light brown sugar
finely grated zest of 1 large lemon
60 ml /4 tbls finely chopped almonds
zest of ½ orange, thinly sliced
chilled whipped cream, to serve

1 Heat the oven to 180C /350F /gas 4. Wash, dry and core the apples. With a sharp knife, enlarge the cavity in each apple to 2.5–4 cm /1–2 in diameter.
2 Lightly butter a baking dish large enough to hold the apples side by side.
3 In a mixing bowl, cream together the softened butter with the brown sugar; stir in the grated lemon zest and the finely chopped almonds. Use some of the mixture to fill the apple cavities. Arrange the apples in the prepared baking dish and pile the remaining butter and sugar mixture over the top of each individual apple. Scatter half the orange zest over the top.
4 Bake for 35–40 minutes, or until the apples are soft but not disintegrating and the butter and sugar mixture has melted down the sides and caramelized.
5 Serve the apples lukewarm, topped with chilled whipped cream and decorated with the remaining thinly sliced orange zest.

 1 hour

Peach amaretti

Serves 8
8 firm peaches
275 ml /10 fl oz thick cream, whipped and chilled
75 g /3 oz amaretti (small Italian macaroons), crumbled, plus extra
*   for serving*
For the crème pâtissière
575 ml /1 pt milk
5 cm /2 in piece vanilla pod, split
50 g /2 oz cornflour
60 ml /4 tbls caster sugar
4 egg yolks
15 g /½ oz butter
60 ml /4 tbls Amaretto di Saronno liqueur

1 Make the crème pâtissière. Put the milk and the split vanilla pod into a heavy-based saucepan and bring to boiling point. Remove it from the heat, cover and leave to infuse for 10–15 minutes.
2 In a large bowl, mix the cornflour and caster sugar. Add the egg yolks and whisk the mixture until pale and thick.
3 Remove the vanilla pod from the milk and pour the milk in a thin stream onto the egg and sugar mixture, whisking until blended.
4 Return the mixture to a clean saucepan. Bring it to the boil over a medium heat, stirring constantly. Simmer the custard for 3 minutes, beating vigorously.
5 Remove it from the heat and beat in the butter. Strain the crème pâtissière through a fine sieve into a bowl. Cover it with buttered greaseproof paper to prevent a skin forming, and leave it until cold.
6 Mix the Amaretto liqueur into the crème pâtissière when it is cold and set it aside until required.
7 Put the peaches in a bowl and pour boiling water over them to cover. Leave them for about 30 seconds, then drain and slip the skins off the peaches. Slice the peaches in half and remove the stones.
8 Gently fold the whipped, chilled cream into the cold crème pâtissière.
9 To assemble, place 2 peach halves on each plate. Top with the Amaretto-flavoured crème pâtissière and sprinkle crumbled amaretti biscuits over the top. Serve with extra amaretti biscuits.

● This dessert can also be made with large, canned peaches if they are well drained.

    25 minutes,
    plus cooling

Pineapple Romanoff

Serves 4–6
1 medium-sized ripe pineapple
30–45 ml /2–3 tbls icing sugar
30–45 ml /2–3 tbls Cointreau
30–45 ml /2–3 tbls rum
200 ml /8 fl oz thick cream
30–45 ml /2–3 tbls kirsch
finely grated zest of 1 orange
To garnish
orange slices
maraschino cherries

1 To prepare the pineapple shell, slice off the top of the pineapple and reserve it. With a sharp knife, carefully cut down the sides of the pineapple, about 12 mm /½ in inside the pineapple skin, being careful not to pierce the skin.
2 Now, with the point of the knife, cut into the pineapple, from the outside, in 2 places 25 mm /1 in from the bottom of the shell and loosen the central core so you can remove the pineapple flesh in one piece. Do this by pushing the knife blade into the pineapple from these 2 small slits, being careful not to increase the size of the slits. Work the knife to the left and right; try not to pierce the shell anywhere else.
3 Slice the pineapple flesh into 8–12 slices. Cut out the core from each slice and cut each slice into even-sized segments.
4 Toss the pineapple segments in the icing sugar, then arrange the segments in a bowl and pour over them a mixture of Cointreau and rum. Chill the fruit and the pineapple shell in the refrigerator.
5 One hour before serving, whip the cream and flavour it with kirsch. Keep it cold until you are ready to serve it.
6 Just before serving, spoon the whipped cream into the marinated pineapple pieces, tossing them until every piece is coated with the creamy liqueur mixture. Taste and add a little more icing sugar, if desired. Pile the pineapple mixture into the prepared pineapple shell. Top it with finely grated orange zest and replace the pineapple top. Arrange the orange slices and maraschino cherries attractively around the pineapple.

● The Romanoffs, after whom this dish is named, were the imperial family that ruled Russia from 1613 until 1917.

    20 minutes, plus chilling,
    then 5 minutes, plus chilling

Vanilla and raspberry brioches

Serves 6

275 ml /10 fl oz vanilla ice cream
6 individual small brioches
125 ml /4 fl oz thick cream
30–45 ml /2–3 tbls rum
100 g /4 oz raspberries

For the raspberry sauce
350 g /12 oz raspberries
60 ml /4 tbls icing sugar, sifted
30 ml /2 tbls crème de cassis
15 ml /1 tbls lemon juice

1 To make the raspberry sauce, place the raspberries in a blender and purée them. Press the purée through a sieve to remove the pips. Stir in the sifted icing sugar, crème de cassis and lemon juice. Chill.
2 About 30 minutes before serving, transfer the vanilla ice cream to the main part of the refrigerator, to soften slightly.
3 Using a sharp knife, cut the top off each brioche and hollow out the inside. Discard the inside or reserve it for another recipe. Arrange the brioches on a serving plate.
4 Whisk the thick cream until firm, add rum to taste and whisk it again until the cream holds up in stiff peaks. Fit a piping bag with a 15 mm /½ in star nozzle and spoon in the cream.
5 Using an ice-cream scoop, scoop one ball of vanilla ice cream into each brioche. Top each one with fresh raspberries.
6 Pipe the whipped cream in a shell design around the vanilla ice cream balls and raspberries. Replace the lids at an angle on the top. Serve immediately, accompanied by the chilled, fresh raspberry sauce.

● If brioches are unobtainable, shortcrust pastry tartlets 10 cm /4 in in diameter can be used instead.
● Try this recipe with sliced fresh peaches or strawberries, which are also delicious with fresh raspberry sauce.

 40 minutes,
including chilling

English spring pudding

Serves 6

1.1 kg /2½ lb young rhubarb
juice of 1 lemon
150 g /5 oz soft, light brown sugar
a few drops of red food colouring
8 slices white bread, crusts removed
butter, for greasing

For the English custard
950 ml /1½ pt milk
5 cm /2 in piece of vanilla pod, split
90–120 ml /6–8 tbls caster sugar
10 ml /2 tsp cornflour
6 egg yolks

1 Cut off the thick ends and the leaves of the rhubarb. Wash and slice the rhubarb stalks into 5 cm /2 in pieces. Place it in a large saucepan with the lemon juice, brown sugar, red food colouring and 60 ml /4 tbls water. Simmer over a gentle heat, turning the rhubarb occasionally, for 25–30 minutes, or until tender.
2 Strain the rhubarb and cool it, reserving the liquid.
3 Cut 4 bread slices into 2 strips each and arrange the strips around the sides of a well-buttered 1.7 L /3 pt charlotte mould.
4 Cut 2 slices of bread in half to form 4 triangles to fit the base of the charlotte mould. Fit them into the mould, trimming them, if necessary.
5 Press the rhubarb firmly into the bread-lined charlotte mould. Pour enough of the reserved liquid onto the rhubarb to soak the bread down the sides of the charlotte mould.
6 Cut the remaining 2 slices of bread in half to form 4 triangles to fit the top of the charlotte mould and press gently into place. Chill until quite firm.
7 To make the English custard, pour the milk into a saucepan, add the split vanilla pod. Scald the milk, remove the pan from the heat, cover it and leave it to infuse for 10 minutes.
8 Mix together the sugar and cornflour and add the egg yolks. Whisk the ingredients together until they are pale and creamy. Add the hot milk in a stream, whisking continuously.
9 Put the egg mixture in the top pan of a double boiler over simmering water and cook for 10 minutes, stirring all the time. When the custard has thickened sufficiently, remove it from the heat and then plunge the base of the saucepan into cold water to stop the cooking process.
10 Strain the custard through a fine sieve into a bowl. Keep warm.
11 Carefully unmould the pudding onto a serving platter and pour some custard over it. Serve accompanied by the rest of the custard.

 55 minutes, plus cooling,
chilling and making the custard

A Slice of Sweetness

CHEESECAKES

Slice into a satisfying, smooth, thick cheesecake for your dessert. Here I provide an exciting range of recipes from several different countries and a variety of toppings and a selection of bases.

Whilst often thought of as a modern recipe, in actual fact cheesecake has a long history. It is said to have been one of Socrates' favourite desserts, and it certainly figures strongly in traditional Russian and Eastern European cookery. Nowadays cheesecake seems to be popular worldwide.

The ingredients for a traditional cheesecake are fresh, unripened cheeses, enriched with eggs and extra cream, and flavoured or scented with dried or fresh fruit, lemon, vanilla and spices. The exception in this chapter is the recipe for the unusual Wilfra cheesecakes which do not actually contain cheese in the ingredients. They may have got their name from the fact that the eggs set the milk in a curd.

Types of cheesecake

There are two basic kinds of cheesecake: the European cooked cheesecake, often baked in a pastry case of some kind, and the American-inspired 'uncooked' cheesecake, which relies on gelatine instead of flour and/or eggs to set it. The latter often has a shell or a base of crushed biscuits mixed together with butter, replacing the traditional pastry case.

An example of the former type of cheesecake is the Viennese cheesecake, the recipe for which is included here. It certainly lives up to the Austrians' reputation for being discriminating cake- and pastry-eaters. Made with a traditional shortcrust pastry base, the filling includes curd cheese, dried fruit, lemon and vanilla. Pear and cottage cheese cake is a biscuit-base cheesecake. Made with firm, ripe pears, ratafia liqueur and kiwi fruit, it is moist and fresh tasting.

Store-cupboard lemon cheesecake, made with commercial jelly tablets, is one of the simplest 'uncooked' cheesecakes to make. Chocolate-cherry cheesecake is another, but it is richer to the taste and is impressively decorated with chocolate curls and luscious, stoned black cherries.

Suitable cheeses

The cheeses used for cheesecakes are curd cheese, cream cheese or cottage cheese.

Curd cheese is my favourite; it has the most pronounced cheese flavour of the three and is made from full-cream milk. This unripened cheese has a slightly granular texture and is often sieved or whisked before use to make it smooth. It contains more moisture than is desirable for a cheesecake, so to correct this, wrap the cheese tightly in a double thickness of muslin; shape it into a ball and leave it to drain overnight with a heavy weight on top. You will be surprised at the amount of moisture this forces out. The following day, finish the operation by twisting the ends of the muslin and squeezing the ball of cheese until no more beads of moisture spring to the surface. For some recipes the moisture content is less important and you can just squeeze the cheese, without the overnight draining.

Cream cheese: this is also an unripened cheese, made from full milk with extra cream added to increase the fat content. Some brands have thick cream added, giving the maximum fat content; these are known as full-fat cream cheeses and are the type used in my recipes. Medium-fat cream cheeses have thin cream added, which of course is not so rich and will give a different texture to the finished cheesecake. Cream cheese is less tasty than curd cheese, but gives a cheesecake with a superb texture.

Cottage cheese: this is often made from skimmed milk, so it is a low-fat product. The simplest type of cheese made, the flavour is very mild and the texture very light. Cottage cheese is lumpy so will always need sieving or beating before using in cheesecake. Often cottage cheese is used with cream cheese to lighten the mixture.

Combining the ingredients

Coming from old recipes, most cheesecakes can be made by simply beating the ingredients together with a wooden spoon. But, as with so many foods, an electric whisk, mixer or food processor makes it easier and gives a smoother, lighter result.

Making the tart case

I always use my favourite shortcrust pastry recipe (see page 58) when I need a pastry base for cheesecakes, but a cheesecake is usually deeper than a normal tart, so I make it in a spring-release cake tin or a cake tin with a removable bottom. To line a deep tin like this, it is easiest to do it in two operations — roll out the pastry and cut a disc to fit the base, then cut a strip of the appropriate depth to make the side of the case. Use beaten egg to join the strip and also to make it adhere to the base.

If the case is a crumbly biscuit shell you may find it easier to lift the shell out if you first line the tin with cling film (yes, you can put it in the oven without it melting). You can then lift the case free of the tin with the help of the cling film.

Baking cheesecakes

Most cooked cheesecakes are baked at a moderate temperature. This gives them a smooth, uncurdled texture and stops them cracking on the surface. It also prevents the cake from rising excessively, which usually results in it sinking in the middle as it cools. A tiny amount of flour in the cheese mixture helps to prevent this by strengthening the structure of the cake, but, basically, controlled heat is the answer.

If a cheesecake persists in sinking, it may be that the cheese has not been drained well enough and the raw mixture was too wet for the eggs and flour to set it firmly.

Serving cheesecakes

Like most cakes, cheesecakes are best eaten the day they are made. If, however, you are

Pear and cottage cheese cake

keeping them overnight, then put them in the refrigerator until they are needed, but serve your baked cheesecakes at room temperature. Uncooked, gelatine-set cheesecakes may be served while still lightly chilled.

Pear and cottage cheese cake

1 hour 20 minutes, plus cooling

Serves 6–8
225 g /8 oz sugar
6 firm, ripe pears
25 g /1 oz raisins
25 g /1 oz sultanas
225 g /8 oz plain, sweet biscuits
75 g /3 oz butter, softened
225 g /8 oz cottage cheese
50 g /2 oz caster sugar
3 egg yolks, beaten
juice and grated zest of ½ lemon
15 ml /1 tbls ratafia liqueur (optional)
4 kiwi fruit
5 ml /1 tsp cornflour

1 Put the sugar in a saucepan with 425 ml / 15 fl oz cold water; stir it over a gentle heat until the sugar is dissolved. Bring it to the boil. Peel and core the pears and place them in the syrup. Reduce the heat and simmer the pears for 10 minutes until they are soft but still firm. Drain the pears, reserving the liquid.
2 Put the raisins and sultanas in a bowl and cover them with hot water. Leave them to swell while you continue the preparation.
3 Heat the oven to 190C /375F /gas 5. Crush the biscuits to fine crumbs and add the softened butter. Line a 19 cm /7½ in sandwich tin with cling film and line the base and sides with the biscuit mixture.
4 Reserve 3 poached pears for the decoration. Slice enough pear to cover the base of the lined tin and dice the remainder.
5 Whisk the cottage cheese with the drained raisins and sultanas, the caster sugar, egg yolks, lemon zest and juice and ratafia, if using, until well mixed. Fold in the diced pears and fill the biscuit and pear-lined tin with the mixture. Bake in the oven for 25 minutes. Remove and leave to become cold.
6 Slice the 3 reserved pears and the kiwi fruit. When the cheesecake is cold, decorate the top with a thin layer of pear slices interspersed with kiwi fruit in overlapping circles. In the centre, place 4 overlapping slices of kiwi fruit to finish the decoration.
7 Boil the poaching liquid until it is reduced to 150 ml /5 fl oz. Mix 5 ml /1 tsp cornflour with 5 ml /1 tsp water and stir it into the syrup. Boil, stirring constantly, for 1–2 minutes or until the glaze has thickened. Allow the glaze to cool and then spoon it over the decorated cheesecake. Serve the pear and cottage cheese cake cold.

Viennese cheesecake

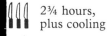
2¾ hours, plus cooling

Viennese cheesecake

Serves 8
25 g /1 oz flour, plus extra for dusting
½ × Shortcrust pastry (see page 58)
500 g /1 lb curd cheese
125 g /4 oz butter, softened
4 eggs, separated
150 g /5 oz icing sugar, sifted
juice and finely grated zest of 1 lemon
2.5 ml /½ tsp vanilla essence
25 g /1 oz raisins or coarsely chopped sultanas
25 g /1 oz chopped candied peel
sifted icing sugar, to decorate

1 Heat the oven to 200C /400F /gas 6.
2 Flour a board and rolling pin lightly and roll the pastry out to approximately 3 mm /⅛ in thick.
3 Line the base and sides of a 22 cm / 8½ in spring-release cake tin, leaving a 15 mm /½ in border at the top. Flute the top edge and prick the base all over with a fork. Cover the pastry with a sheet of greaseproof paper and weight it down with dried beans. Chill the pastry case in the refrigerator for at least 30 minutes to allow the uncooked pastry to relax.
4 Put the lined tin in the oven and bake blind for 10 minutes. Then remove the beans and paper, reduce the oven temperature to 180C /350F /gas 4 and continue to bake the case for 10 minutes longer, or until the pastry is both cooked through and lightly coloured.
5 Remove the pastry from the oven and leave it to cool. Raise the oven temperature to 190C /375F /gas 5.
6 Squeeze out as much moisture from the cheese as possible. Wrap the cheese in a double thickness of muslin, twist the ends of the cloth as hard as you can and squeeze the ball of cheese between your hands until the milky liquid stops oozing out of it.
7 Whisk the softened butter until it is light and fluffy.
8 Add the egg yolks, the sifted icing sugar and the curd cheese alternately to the butter, a little at a time, whisking the mixture between each addition. Next, continue to whisk until the mixture is blended.
9 Sharpen the flavour of the cheese mixture with the lemon juice and grated zest and add vanilla to taste, bearing in mind that the flavours are weakened as the cheesecake cooks. It should be rather lemony.
10 Sift the flour over the raisins or sultanas and candied peel. Toss the fruit and peel to coat them thoroughly and fold them into the cheese mixture.
11 Whisk the egg whites until they are stiff but not dry. With a large metal spoon, fold them gently into the cheese mixture.
12 Fill the pastry case with the cheese mixture, piling it up in the centre, as this part will sink slightly when the cake cooks.
13 Bake it for 50–55 minutes until it is firm in the centre and evenly risen. Remove it from the oven and cool it in the tin before unmoulding it carefully onto a serving dish. To decorate the cheesecake, lightly sift icing sugar over the top.

Store-cupboard lemon cheesecake

This easy-to-make cheesecake uses two commercial jelly tablets for setting. Use a bought sponge cake for convenience. Serve this dessert with a jug of thick cream, for a touch of luxury.

🍴 1 hour,
plus cooling and chilling

Serves 10–12
2 tablets lemon jelly
3 eggs, separated
150 ml /5 fl oz milk
grated zest and juice of 2 lemons
25 g/1 oz caster sugar
17.5 cm /7 in bought. whisked sponge cake
450 g /1 lb cream cheese
150 ml /5 fl oz thick cream
icing sugar, to dust

Store-cupboard lemon cheesecake

1 Cut the jelly tablets into small pieces and place them in a saucepan with 60 ml /4 tbls of water. Place over a low heat and dissolve, stirring occasionally.
2 Beat the egg yolks with the milk. Take the jelly off the heat and stir in the egg and milk mixture. Return it to the heat for 2 minutes. Stir but do not allow it to boil.
3 Stir in the lemon zest, juice and sugar. Allow it to cool until on the point of setting.
4 Divide the sponge cake in half horizontally and place the bottom half in the base of a 17.5 cm /7 in spring-release cake tin.
5 Beat the cream cheese until it is smooth and beat in the jelly mixture a little at a time.
6 Lightly whip the cream and fold it into the jelly mixture. Whisk the egg whites until they stand in stiff peaks, then fold them into the jelly mixture, too.
7 Spoon the mixture on top of the cake in the tin. Level and top with the other cake half. Chill until firm.
8 Serve dusted with icing sugar.

● To make this cheesecake extra special, serve it with raspberries or strawberries.

Chocolate-cherry cheesecake

🕐🍴 1 hour 10 minutes,
plus overnight chilling

Serves 8–10
425 g /15 oz canned, stoned black cherries in syrup
350 g /12 oz full-fat soft cheese
75 g /3 oz caster sugar
2 medium-sized eggs, separated
15 ml /1 tbls kirsch
15 g /½ oz gelatine
300 ml /10 fl oz whipping cream or a combination of whipping and thick cream
15 ml /1 tbls arrowroot
kirsch or lemon juice, to taste
125 g /4 oz plain chocolate, to decorate
For the base
75 g /3 oz plain chocolate, broken up
65 g /2½ oz butter, plus extra for greasing
250 g /9 oz plain chocolate digestive biscuits, crumbled

1 First make the base. Line and grease the base of a 23 cm /9 in loose-bottomed cake tin. In a small saucepan, melt the chocolate and butter over low heat, then mix them with the biscuit crumbs.

2 Spread the mixture evenly over the base of the tin and press down well. Chill the biscuit base in the refrigerator while you make the filling.

3 Drain the cherries, reserving the syrup. Cut them in half and spread one-third of them over the crumb base. Reserve the rest.

4 In a large bowl, thoroughly cream together the cheese and sugar. Beat in the egg yolks and the kirsch.

5 Pour 30 ml /2 tbls cold water into a small, heatproof bowl and add the gelatine. Leave for a few minutes to soften, then stand the bowl in very hot water and stir until the gelatine dissolves. Leave it to cool slightly.

6 Whip the cream until it just holds soft peaks. Whisk the egg whites until they are stiff. Beat the gelatine mixture slowly into the cheese without letting lumps form. Fold in the cream, then the egg whites, using a metal spoon.

7 Turn the cheese mixture gently onto the chilled base and spread it evenly. Chill it for several hours or overnight.

8 Make a cherry sauce: blend the arrowroot to a cream with a little of the reserved syrup. Pour the remaining syrup into a pan, adding kirsch or lemon juice to taste. Bring it slowly to the boil, then stir in the arrowroot mixture. Continue stirring until the liquid thickens and clears. Remove the sauce from the heat and allow it to cool under a piece of damp greaseproof paper, which will prevent a skin forming.

9 Shortly before serving, remove the cheesecake from the tin and decorate it with a ring of the remaining halved cherries. Spoon a little of the sauce over them. Shave long, thin curls of chocolate off the block with a potato peeler or sharp knife and arrange the curls around the edge of the cake.

10 Serve the cheesecake with the rest of the cherry sauce in a sauce-boat.

New York cheesecake

This is a rich and elegant dessert. Made famous by Lindy's restaurant in New York's Times Square area, this particular style of cheesecake is thick, smooth and creamy. It is a good idea to make it a day ahead and chill it overnight, but you will also find it irresistibly delicious when still warm.

 10 minutes, chilling, then 2 hours baking and cooling

Serves 10–12
1 kg /2¼ lb Philadelphia cream cheese, at room temperature
150 g /5 oz sugar
45 ml /3 tbls flour
7.5 ml /1½ tsp grated lemon zest
a large pinch of the inside pulp of a vanilla bean or 1.5 ml /¼ tsp vanilla extract
5 eggs, plus 2 yolks
50 ml /2 fl oz thick cream

For the crust
100 g /4 oz sifted flour
50 g /2 oz sugar
5 ml /1 tsp grated lemon zest
a pinch of salt
a pinch of the inside pulp of a vanilla bean or 1.5 ml /¼ tsp vanilla extract
100 g /4 oz butter, diced, plus extra for greasing
1 medium-sized egg yolk, lightly beaten
25–35 ml /1–1½ fl oz cold milk

1 To make the crust, combine the flour, sugar, lemon zest, salt and vanilla in a bowl. Cut in the butter with a pastry blender or 2 knives until the mixture resembles oatmeal.

2 Stir in the egg yolk with a fork and then work in enough milk to form a soft dough. Wrap the dough in greaseproof paper and chill it for 1 hour.

3 Heat the oven to 225C /425F /gas 7. Roll out the pastry 3 mm /⅛ in thick and place it on the buttered base of a 25 cm /10 in spring-form cake tin with the sides removed. Bake it for 18 minutes, then set it aside to cool.

4 Turn up the oven to 230C /450F /gas 8. Mash the cream cheese with sugar, flour, lemon zest and vanilla in a very large bowl. With an electric beater, blend in the eggs and yolks, one a time, to create a thick, smooth mixture. Stir in the cream.

5 Butter the sides of the spring-form tin and set them in place around the base. Pour the cheese mixture onto the crust and bake it for 10 minutes.

6 Reduce the heat of the oven to 150C /300F /gas 2 and continue to cook the cheesecake for 45 minutes, or until the edges are golden brown and the centre is set.

7 Turn off the heat and let the cake cool in the oven for 1 hour. Then leave it, still in the tin, on a wire rack until cold. Chill it. To serve, run a knife around the sides and then

Chocolate-cherry cheesecake

release the spring. Serve the cheesecake on the tin base; cut out the portions with a serrated knife and serve immediately.

Wilfra cheesecakes

Wilfra week, celebrated at the beginning of August, commemorated the patron saint of Ripon, Yorkshire — St Wilfred. During the festivities women used to bake large quantities of these pastry tarts to hand out to passers-by to eat.

40 minutes

Makes 12
200 ml /7 fl oz milk
25 g /1 oz fresh breadcrumbs
1 × Shortcrust pastry (see page 58)
75 g /3 oz butter, softened, plus extra for greasing
20 g /¾ oz caster sugar
40 g /1½ oz ground almonds
finely grated zest of 1 small lemon
2 eggs, lightly beaten

1 Heat the oven to 180C /350F /gas 4. Bring the milk to boiling point; stir in the breadcrumbs. Allow to stand for 10 minutes.

2 Meanwhile, thinly roll out the pastry and use it to line 12 greased deep patty tins.

3 Mix together the butter, sugar, almonds and lemon zest. Add them to the milk mixture, together with the eggs, and beat them well with a wooden spoon.

4 Divide the filling among the pastry cases and bake them in the oven for 20–25 minutes, until the filling is golden brown. Serve warm or cold.

Apricot cheesecake

Canned apricots can be used here instead of dried, but if so, sharpen the flavour of the glaze with a little lemon juice.

overnight soaking,
then 2 hours, plus cooling

Serves 6–8
175 g /6 oz wholemeal biscuits
50 g /2 oz butter, softened
For the filling
225 g /8 oz dried apricots, soaked overnight
175 g /6 oz full-fat soft cream cheese
225 g /8 oz cottage cheese
60 ml /4 tbls caster sugar
5 ml /1 tsp vanilla essence
juice and grated zest of 1 lemon
2 egg yolks, beaten
15 g /½ oz gelatine
300 ml /10 fl oz thick cream, whipped
3 egg whites
For the topping
30 ml /2 tbls apricot jam, sieved
5 ml /1 tsp cornflour
400 g /14 oz canned apricot halves, drained

1   Heat the oven to 170C /325F /gas 3.
2   To make the crust, crush the biscuits to fine crumbs and combine them with the softened butter. Line a 22 cm /8½ in loose-bottomed cake tin with cling film. Press the mixture evenly over the base and up the sides. Bake for 10 minutes, remove the base from the oven and allow it to cool.
3   Put the soaked apricots and their juice in

Apricot cheesecake

a saucepan. Add extra water, if necessary, to cover and then cook them for 20 minutes or until tender. Drain, reserving the juices. Purée the apricots in a blender and press them through a sieve into a bowl. Leave the purée to become cold.
4   Combine the cheeses, sugar and vanilla essence in a large bowl. Add the lemon juice, grated lemon zest and beaten egg yolks and whisk until smooth.
5   In a small bowl, sprinkle the gelatine over 45 ml /3 tbls cold water and leave it to soften. Place the bowl in a saucepan of simmering water until the gelatine is completely dissolved. Leave it to cool slightly, then add it to the cheese mixture and blend.
6   With a large metal spoon, fold the whipped cream into the mixture, together with the apricot pulp. Whisk the egg whites until they are stiff but not dry and fold them gently into the cheese mixture.
7   Spoon the mixture over the crumb base and chill it in the refrigerator until set.
8   Remove the cheesecake carefully from the tin and place it on a serving platter.
9   Put 300 ml /10 fl oz of the strained apricot juice in a saucepan and boil for 10–15 minutes until it is reduced to half the original volume. Add the sieved apricot jam and stir until it is melted. Mix the cornflour with 5 ml /1 tsp cold water and add it to the syrup. Boil for 1–2 minutes or until the syrup has thickened. Allow it to cool slightly. In the meantime, arrange the apricot halves on top of the cheesecake and then glaze them with the tepid syrup. Serve chilled.

Strawberry cheesecake

1 hour,
plus setting

Serves 6–8
40 g /1½ oz butter, melted, plus extra for greasing
100 g /4 oz shortbread biscuits, finely crushed
225 g /8 oz strawberries, hulled
30 ml /2 tbls orange juice
grated zest of ½ orange
10 ml /2 tsp powdered gelatine
175 g /6 oz curd cheese
75 g /3 oz caster sugar
1–2 drops vanilla essence
30 ml /2 tbls yoghurt
150 ml /5 fl oz thick cream, lightly whipped
1 medium-sized egg white, stiffly whisked
halved strawberries, to decorate

1   Heat the oven to 180C /350F /gas 4. Lightly butter an 18 cm /7 in spring-form tin and reserve it while you prepare the base.
2   Add the crushed biscuits to the melted butter and stir until evenly coated. Spoon it into the tin and press it firmly and evenly over the base. Bake for 8–10 minutes until golden brown and then leave until it is cold.
3   Place the strawberries in a bowl and sprinkle them with the orange juice and orange zest. Using a fork, crush the mixture to a pulp. Set aside. Sprinkle the gelatine over 45 ml /3 tbls warm water in a small, heavy-based saucepan and leave it to soak.

4 Using a wooden spoon, beat the curd cheese until it is soft and smooth. Gradually beat into the curd cheese, the caster sugar, vanilla essence, yoghurt, whipped thick cream and pulped strawberries.

5 Set the soaked gelatine over a very low heat for 2–3 minutes until it is completely dissolved, then remove it from the heat. Stir a little of the curd cheese mixture into the dissolved gelatine, then pour onto the rest of the cheese mixture in the bowl, stirring constantly until it is well incorporated.

6 Allow the cheese mixture to stand for 5 minutes, then fold in the stiffly whisked egg white with a metal spoon. Turn the mixture onto the biscuit base inside the tin and gently tilt the tin to level the surface. Cover the cake loosely and refrigerate for 3–4 hours until the cheese mixture is set.

7 Just before serving, remove the sides of the tin and decorate the top of the cheesecake with halved strawberries.

Blackcurrant cheesecake

1 hour,
plus 1 hour setting

Blackcurrant cheesecake

Serves 6
200 g /7 oz digestive biscuits
75 g /3 oz butter
1.5 ml /¼ tsp vanilla essence
oil, for greasing
For the topping
375 g /12 oz canned blackcurrants in syrup
15 g /½ oz powdered gelatine
juice of ½ lemon
175 g /6 oz cream cheese
2 eggs, separated
50 g /2 oz caster sugar
200 ml /7 fl oz thick cream
10 ml /2 tsp arrowroot

1 Heat the oven to 200C /400F /gas 6. Put the biscuits between 2 pieces of greaseproof paper or in a polythene bag and crush them with a rolling pin. Put them in a bowl.

2 Melt the butter in a small saucepan and stir the crumbs into it, together with the vanilla essence.

3 Press the crumb mixture into the base of a deep 18 cm /7 in cake tin with a loose base. Bake the crumb case for 15 minutes and then leave until it is cold. Line the sides of the cake tin with greaseproof paper which has been oiled on both sides.

4 Drain the blackcurrants and reserve the syrup. Sprinkle the powdered gelatine over the lemon juice and 30 ml /2 tbls water in a small bowl and leave aside to soak.

5 Put the cream cheese in a bowl and beat in the egg yolks and caster sugar. When the mixture is smooth, gradually beat in the thick cream and 60 ml /4 tbls of the reserved blackcurrant syrup. Fold in half of the blackcurrants. Stiffly whip the egg whites and fold them into the mixture.

6 Set the bowl containing the gelatine over a saucepan of hot water on a low heat until the gelatine is melted. Stir it into the blackcurrant and cream mixture. Pour it onto the biscuit base in the cake tin and put it into the refrigerator to set.

7 Mix the arrowroot with 30 ml /2 tbls of the remaining blackcurrant syrup. Put the rest of the syrup into a saucepan and bring it to the boil. Add the arrowroot and cook it, stirring all the time, until the syrup is thick and transparent. Remove the pan from the heat and stir in the remaining blackcurrants. Leave it to cool.

8 Stand the cake tin on an upturned jam jar and slide away the ring. Transfer the cheesecake from the base of the tin to a serving plate. Carefully pour the thickened blackcurrant syrup evenly over the top of the cheesecake. Serve it chilled.

● Try this cheesecake for an attractive supper party dessert.
● Use ginger biscuits as a substitute for the digestive biscuit base.

Austrian cheesecake with cherry topping

Serves 8
100 g /4 oz wholemeal biscuits
25 g /1 oz unsalted butter,
* softened*
For the cheese filling
550 g /1¼ lb curd cheese
175 g /6 oz caster sugar
finely grated zest of 2 lemons
finely grated zest of 1 orange
3 medium-sized eggs, separated

22 ml /1½ tbls self-raising flour
60 ml /4 tbls thick cream
For the cherry topping
2 × 400 g /14 oz cans stoned, black
* cherries*
22 ml /1½ tbls cornflour
30 ml /2 tbls lemon juice
15 ml /1 tbls sugar
150 ml /5 fl oz thick cream,
* whipped*

1 Put the biscuits in a strong polythene bag and crush them with a rolling pin. Alternatively, crush them in a blender. Put the crushed biscuits in a bowl and work in the softened butter until it is thoroughly dispersed throughout the mixture.
2 Press the biscuit mixture evenly over the base of a loose-bottomed, 20 cm /8 in diameter cake tin. Heat the oven to 200C /400F /gas 6.
3 To make the cheese filling, put the curd cheese in a double thickness of muslin and squeeze it to extract the moisture.
4 Put the cheese in a bowl. Add the caster sugar and beat it until soft and creamy. Beat in the finely grated lemon and orange zests, then add the egg yolks, one at a time, beating well.
5 Sift the flour into the bowl, add the thick cream and mix gently, just enough to blend in the ingredients. Whisk the egg whites until they form stiff peaks and fold them into the mixture with a metal spoon. Spoon the cheese mixture over the prepared base.
6 Bake the cheesecake for 5 minutes, then reduce the heat to 140C / 275F /gas 1 and bake it for 1½ hours or a little longer, until the cake is an even, golden colour and feels firm when pressed in the centre.
7 Allow the cheesecake to cool in its tin. Chill it for 3 hours.
8 To decorate the cake, drain the canned cherries, reserving the syrup. Cover the top of the cheesecake with cherries, leaving a clear, thin border around the edge. Combine the reserved cherry syrup, cornflour, lemon juice and sugar in a saucepan and bring to the boil. Boil it for 2 minutes. Cool it for 2–3 minutes, then pour the cooled glaze over the cherries. Fit a piping bag with a size 8 star nozzle and fill the bag with whipped cream. Pipe the cream decoratively around the outer edges of the cheesecake. Refrigerate before serving.

 2 hours 20 minutes,
plus chilling and decorating

Chocolate cheesecake

Serves 6
150 g /5 oz chocolate-covered wheatmeal biscuits
45–60 ml /3–4 tbls melted butter
For the filling
75 g /3 oz plain chocolate
225 g /8 oz cream cheese
45 ml /3 tbls caster sugar
2 egg yolks, beaten
3 egg whites
150 ml /5 fl oz thick cream
For the decoration
50 g /2 oz plain or milk chocolate, grated

1 Heat the oven to 170C /325F /gas 3. Make the crust. To crush the biscuits finely, put them in a polythene bag and roll it with a rolling pin. Check with your fingers that there are no large pieces. Turn out the crumbs into a bowl and stir in the melted butter.
2 Press the mixture into the base of an 18 cm /7 in loose-bottomed cake tin. Bake in the oven for 10–15 minutes, then leave it to cool.
3 Meanwhile, make the filling: melt the chocolate in the top pan of a double boiler, then leave it to cool slightly. Put the cream cheese in a bowl and blend it with the caster sugar. Add the beaten egg yolks and the slightly cooled chocolate and beat them with a wooden spoon until the mixture is smooth.
4 Whisk the egg whites until stiff peaks form. Whisk the cream until it is thick and fold it into the cream cheese mixture using a large metal spoon. Gently fold in the whisked egg whites.
5 Spoon the mixture over the chocolate crumb crust and smooth the top with a palette knife. Chill it in the refrigerator until set.
6 Remove the cheesecake from the tin and slide it onto a serving plate. Decorate the rim with grated chocolate.

● Take care not to 'over fold' the whisked egg whites into the cheese mixture as this will prevent the mixture from setting.

 45 minutes,
plus chilling

Siphnos cheese and honey cake

Serves 8
25 g /8 oz flour
2.5 ml /½ tsp salt
225 ml /8 oz butter, chilled
For the filling
450 g /1 lb ricotta or curd cheese
4 medium-sized eggs
10 ml /2 tsp powdered cinnamon
125–150 ml /4–5 fl oz clear honey

1 To prepare the crust, first sift the flour and salt together. Cut the chilled butter into tiny pieces and drop them into the flour. Work the butter into the flour very lightly with your fingertips, or use a pastry blender. Gradually add just enough water to make the dough hold together in a soft ball — about 45 ml /3 tbls. Wrap the dough in cling film and chill for 30 minutes.
2 Heat the oven to 180C /350F /gas 4 and place a baking sheet on the top shelf. Press the dough into the sides and bottom of a 25 cm / 10 in flan dish with your hands and bake it on the hot baking sheet for 10 minutes.
3 In the meantime, make the filling. Mix together the cheese, eggs, 5 ml /1 tsp of the cinnamon and 125 ml /4 fl oz honey (add more honey if needed.) Blend well.
4 Cool the empty, baked shell before filling it or it will disintegrate. Turn the oven up to 190C /375F /gas 5. Pour the cheese mixture gently into the pastry case and place in the oven for 35 minutes or until the pie is firm and the top is golden. Dust the pie with the rest of the cinnamon and let it cool.

● This recipe comes from the Greek island of Siphnos. It uses, traditionally, *mizithra*, a soft cheese made from goat's milk.

45 minutes for making the pastry,
plus cooling, then 50 minutes

Cassata siciliana

Serves 8
400 g /14 oz ricotta cheese
175 g /6 oz caster sugar
200 g /7 oz crystallized fruit
a pinch of ground cinnamon
75 g /3 oz bitter chocolate, cut into small pieces
25 g /1 oz pistachio nuts, blanched, peeled and chopped
100 ml /4 fl oz Maraschino or another sweet liqueur
450 g /1 lb bought Madeira cake
non-toxic green leaves, to garnish
For the icing
600 g /1¼ lb icing sugar, sifted
15 ml /1 tbls lemon juice

1 Press the ricotta cheese through a fine-mesh sieve and set it to one side. Simmer the caster sugar and 150 ml /5 fl oz water in a heavy saucepan over a very low heat until the syrup is clear but not coloured. Do not stir the mixture during cooking.
2 Meanwhile, cut 100 g /4 oz of the crystallized fruit into small pieces, reserving the best pieces for decoration.
3 When the sugar has dissolved, pour it over the ricotta and stir it hard until the mixture is smooth. Add the cinnamon, chocolate, crystallized fruit, pistachios and half the liqueur and mix.
4 Line an 18 cm /7 in round cake tin with greaseproof paper. Cut the Madeira cake into thin slices and use these to line the bottom and the sides of the tin. Use the trimming to fill in any gaps. Moisten the cake by sprinkling some of the liqueur over it.
5 Spoon in the ricotta mixture and cover it with a layer of sliced cake. Moisten the top layer with the remaining liqueur. Cover it with cling film and chill for at least 3 hours.
6 To make the icing, melt the icing sugar with 100 ml /3½ fl oz water and the lemon juice in a heavy saucepan over a low heat. Do not let the icing get too hot. When it evenly coats the back of a spoon, turn out the cake onto a flat plate or cake board and pour the icing over the cake and allow it to run down the sides.
7 Put the cake back into the refrigerator to allow the icing to set. Decorate the cake with the reserved crystallized fruit and some non-toxic leaves. Serve chilled.

● This Sicilian dessert is sold throughout Italy. The genuine cassata has an outside layer of sponge cake and an inner one of cream cheese; it is chilled but not frozen.

1 hour,
plus 3 hours chilling

GATEAUX & CAKES

Cover and fill them with jams and creams, chocolate and fruit, and you'll have gateaux and cakes for every taste and occasion. Some of the recipes in this chapter are simpler than others, but they are all well worth making.

This chapter covers a wide range of cakes based on sponge or pastry recipes. They can be fairly elaborate, such as my Strawberry torte, or simpler like my Plum cake. Serve them at family lunches, formal dinner parties — and at any time when you want a treat.

Usually, when we think of gateaux, we think of beautifully decorated, creamy cakes, but I have also included recipes for Croquembouche and Profiteroles. Croquembouche, a spectacular mountain of choux pastry puffs, filled with a delicate crème pâtissière, is time-consuming to make, but prepared as a grand finale to a meal for a large number of people, the extra effort is well worthwhile. My recipe for Profiteroles is based on the same principles as the Croquembouche, but they are easier to make, and are better served at the end of a more intimate meal, or as a family dessert.

Of course, no chapter on cakes would be complete without chocolate gateaux, and I have included several of my favourite recipes for these, as well as recipes for savarins, delicious, fruit-filled, alcohol-soaked rings.

And last, but not least, why not try the Chocolate cherry roll or Mandarin roll — both guaranteed to satisfy the sweetest tooth!

Savarin with fruit and cream

🔪🔪🔪 3¼ hours, plus cooling, 2–3 hours soaking, then 1 hour

Serves 8
75 ml /3 fl oz milk
25 g /1 oz fresh yeast
50 g /2 oz sugar
25 g /1 oz butter, softened
2 eggs, beaten
225 g /8 oz strong flour
3 egg yolks
melted butter, for greasing
150 ml /5 fl oz thick cream, whipped
For the syrup
225 g /8 oz sugar
45 ml /3 tbls brandy
45 ml /3 tbls Cointreau
For the filling
1 banana, sliced
2 oranges, peeled and segmented
2 kiwi fruit, peeled and sliced
10 strawberries, hulled
10 white grapes, seeded
10 black grapes, seeded
For the glaze
90–120 ml /6–8 tbls apricot jam
15 ml /1 tbls lemon juice

1 In a pan, warm the milk until it is lukewarm (37C /99F), then crumble the yeast over the milk and stir until dissolved.
2 Put the milk mixture into a large bowl and add the sugar, the softened butter and the beaten eggs; sift in the flour. Mix well with one hand, then add the egg yolks and mix to form a soft dough. Cover it with cling film and leave in a warm place until it has doubled in size.
3 In the bowl, knead the savarin dough until it returns to its original size.
4 Brush a 1.6 L /2¾ pt savarin mould with the melted butter and fill it with the dough to one-third full. Cover it with cling film and leave it in a warm place to rise until the dough has filled the mould.
5 Heat the oven to 170C /325F /gas 3.
6 Bake the dough in the oven for 30–40 minutes or until it is golden brown.
7 Remove the savarin from the oven, allow it to stand for 5 minutes in the tin, then turn it onto a wire rack to cool to lukewarm.
8 To make the syrup, put the sugar in a saucepan with 300 ml /10 fl oz water, stir over a gentle heat until the sugar is dissolved, then bring it to the boil for 5 minutes. Remove and add the brandy and Cointreau.
9 Place the savarin on a flat serving dish, the right way up, and prick it all over with a fork. Spoon three-quarters of the warm syrup evenly over the savarin, then leave it for 2–3 hours. Let the remaining syrup cool.
10 Put the fruit in a bowl and pour the cooled syrup over it. Leave it to macerate.
11 To make the glaze, in a saucepan combine the apricot jam with 30 ml /2 tbls water and the lemon juice, and heat until the jam is melted. Bring it to the boil and then sieve it to remove any lumps from the jam. Brush the glaze evenly over the savarin.
12 Spoon the macerated fruit into the centre of the savarin; pipe the whipped cream decoratively around it and then serve.

Rum savarin

🍴🍴🍴 10 minutes, 3–4 hours rising, then 1½ hours

Serves 10–12
225 g /8 oz strong white flour, plus extra for dusting
a large pinch of salt
30 ml /2 tbls caster sugar
15 g /½ oz fresh yeast (see notes)
2 medium-sized eggs, beaten
50 g /2 oz unsalted butter, melted and slightly cooled, plus extra for greasing
For the rum syrup
225 g /8 oz sugar
125–150 ml /4–5 fl oz dark rum
For the glaze and filling
30 ml /2 tbls dark rum
45 ml /3 tbls apricot jam, sieved and dissolved in 15 ml /1 tbls boiling water
275 ml /10 fl oz thick cream, whipped
225 g /8 oz mixed fresh fruit or drained canned fruit, diced

1 Sieve the flour and salt into a large, warmed mixing bowl and stir in the sugar. Blend the yeast with 10 ml /2 tsp warm water and pour it onto the flour. Add the eggs and the butter and mix to form a soft, slightly sticky dough.
2 Turn the dough onto a very lightly floured surface and knead it vigorously for about 5 minutes, until it is smooth, elastic and no longer sticky. Shape the dough into a ball and return it to a clean, lightly floured mixing bowl. Cover the bowl with cling film or a clean, damp cloth and leave it in a warm place for 1½–2 hours, until the dough has doubled in bulk.
3 Knock back the risen dough and form it into a long sausage shape. Place the dough in a generously buttered 1.1 L /2 pt capacity metal savarin or ring tin. Lightly and evenly press the dough into the tin and seal the join. Cover it loosely with cling film or a clean, damp cloth and leave it in a warm place for 1½–2 hours until the dough has risen almost to the top of the tin.
4 Heat the oven to 190C /375F /gas 5. Bake the risen savarin for about 30 minutes, or until it is well browned and just shrinking from the sides of the tin. Cover it with foil for the last 10 minutes of baking to prevent the savarin from becoming over brown.
5 For the rum syrup, dissolve the sugar in 425 ml /15 fl oz water over a low heat. Then boil, without stirring, for 5 minutes. Remove it from the heat, allow the syrup to cool slightly, then stir in the rum.
6 Cool the baked savarin in the tin for 5 minutes, then turn it out onto a wire rack and prick it all over with a fork or a fine skewer. Place the savarin, rounded side up, in a large, fairly deep dish, and slowly pour the warm rum syrup over it. Leave it to soak for about 30 minutes, basting frequently, until all the syrup is absorbed.
7 Carefully transfer the savarin to a large serving plate. Sprinkle 30 ml /2 tbls rum over the top, boil the apricot glaze and brush it over the entire surface of the savarin. Spoon or pipe the whipped cream into the centre of the savarin and pipe a border around the base if wished. Arrange the fruit on top of the cream in the centre, to show each piece to its best advantage.

● Use 10 ml /2 tsp dried, active baking yeast instead of fresh yeast: dissolve a large pinch of caster sugar in 15 ml /1 tbls lukewarm (37C /99F) water, whisk in the dried yeast and leave it in a warm place for 10 minutes until the mixture becomes frothy; blend this mixture with the beaten eggs and pour it onto the sifted flour mixture with the melted butter.

● For a smaller savarin, use 1 sachet (7 g /¼ oz) 'easy blend' dried yeast instead of fresh yeast: stir the yeast into the sifted flour mixture; beat the eggs with 15 ml /1 tbls lukewarm (37C /99F) water and add to the flour with the butter. Use an 850 ml /1½ pt ring tin and bake in the oven for 20 minutes. To decorate, make the syrup with 100 g /4 oz sugar, 225 ml /8 fl oz water and 60 ml /4 tbls rum. Use 100 g /4 oz fruit and 150 ml /5 fl oz cream. This serves 6–8.

Savarin with fruit and cream

48

Profiteroles

‖ 2 hours,
including chilling

Serves 4
For the choux paste
50 g /2 oz butter, diced
65 g /2½ oz flour
5 ml /1 tsp sugar
2 eggs, beaten
a few drops of vanilla essence
275–425 ml /10–15 fl oz
thick cream, whipped
For the chocolate sauce
75 g /3 oz plain chocolate
10 ml /2 tsp cocoa powder
60 ml /4 tbls sugar
5 ml /1 tsp vanilla essence
2 egg yolks

1 Heat the oven to 220C /425F /gas 7, and butter a baking sheet. Sift the flour onto a sheet of greaseproof paper. Put the diced butter and the sugar in a small heavy saucepan, with 150 ml /5 fl oz water. Bring to the boil slowly.
2 When the liquid boils briskly, remove the pan from the heat. Quickly pour in the flour, all at once, and beat it vigorously.
3 Return the pan to a low heat and continue to beat the paste for 2 minutes, until it forms itself around the spoon in a smooth ball, leaving the bottom and sides of the pan clean. Remove from the heat.
4 Add the beaten eggs, a little at a time, beating vigorously. Continue to beat until the paste is glossy. Beat in a few drops of vanilla essence.
5 Stand a piping bag fitted with a large plain nozzle in a tall tumbler, and fold back the bag top: like this, it is easier to spoon in the paste. Pipe walnut-sized puffs onto the greased baking sheet.
6 Bake in the oven for 10 minutes, then remove the tray from the oven and reduce the heat to 190C /375F /gas 5. Pierce each profiterole in the side with a knife, return them to the oven and bake them for a further 10 minutes or until they are firm and dry. Leave them to cool on a wire rack.
7 Meanwhile, make the chocolate sauce. Break the chocolate into a heavy-based saucepan. Measure 150 ml /5 fl oz water. Blend the cocoa powder with 30 ml /2 tbls water from the measured amount, and add this to the chocolate, together with the sugar and the remaining water. Bring to the boil, stirring with a wooden spoon until well blended. Boil, stirring occasionally, for about 15 minutes or until the mixture becomes thick and syrupy. Remove the chocolate mixture from the heat and leave it to cool slightly. Whisk the vanilla essence and the egg yolks into the chocolate mixture, then cool and chill the sauce.
8 Split the cold profiteroles almost in half. Using a piping bag fitted with a large star nozzle, pipe the whipped thick cream into them. Arrange the filled profiteroles on top of each other on a large serving plate, and pour some of the chilled chocolate sauce over them. Serve the remaining sauce separately in a jug. Serve immediately.

Croquembouche

⏲‖‖ 4½ hours,
plus cooling and chilling

Serves 20–25
½ × Shortcrust pastry (see page 58 for
ingredients and method)
flour, for dusting
2 × Choux paste (see previous recipe for
ingredients and method)
For the crème pâtissière
775 ml /1 pt 8 fl oz milk
a piece of vanilla pod, 5 cm /2 in long, split
8 egg yolks
125 g /4 oz caster sugar
60 ml /4 tbls flour
30 ml /2 tbls cornflour
25 g /1 oz butter

For the white praline
oil, for greasing
125 g /4 oz caster sugar
25 g /1 oz blanched, chopped almonds
For the caramel
225–350 g /8–12 oz sugar

1 Roll out the sweet shortcrust pastry on a lightly floured board, or between sheets of cling film, to a 23–25 cm /9–10 in circle. Transfer to a baking sheet, flute the edges, prick the base and chill for 30 minutes.
2 Heat the oven to 220C /425F /gas 7. Lightly dampen 1 or more baking sheets. Spoon the choux paste into a piping bag fitted with a 15 mm /½ in plain nozzle. Pipe the paste onto the damp baking sheet or sheets in 25 mm /1 in diameter circles to begin with, gradually making some of the circles larger. Smooth down any sharp points

diameter. In a heavy saucepan, heat the sugar with 30 ml /2 tbls water. Spread the blanched, chopped almonds on the oiled baking sheet.

10 Stir the sugar and water over a gentle heat until the sugar dissolves, then boil it until the syrup becomes a light, golden caramel and pour it over the nuts. Lift the thin edges of the caramel onto the nuts with the oiled palette knife, but do not stir the mixture or it will crystallize.

11 As the mixture cools, cut two 6 cm /2½ in circles and 6 equal-sized crescents with the 4 cm /1½ in biscuit cutter. If the praline does not cut easily, let it cool a little more, then work rapidly as it will set quickly. Should the caramel set too quickly, warm it over a pan of boiling water for a few minutes.

12 To assemble the croquembouche, fill the choux puffs with the crème pâtissière, using a piping bag and a small plain nozzle. Place the cooked shortcrust circle on a large, flat serving dish.

13 Make the caramel: in a small saucepan, heat 125 g /4 oz sugar with 30 ml /2 tbls cold water, stirring until the sugar is dissolved. Bring it to the boil, and boil until the syrup becomes a light, golden caramel. Set the base of the saucepan in cold water to stop the caramel cooking.

14 Working as quickly as possible, start to make a pyramid of puffs on the shortcrust base; using a 2-pronged fork dip one of the large puffs in the caramel so that it is coated on the top and round the sides. Place it 5 cm /2 in in from the edge of the pastry base with the uncoated side inwards. Continue coating the largest puffs and placing them on the pastry base to form a ring, leaving the centre empty. The caramel will act as a glue.

15 Place a second ring of choux puffs on top of the first and continue to build a cone that is about 12 cm /4½ in in diameter at the top and 37–45 cm /15–18 in high. Use the smaller puffs as you get to the top.

16 If the caramel becomes too firm, warm it gently. Do not reboil it as it will crystallize. Make further batches of caramel as you find you need them — don't make the caramel all at once as it will harden before you can use it.

17 To decorate, with the tip of a knife, rub a little caramel onto the edge of one praline circle and place it, caramel side down, on top of the choux pyramid. Dip the tips of 4 crescents in the caramel and stand them back edge to back edge on the praline base. Dip the remaining praline circle in the caramel and place it, caramel side down, on top of the 4 crescents. Dip the tips of the remaining 2 crescent shapes in the caramel and place them back edge to back edge on top of the second circle. Serve the croquembouche as soon as possible.

● The crème pâtissière can be made in advance and kept, covered, in the refrigerator. The praline can be made the day before and kept in an airtight tin. The choux puffs and pastry base can be made 6–8 hours ahead. The whole thing should be assembled only a couple of hours before it is needed or the choux may go soggy.

● The caramel-covered puffs 'crunch in the mouth', thus giving the dessert its name.

with a knife dipped in water, otherwise they will burn. Space the circles about 25 mm / 1 in apart on the baking sheet or sheets.

3 Bake in the oven for 10 minutes, then reduce the heat to 170C /325F /gas 3 and continue to bake them for 15–20 minutes, until the puffs are crisp, light and golden. Remove them from the oven and slit them with a sharp knife to allow the steam to escape. If necessary, scrape out any uncooked paste with a teaspoon. Leave the puffs to cool on a wire rack.

4 Raise the oven temperature to 190C / 375F /gas 5. Cook the shortcrust pastry in the oven for 15–18 minutes until it is lightly browned. Transfer it to a rack to cool.

5 Meanwhile, make the crème pâtissière: put the milk and the split vanilla pod in a saucepan and place it over a low heat. Bring it slowly to boiling point, then remove it

Profiteroles

from the heat, cover the pan and set the milk aside to infuse.

6 In a large bowl, whisk the egg yolks and sugar until thick and light. Gradually whisk in the flour and cornflour.

7 Remove the vanilla pod from the milk and gradually pour the flavoured milk onto the egg yolk mixture, whisking until blended.

8 Add the butter to the eggs and milk and beat for 1–2 minutes longer to cool the cream, then beat in the kirsch. Pass the cream through a fine sieve into a clean bowl, cover it with a sheet of lightly buttered greaseproof paper and set it aside to cool. When cold, chill it until required.

9 Prepare the praline: oil a marble slab or baking sheet, a palette knife and 2 biscuit cutters 6 cm /2½ in and 4 cm /1½ in in

Plum cake

Beautiful golden plums called mirabelles grow in the Lorraine region of France and are used for this delicious batter cake, which makes a lovely dessert. Mirabelle plums may be difficult to obtain, in which case substitute canned red or purple plums.

 1 hour

Serves 8–10
butter and flour, for the tin
4 medium-sized eggs, separated
150 g /5 oz icing or caster sugar
600 ml /1 pt yoghurt
150 ml /5 fl oz mirabelle or other plum brandy
10 ml /2 tsp baking powder
200 g /7 fl oz flour
300 g /11 oz mirabelle plums, preserved in syrup, well drained

1 Heat the oven to 180C /350F /gas 4. Butter and flour a 25 cm /10 in spring-release cake tin.
2 Whisk together the egg yolks and the

Plum cake

sugar until they are thick and creamy. Now, whisk in the yoghurt and then the plum brandy.
3 Sift the baking powder with the flour, then whisk the egg whites until stiff. Fold the flour mixture into the yoghurt mixture, alternately with the egg whites.
4 Pour half the mixture into the cake tin. Cover the mixture with the drained plums, then pour the rest of the mixture over the top, levelling it with a rubber spatula.
5 Bake the cake for 35–40 minutes. Let it cool for a few minutes in the cake tin, then turn it out carefully and cool it on a wire rack before serving.

● Canned apricots can be used in this recipe, instead of the mirabelles, but if using apricots, I suggest that you use an apricot brandy instead of plum brandy.

Chocolate cherry roll

 1¾ hours

Serves 8
oil, for greasing
50 g /2 oz flour
25 g /1 oz cocoa
3 eggs
75 g /3 oz caster sugar, plus extra for sprinkling
450 g /1 lb canned, stoned cherries, drained and juice reserved
30 ml /2 tbls kirsch
275 ml /10 fl oz thick cream
To decorate
icing sugar, for sprinkling

1 Heat the oven to 220C /425F /gas 7. Oil and line a 20 × 30 cm /8 × 12 in Swiss roll tin with greaseproof paper and oil it lightly.
2 Sift the flour and the cocoa together onto a sheet of greaseproof paper.
3 Break the eggs into a medium-sized bowl which fits over a saucepan and add the sugar. Stand the bowl over a pan containing 25 mm /1 in hot water and whisk continuously (preferably with an electric whisk) until the mixture is thick and creamy and doubled in bulk. Alternatively, whisk the mixture in the bowl of a table-top electric mixer at high speed for 5 minutes.

4 Sprinkle the sifted flour and cocoa over the mixture and fold it in lightly with a metal spoon. Stir in 15 ml /1 tbls water.
5 Spread the mixture evenly in the Swiss roll tin and bake until it is risen and firm to the touch — about 10 minutes.
6 Place all but 8 of the cherries in a bowl and sprinkle them with the kirsch. Leave them to marinate for 1 hour. Reserve the 8 cherries in the cherry juice.
7 Sprinkle a big sheet of greaseproof paper with sugar. Turn the Swiss roll out of the tin onto it, and peel away the lining paper. Trim any crisp edges from the sponge and roll up the cake immediately with the paper inside. Leave it to cool.
8 When the sponge is cold, whip the cream until it holds its shape. Spoon about 45 ml /3 tbls into a piping bag fitted with a rosette nozzle and set it aside.
9 Unroll the sponge. Drain the marinated cherries and sprinkle the juices over the sponge. Fold the cherries into the remaining cream and spread it over the sponge. Roll up the sponge and ease away the greaseproof paper. Sprinkle the chocolate cherry roll with icing sugar and then serve.

Mandarin roll

 35 minutes,
 plus cooling

Serves 8
butter, for greasing
3 eggs
75 g /3 oz caster sugar, plus extra for dredging
65 g /2½ oz flour
5 ml /1 tsp ground mixed spice
a pinch of salt
15 g /½ oz ground almonds
175 g /6 fl oz whipping cream
100 g /4 oz canned mandarin segments, well
  drained and chopped
icing sugar, to garnish
fresh orange slices, to garnish

1 Heat the oven to 200C /400F /gas 6. Grease a 23×33 cm /9×13 in Swiss roll tin and line it carefully with buttered grease-proof paper.
2 Whisk together the eggs and the sugar until the mixture is pale and the whisk leaves a trail on the surface.
3 Sift together the flour, the mixed spice and the salt and stir in the ground almonds. Lightly fold this into the egg mixture.
4 When the mixtures are evenly combined, pour it into the prepared tin, level the surface and bake it for 8–10 minutes, until the cake is just firm to the touch.
5 Invert the cake onto a sheet of sugared greaseproof paper, peel away the lining paper and trim the edges. Roll it up firmly with the sugared paper inside and let it cool.
6 Just before serving, lightly whip the cream. Carefully unroll the cake and spread the cream evenly over the surface, leaving a border of 5 mm /¼ in around the edge.
7 Scatter the mandarins over the cream. With the aid of the paper, re-roll the cake. Sift icing sugar over the top and serve it as soon as possible, garnished with orange slices cut into quarters.

Sachertorte

The original recipe for this elegant cake was claimed by both the Hotel Sacher and Demels, the famous Viennese baker, but every Austrian housewife has her favourite version of the recipe. Like many gateaux, this one is turned bottom uppermost before icing to give it a smooth surface.

 3¼ hours,
 plus cooling

Makes 12 slices
butter and flour, for the cake tin
150 g /5 oz plain chocolate
15 ml /1 tbls rum or Madeira
150 g /5½ oz butter
150 g /5½ oz icing sugar
6 eggs, separated
10 ml /2 tsp Vanilla sugar (see page 10)
120 g /4½ oz flour, sifted twice
For the apricot icing
75 g /3 oz apricot jam
120 g /4½ oz plain chocolate, broken into pieces
120 g /4½ oz caster sugar
2 drops refined olive oil

1 Heat the oven to 180C /350F /gas 4. Butter and flour a 23 cm /9 in round cake tin. Break the chocolate for the cake into small pieces in a bowl. Add 15 ml /1 tbls water and place the bowl over a saucepan of hot, but not boiling, water and place the saucepan over a low heat. When the chocolate melts, remove the pan from the heat and stir in the rum or Madeira. Allow the mixture to cool a little.

2 Beat the butter in a mixing bowl until it is soft and light. Add 120 g /4½ oz of the icing sugar and beat until the mixture is light and fluffy. Gradually stir in the egg yolks and then beat in the barely warm chocolate mixture into it.
3 Whisk the egg whites until they are stiff, then whisk in the remaining sugar and the vanilla sugar. Fold spoonfuls of the beaten egg whites into the butter mixture alternately with the flour. Pour the mixture into the prepared tin. Bake the cake in the centre of the oven for 1 hour, or until the cake has evenly risen and springs back if pressed.
4 Allow the cake to cool in the tin for 5 minutes before turning it out onto a wire rack, and leave it to become cold (24 hours). The cake is then iced bottom uppermost because the surface is smoother.
5 Warm the apricot jam in a small saucepan over a very low heat. Sieve the jam and then spread it over the sides and 'top' of the cake, so the jam is about 6 mm /¼ in thick.
6 For the icing, melt the chocolate in a bowl over a saucepan of hot, but not boiling, water. Remove it from the heat.
7 Put the caster sugar in a saucepan with 60 ml /4 tbls water, bring it to the boil, cook for 1 minute and then remove it from the heat. When the sugar syrup is lukewarm, stir it into the melted chocolate with two drops of olive oil.
8 Spread the icing, while it is still warm, evenly over the cake, using a palette knife dipped in hot water. Allow the icing to cool before cutting the cake, but do not chill it.

Mandarin roll

Orange marble cake

Serves 8–10
For the vanilla mixture
225 g /8 oz flour
350 g /12 oz caster sugar
12 medium-sized egg whites, at
* room temperature*
2.5 ml /½ tsp salt
7.5 ml /1½ tsp cream of tartar
7.5 ml /1½ tsp vanilla essence
For the orange mixture
6 medium-sized egg yolks
15 ml /1 tbls flour
15 ml /1 tbls cornflour
30 ml /2 tbls caster sugar
30 ml /2 tbls grated orange zest
60 ml /4 tbls orange juice
10 drops of yellow food colouring
For the apricot sauce
400 g /14 oz canned apricot
* halves in syrup*
15 ml /1 tbls caster sugar
5 ml /1 tsp arrowroot
about 15 ml /1 tbls lemon juice
5 ml /1 tsp kirsch
For the decoration
icing sugar

1 To make the vanilla mixture, sift the flour and sugar separately 3 times. Whisk the egg whites with the salt and the cream of tartar, using a mixer at a high speed, until soft peaks form.
2 Whisk in the sugar, 60 ml /4 tbls at a time, until stiff peaks form. Fold in the vanilla essence.
3 Sift the flour, a quarter at a time, over the egg whites and fold in gently. Turn two-thirds of the mixture into a bowl and reserve.
4 Heat the oven to 190C /375F /gas 5. To make the orange mixture, whisk the egg yolks, the flour, the cornflour and the sugar until very thick. Add the orange zest, the orange juice and the food colouring. Fold the yolk mixture into the remaining one-third of the vanilla mixture.
5 To marble the cake, spoon half of the vanilla mixture into a 3.3 L / 5¾ pt Gugelhupf ring mould. Layer the orange mixture on top of this, and finish with the remaining vanilla mixture. Cut down through the mixtures twice with a spatula. Level the top.
6 Bake the cake on a low shelf in the oven for 35–40 minutes, or until it springs back when pressed. Allow to cool for at least 2 hours.
7 Meanwhile, make the apricot sauce: drain the apricot halves, reserving the syrup, and purée them through a fine sieve. Mix in the caster sugar and pour into a saucepan. Blend 45 ml /3 tbls apricot syrup with the arrowroot, and add the apricot purée, together with the lemon juice. Boil, then simmer, stirring occasionally, for 5–6 minutes. Cool the sauce, then add the kirsch.
8 Loosen the cake using a round-bladed knife, then remove it from the tin. Sprinkle it with icing sugar and serve with the apricot sauce.

 1¼ hours,
plus cooling

Gâteau Esterel

Serves 6
15 ml /1 tbls dried yeast
150 g /5 oz butter
flour, for dusting
4 eggs
225 g /8 oz caster sugar
225 g /8 oz flour
a pinch of salt
120 ml /8 tbls orange marmalade
225 g /8 oz plain chocolate
15 ml /1 tbls Cointreau
For the syrup
100 g /4 oz sugar
45 ml /3 tbls Cointreau

1 Heat the oven to 200C /400F /gas 6. In a small bowl, sprinkle the yeast into 60 ml /4 tbls lukewarm (37C /99F) water. Stand it for 6 minutes, covered, in a warm place, then stir until dissolved.
2 Melt the butter in the top of a double boiler. Grease a 20 cm /8 in savarin mould with melted butter, and dust the mould with flour.
3 In a small bowl, whisk the eggs and the sugar until they are light and fluffy. Sift the flour with the salt and fold into the egg and sugar mixture using a large metal spoon. Fold in the remaining melted butter and the dissolved yeast mixture. Pour the mixture into the prepared savarin mould and bake it in the oven for 10 minutes.
4 Lower the oven temperature to 180C /350F /gas 4 and cook the cake for a further 25 minutes, or until it is golden brown. Unmould it onto a wire rack and leave to cool.
5 Meanwhile, make the syrup. In a small saucepan, dissolve the sugar in 225 ml /8 fl oz water over a low heat, bring it to the boil and boil until the temperature reaches 108C /220F — this takes about 10 minutes. Remove the syrup from the heat, flavour it with the Cointreau and leave it to cool.
6 Cut the cake in half horizontally and moisten the cut sides of both halves with the syrup, reserving 45 ml /3 tbls. Spread the cut sides with orange marmalade, then re-form the cake.
7 Melt the chocolate in the top of a double boiler over simmering water, add the reserved syrup and Cointreau, beating until smooth.
8 Place the cake on a serving platter, cover it with the chocolate mixture, using a palette knife to spread the chocolate. Allow the chocolate mixture to cool, and then serve.

 1 hour 40 minutes

Winter lemon cake

Serves 8–12
butter, for the cake tins
flour, for the cake tins
6 eggs, separated
175 g /6 oz caster sugar
finely grated zest of 1 lemon
a large pinch of salt
75 g /3 oz flour
25 g /1 oz cornflour

For the filling and topping
2 eggs
275 g /10 oz caster sugar
finely grated zest and juice of
 2 lemons
50 g /2 oz flour, sifted
575 ml /1 pt thick cream, whipped
crystallized orange and lemon
 slices, to decorate

1   Heat the oven to 180C /350F /gas 4. Butter 3×20 cm /8 in
diameter sandwich cake tins and dust them with flour.
2   Combine the egg yolks, the sugar, the lemon zest and the salt in a
large mixing bowl with 30 ml /2 tbls cold water. Using an electric
mixer set at high speed, beat the ingredients together for 5 minutes
until they are light and fluffy.
3   Sift together the flour and the cornflour, then gradually fold them
into the egg yolk mixture using a large metal spoon or a spatula. In a
clean dry bowl, whisk the egg whites until they are stiff but not dry.
Fold the whisked whites into the cake batter.
4   Divide the cake batter equally among the prepared tins. Bake it
immediately, for 45 minutes, or until it is risen and golden.
5   Remove the tins from the oven and invert them onto a wire rack.
Leave them until cool, then run a palette knife around the inside rim
of the tins and turn out the cakes.
6   Meanwhile, make the filling and topping. In a mixing bowl, whisk
together the eggs, the sugar and the lemon zest until the mixture is
foamy. Measure the lemon juice and make it up to 275 ml /10 fl oz
with water, then beat it into the egg and sugar mixture, together with
the sifted flour.
7   Turn the lemon mixture into a heavy-based saucepan and bring it
to the boil over a low heat, stirring constantly. Cook the mixture,
stirring, for 5–7 minutes until it is smooth and thick. Remove the pan
from the heat and leave the lemon mixture to cool completely.
8   Fold the whipped cream into the cold lemon mixture. Use some of
the creamy lemon mixture to sandwich the layers of cake together.
Spread the remainder over the top and the sides of the cake to cover it
completely. Decorate the top of the cake with crystallized orange and
lemon slices.

 1½ hours,
plus cooling

Strawberry torte

Serves 6–8
16 trifle sponges
butter, for greasing
700 g /1½ lb strawberries
600 ml /1 pt thick cream
5 ml /1 tsp vanilla essence
For the glaze and decoration
800 g /1¾ lb strawberries
45 ml /3 tbls sugar
7.5 ml /1½ tsp cornflour
5 ml /1 tsp lemon juice
300 ml /10 fl oz thick cream, whipped
100 g /4 oz flaked almonds, toasted

1   Cut each sponge into 6 pieces. Grease a 22 cm /8½ in spring-
release, loose-bottomed cake tin and line the bottom and sides with
half of the sponge pieces, cut sides against the tin.
2   Purée 225 g /8 oz of the strawberries in a blender, then sieve to
remove the seeds. Slice 450 g /1 lb strawberries. Whip the cream in a
large bowl until it is stiff and fold in the purée, the vanilla essence
and the sliced strawberries.
3   Spoon half the cream mixture into the sponge-lined tin, smoothing
the surface. Using half of the remaining sponge pieces, cover the
strawberry cream. Repeat with the remaining strawberry cream and
sponge pieces. Cover the surface with greaseproof paper, then a plate
which fits inside the tin exactly, and place a weight on top. Chill
overnight.
4   Meanwhile make the glaze: purée 175 g /6 oz of the ripest
strawberries in a blender and then sieve them. In a small saucepan,
mix the sugar and the cornflour in 30 ml /2 tbls water. Stir in the
strawberry purée. Simmer, stirring, over a gentle heat for 1–2
minutes or until it is thickened. Stir in the lemon juice and allow the
mixture to cool.
5   Turn the strawberry torte out onto a flat serving platter. Coat the
sides of the torte with half the whipped cream. Press toasted flaked
almonds around the sides, using a clean palette knife.
6   Arrange the remaining whole strawberries on the top of the torte.
Spoon the cooled glaze over the fruit and chill.
7   To serve, pipe the remaining whipped cream around the top of
the torte using a large star nozzle.

 40 minutes,
then chilling and decorating

Gâteau à l'orange

Serves 6–8
15 g /½ oz butter
100 g /4 oz flour, plus extra for
dusting
4 eggs
100 g /4 oz sugar
grated zest of 1 orange
60 ml /4 tbls orange juice
100 ml /4 oz butter, melted
For the icing
100 g /4 oz unsalted butter
15 ml /1 tbls Cointreau

100 g /4 oz sugar
2 egg yolks
grated zest of 1 orange
For the filling
150 ml /5 fl oz thick cream
15 ml /1 tbls Cointreau
25 g /1 oz ginger biscuits, ground
For the decoration
50 g /2 oz ginger biscuits, ground
2 oranges, cut into segments
1 orange slice
2 pieces of green glacé cherry

1 Heat the oven to 190C /375F /gas 5. Butter a loose-bottomed
18 cm /7 in cake tin and dust it with the flour.
2 In a large mixing bowl, combine the eggs and the sugar. Place the
bowl over a pan of simmering water, over a low heat. Whisk the
mixture until it is light and pale. Remove from the heat and continue
whisking until cool. Fold in the orange zest and juice.
3 Sift the remaining flour onto the egg mixture, and fold it in. Pour
in the melted butter and fold it in. Pour the mixture into the cake tin,
set the tin on a baking sheet and bake in the centre of the oven for
20–30 minutes, or until the cake springs back when lightly touched.
4 Remove the cake from the oven and cool it in the tin for 5
minutes. Turn it out onto a wire rack to cool completely.
5 To make the icing, cream the butter until it is light and fluffy,
then beat in the Cointreau.
6 Dissolve the sugar in 25 ml /1 fl oz water over a moderate heat,
stirring constantly. Bring it to the boil. Without stirring, continue
boiling the syrup until it reaches 110C /225F on a thermometer.
Remove it from the heat.
7 Whisk the egg yolks until they are pale and thick. Add the hot
syrup, a little at a time, whisking constantly until the mixture is thick
and smooth. Add the orange zest and whisk until cold. Beat in the
butter and Cointreau a little at a time, until blended.
8 To make the filling, whisk the cream and the Cointreau until the
cream holds stiff peaks. Fold in the ground biscuits. Cut the cake into
2 layers and sandwich them with the filling.
9 Spread the cake with the icing and press the ground ginger
biscuits around the sides. Decorate the top with the orange segments.
Place an orange slice and 2 pieces of cherry in the centre.

 1½ hours, cooling,
then 20 minutes decorating

Danish layer cake

Serves 6
575 ml /1 pt thick cream, whipped
125 g /4 oz raspberry jam
½ × Crème pâtissière (page 50)
15 ml /1 tbls kirsch
For the pastry
225 g /8 oz butter, plus extra for greasing
200 g /7 oz caster sugar
225 g /8 oz flour

1 Heat the oven to 220C /425F /gas 7. Line 3 baking trays with
greaseproof paper and butter them well.
2 To make the pastry, in a bowl and using an electric beater, cream
the butter and the sugar until they are pale and creamy. Beat in
the flour and then work with your hands until the dough forms a
smooth ball.
3 Divide the dough into 3 portions. Roll out each portion between
2 pieces of cling film to a 25 cm /10 in diameter circle. Remove the
cling film and lay a circle of pastry on each baking tray. Prick all over
with a fork and leave the pastry to relax in the refrigerator for at least
15 minutes.
4 Bake 2 layers in the oven for 6–8 minutes, or until they are golden
brown. Remove them from the baking sheets, but do not remove the
greaseproof paper until the cake is to be assembled. Now bake the
third layer.
5 About 2 hours before serving, assemble the cake. Place one layer
of pastry upside down on a large, flat cake plate (it helps if you
anchor the pastry to the plate with a little whipped cream). Spread the
pastry with a thin layer of raspberry jam. Top it with half the crème
pâtissière. Spread the second layer of pastry with a thin layer of
raspberry jam. Place it on top of the first and spread with the
remaining crème pâtissière. Place the final pastry layer on top.
6 Spread a thin layer of whipped cream on the top of the cake.
Using a piping bag fitted with a star nozzle, pipe the remaining cream
to cover the sides and decorate the outer border at the top of the cake.
7 Heat the remaining raspberry jam with the kirsch. Rub the melted
jam through a sieve, then leave it to cool a little. Put the cooled jam
into a piping bag fitted with a small round nozzle, and pipe parallel
lines on the top of the cake. Draw a skewer across the lines to make a
pattern. Chill the cake until ready to serve it.

1½ hours,
plus chilling

Chocolate rum cake

Serves 8–10
butter, for greasing
225 g /8 oz flour, plus extra for
  dusting
a pinch of salt
10 ml /2 tsp baking powder
1.5 ml /¼ tsp bicarbonate of
  soda
150 g /5 oz butter, softened
100 g /4 oz caster sugar
2 eggs, separated
5 ml /1 tsp grated orange zest
125 ml /4 fl oz orange juice
125 ml /4 fl oz light rum

2.5 ml /½ tsp almond essence
2.5 ml /½ tsp vanilla essence
75 g /3 oz chopped walnuts, to
  decorate
For the chocolate icing
50 g /2 oz plain chocolate
75 g /3 oz butter, softened
150 g /5 oz icing sugar, sifted
1 egg yolk
For the filling
275 ml /10 fl oz thick cream
60 ml /4 tbls icing sugar
45–60 ml /3–4 tbls light rum

1   Heat the oven to 180C /350F /gas 4. Grease two 23 cm /9 in
round sandwich cake tins. Cut out 2 circles of greaseproof paper,
butter them and use them to line the tin bases. Dust them with flour.
2   Sift together the flour, the salt, the baking power and the
bicarbonate of soda.
3   In a bowl, cream the butter and beat in 75 g /3 oz of the sugar
until it is light and fluffy. Beat in the egg yolks and the orange zest.
4   Blend the orange juice with 45 ml /3 tbls of the rum, the almond
essence and the vanilla essence. With a metal spoon, fold the liquid
mixture and the flour mixture alternately into the creamed mixture.
5   Whisk the egg whites to stiff peaks, and whisk in the remaining
sugar. Carefully fold the whites into the cake mixture. Divide the
mixture equally between the cake tins, levelling the tops. Bake for 25
minutes or until the surface springs back when pressed.
6   Remove the cakes from the oven and leave them to cool in the tins
for 5 minutes. Turn out the cakes onto wire racks to cool completely.
7   For the chocolate icing, melt the chocolate with 30 ml /2 tbls
water in the top pan of a double boiler, then beat in the butter. Off
the heat, beat in the icing sugar and egg yolk. Leave it to cool.
8   Cut each cold cake in half horizontally, using a sharp knife, to
make 4 layers. Sprinkle each layer with the remaining rum.
9   For the filling, combine the cream, the icing sugar, and the rum in
a bowl. Whisk until it holds its shape. Spread 3 layers with the filling
and sandwich them together, placing the plain layer on top.
10   Beat the cooled chocolate icing again and, using a palette knife,
coat the sides and top of the cake. Pat the walnuts around the sides
and transfer the cake to a serving plate. Chill it overnight.

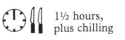   1½ hours,
plus chilling

Caprice Saint Sylvestre

Serves 6–8
100 g /4 oz butter, melted and
  cooled, plus extra for greasing
30 ml /2 tbls toasted almonds,
  coarsely chopped
100 g /4 oz caster sugar
4 medium-sized eggs
100 g /4 oz flour
25 g /1 oz unsweetened cocoa
  powder
For the crème chantilly
300 ml /10 fl oz thick cream
30 ml /2 tbls caster sugar

30 ml /2 tbls iced water
a few drops of vanilla essence
4 glacé chestnuts (marrons
  glacés), coarsely chopped
For the syrup
60 ml /4 tbls Jamaican rum
60 ml /4 tbls syrup from the
  glacé chestnuts
For the garnish
100 g /4 oz chocolate, in small
  pieces
6–8 glacé chestnuts (marrons
  glacés), drained

1   Heat the oven to 200C /400F /gas 6. Prepare a 20 cm /8 in ring
mould by buttering it well and then sprinkling the inside with
chopped, toasted almonds.
2   Beat the sugar and the eggs until they are light and fluffy (if using
an electric mixer, 12–15 minutes at high speed). Sift the flour and the
cocoa powder together and gently fold them into the egg mixture.
Fold in the cooled, melted butter.
3   Pour the mixture into the prepared ring mould. Bake it in the
oven for 25–30 minutes, or until the cake shrinks slightly from the
edges of the mould. Remove it from the oven and, after 5 minutes,
turn it out onto a wire rack to cool.
4   To make the crème chantilly, whip the cream with the sugar until
stiff. Add the iced water and the vanilla essence, and whip it again
until the cream is soft and fluffy. Fold in the coarsely chopped glacé
chestnuts, then chill.
5   Split the cold cake in 2 horizontally. Moisten the 2 cut sides with
the rum and the syrup from the chestnuts. Spread with the crème
chantilly, and sandwich the cake together.
6   Melt the chocolate in a bowl over hot water, then carefully spoon
the melted chocolate over the cake. Surround the cake with whole
glace chestnuts before serving.

●   St Sylvestre was a 4th century pope. His day is celebrated on
New Year's Eve.

   1½ hours,
plus cooling

PIES & TARTS

Mastering the art of making a perfect pastry base will dramatically increase your repertoire to include a whole host of pies and tarts for every occasion. These sweet treats will be ample reward for your efforts.

The secret of successful pastry is to keep everything as cold as possible. Chill all the equipment beforehand and if at any time during the pastry-making the mixture starts to become oily, stop and refrigerate it immediately. Mixing should be done rapidly, especially if your kitchen is warm, so the fat has less time to soften.

Rolling out is something that a lot of people find very difficult to achieve successfully. Pastry thickness is often considered to be the important factor but getting the pastry to fit the chosen tin is, in fact, much more important (generally, it should be rolled about 5 cm /2 in larger all round than your pie tin). Dishes with a heavy filling will be improved by having a thicker, more substantial pastry base to support them.

A light touch is required with pastry and it should be handled as little as possible if a hard, tough result is to be avoided. Do not be discouraged if your first attempts are not melt-in-the-mouth masterpieces, as you will soon achieve this with a little practice.

Gooseberry cream pie

Gooseberry pie is a traditional favourite; a cream filling makes it really special.

 1 hour 25 minutes

Serves 6
250 g /9 oz flour, sifted
a pinch of salt
65 g /2½ oz butter, diced small
65 g /2½ oz lard, diced small
beaten egg, for the glaze

For the filling
500 g /18 oz green gooseberries
75 g /3 oz sugar
5 ml /1 tsp ground cinnamon
1.5 ml /¼ tsp ground mace
60 ml /4 tbls thick cream

1 Heat the oven to 180C /350F /gas 4. Make the pastry by mixing the flour and salt and then rubbing the butter and lard into the mixture with your fingertips. Add enough cold water to mix it. Chill the pastry, wrapped tightly in greaseproof paper and then in a dampened tea-towel, while you prepare the rest of the ingredients.
2 Top and tail the gooseberries. Mix them with the sugar, cinnamon and mace.
3 Roll out two-thirds of the pastry and with it line a 20 cm /8 in flan tin. Put the gooseberries into the flan and spoon the cream over the top. Cover it with the remaining pastry. Seal the edges and brush the top with the beaten egg.
4 Bake the pie for 50 minutes until the top is golden brown. Serve hot or cold.

● If you serve this pie hot, hand round extra whipped cream flavoured with vanilla sugar (see page 10), if you like.

Old-fashioned apple pie

making the pastry, 45 minutes, then 35–40 minutes

Serves 6
700 g /1½ lb cooking apples
juice of ½ lemon
1 × Shortcrust pastry base (see left)
100 g /4 oz sugar
60 ml /4 tbls soft, dark brown sugar
15 ml /1 tbls flour
a good pinch of ground nutmeg
2.5 ml /½ tsp ground cinnamon
finely grated zest of 1 orange
finely grated zest of 1 lemon
30 ml /2 tbls chopped raisins
30 ml /2 tbls chopped sultanas
30 ml /2 tbls orange juice
15 g /½ oz butter
275 ml /10 fl oz thick cream, to serve

1 Heat the oven to 200C /400F /gas 6. Peel, quarter and core the apples and slice them thickly. Place the slices in a bowl of water with the lemon juice to prevent any discoloration.
2 Roll out two-thirds of the pastry on a lightly-floured surface and use it to line a 28 × 15 cm /11 × 6 in oval pie dish, or a deep 23 cm /9 in round pie dish.
3 Mix the sugar, brown sugar, flour, nutmeg and cinnamon in a small bowl. Sprinkle a little of this mixture over the pastry base and rub it in. Add the finely grated orange and lemon zest to the rest of the sugar mixture.
4 Drain the sliced apples and arrange a layer over the pastry base. Sprinkle this with a few chopped raisins and sultanas and a little of the sugar mixture. Repeat the layers until all the ingredients are used up. Sprinkle

Shortcrust pastry base

20 minutes, plus 1 hour resting

Makes 450 g /1 lb (made-weight) pastry
225 g /8 oz flour
5 ml /1 tsp icing sugar
2.5 ml /½ tsp salt
150 g /5 oz butter, chilled
1 medium-sized egg yolk
5 ml /1 tsp lemon juice
30 ml /2 tbls iced water

1 Sift the flour, icing sugar and salt into a large bowl. Cut the butter into 5 mm /¼ in dice and add these to the bowl.
2 Use two knives, cutting across each other like scissor blades, or a pastry blender to cut the diced butter into the flour until the mixture resembles coarse breadcrumbs.
3 Run cold water over the pulse points on your wrists and then pat your hands dry. With some mixture from the bowl and using just your fingertips, rub the fat into the flour. Hold your hands high above the mixture and let it fall back into the bowl. This action will probably only need to be repeated 6–7 times before the mixture resembles fine breadcrumbs.
4 Put the egg yolk, lemon juice and 15 ml / 1 tbls iced water in a small bowl or cup and beat together with a fork.
5 Make a well in the middle of the mixture and pour in the egg, lemon juice and water. Rinse out the small bowl with the remaining iced water and add this to the well.
6 Using a fork, gradually pull the flour into the centre and mix it thoroughly.

7 Continue working with the fork until a dough is formed which can be gathered lightly together to form one piece.
8 Wrap the pastry in a sheet of greaseproof paper, then in a dampened tea-towel and chill for at least 1 hour before using.

● For sweet shortcrust pastry increase the quantity of icing sugar to 30 ml /2 tbls for each 225 g /8 oz of flour.
● Uncooked pastry dough, wrapped airtight in greaseproof paper and then a polythene bag, stores 3 or 4 days in the refrigerator or several weeks in the freezer.
Lining the tart tin: shape the pastry to a ball and flatten it with the palm of your hand. Place the pastry on a lightly-floured surface and start to roll using short, sharp strokes with the rolling pin. Turn the pastry one-eighth turn after each stroke and continue to do this until a circle has been made that is 5 cm /2 in larger all round than your tin (don't forget it has to be large enough to go up the sides as well). Use the rolling pin to help support the pastry as you lift it over the tin and then fold all the edges to the centre. Gently ease the pastry back to line the tin. As much as possible, try to avoid stretching it. Allow the pastry to relax and chill for half an hour before baking.
To bake the pastry case: line the case with crumpled greaseproof paper and fill it with dried beans. Place the tin on a baking sheet and bake the case in a preheated oven set at 200C /400F /gas 6 for 10 minutes. Remove the paper and beans and return the case to the oven for 8–10 minutes to dry the base without colouring it; this gives a half-baked case. For a fully-baked case return it to the oven, after removing the beans, for 10–15 minutes or until set and golden. (Baking an unfilled case is called baking 'blind'.)

the orange juice over the top and dot it with the butter.

5 Roll out the remaining pastry, brush the edges of the pastry base with cold water and cover the pie. Press the edges together to seal them, then trim and flute the pie decoratively. Make decorations with the pastry scraps and stick them to the pie with water. Cut a hole in the middle to allow the steam to escape.

6 Bake the pie in the oven for 10 minutes, then lower the oven temperature to 190C / 375F /gas 5 and bake it for a further 25–30 minutes. The pie is ready when the apples are tender and the pastry is golden brown in colour. Serve the pie warm with a jug of thick cream.

● To reheat the pie, cover it with foil and put it in the oven set at 170C /325 F /gas 3 for 20–30 minutes.

Fresh cherry tart

Fresh cherry tart

10 minutes, plus 1 hour resting, then 45 minutes

Serves 4
225 g /8 oz flour
a pinch of salt
100 g /4 oz butter, diced small
100 g /4 oz caster sugar
a pinch of grated lemon zest
2 medium-sized eggs, separated
45 ml /3 tbls iced water
700 g /1½ lb cherries, stoned
15 ml /1 tbls redcurrant jelly
whipped cream, to serve

1 Sift the flour and salt into a bowl. Work in the butter with the fingertips. Stir in the sugar and zest and make a well in the centre. Add the yolks and iced water to the well.
2 First, with a fork, work together the ingredients in the centre, gradually taking in the flour, then mix with fingertips until the dough is fairly firm. Cover the dough with a cloth and chill for at least 1 hour.
3 Heat the oven to 190C /375F /gas 5. Divide the pastry into two portions, one twice the size of the other. Roll out the larger part and line a buttered and floured 20 cm / 8 in flan tin, letting the pastry edges overlap the tin. Fill the case with the fruit and dot the jelly on top. Roll out the remaining pastry and cover the tart. Fold the overlapping pastry inwards and crimp the edges.
4 Prick a few holes in the top of the pastry with a fork and glaze the top with a little lightly beaten egg white. Bake the tart in the oven for 45 minutes or until lightly golden. Serve warm with whipped cream.

● When fresh cherries are not readily available, substitute 700 g /1½ lb canned or bottled Morello cherries. Stone the fruit and dry it well with absorbent paper first.

Spicy butterscotch pie

Serves 4

175 g /6 oz soft, dark brown sugar
60 ml /4 tbls cornflour
2 eggs, beaten
600 ml /1 pt milk
50 g /2 oz butter
2.5 ml /½ tsp vanilla essence
1.5 ml /¼ tsp ground mixed spice
22 cm /8½ in fully-baked shortcrust pastry case (using the recipe on page 58)
150 ml /5 fl oz thick cream, whipped
pecans or halved walnuts, to garnish

1 Combine the brown sugar, cornflour and beaten eggs in the top pan of a double boiler and blend with a wooden spoon. Stir in the milk and cook over simmering water, stirring constantly, for 10–15 minutes or until the custard is smooth and thick. Do not let the sauce come to the boil or the eggs will curdle. To test the custard, draw your finger over the back of the spoon: it should leave a clear gap which does not close again quickly.
2 Remove the top pan from the heat and beat in the butter a little at a time. Whisk in the vanilla essence and ground mixed spice. Cover the surface with a dampened piece of greaseproof paper to prevent a skin forming, and leave until cold.
3 Whisk the cold butterscotch custard lightly and pour it into the baked pastry case, smoothing the top with a palette knife.
4 Fit a piping bag with a 15 mm /½ in star nozzle. Spoon in the whipped cream and pipe rosettes of cream around the rim of the butterscotch custard. Place a pecan or halved walnut between each rosette and serve.

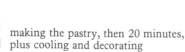 making the pastry, then 20 minutes, plus cooling and decorating

French peach tarts

Serves 4

4 × 10 cm /4 in fully-baked sweet shortcrust tart cases (using the recipe on page 58)
2 large peaches
For the crème pâtissière
50 g /2 oz sugar
25 g /1 oz cornflour
275 ml /10 fl oz milk
3 egg yolks
2.5 ml /½ tsp vanilla essence
5 ml /1 tsp kirsch
For the apricot glaze
60 ml /4 tbls apricot jam
15 ml /1 tbls rum, brandy or kirsch

1 Make the crème pâtissière. In the top pan of a double boiler, combine the sugar and cornflour. Stir in the milk, using a wooden spoon, and cook over direct heat, stirring all the time, until the mixture comes to the boil. Boil for 1 minute, stirring constantly.
2 In a bowl, beat the egg yolks lightly. Add a little of the hot milk mixture, stir to blend, then pour it back into the top pan, stirring well to combine with the rest of the milk mixture.
3 Cook, stirring continuously, over hot, but not boiling, water for 5–10 minutes until the custard is thick enough in consistency to coat the back of a spoon.
4 Strain the crème through a fine sieve, then leave it to get cold. Add the vanilla essence and kirsch. Cover with greaseproof paper and refrigerate until required.
5 Make the apricot glaze. In a small saucepan, gently heat the apricot jam and 30 ml /2 tbls water, stirring continuously with a wooden spoon until the mixture has blended.
6 Strain through a fine sieve. Stir in the rum, brandy or kirsch. Keep the glaze warm until you are ready to use it.
7 Assemble the tarts. Fill each pastry case with cold crème pâtissière, smoothing the top with a palette knife.
8 In a bowl, cover the peaches with boiling water. Leave for 20–30 seconds, then drain and peel. Halve and stone the peeled peaches, then cut each half into 8 slices.
9 Lay 6 overlapping peach slices in the centre of each tart, and 1 slice in the opposite direction on either side.
10 Cover the peach slices with warm apricot glaze and leave to become cold before serving.

 making the pastry, then 40 minutes, plus cooling

Linzertorte

Serves 4–6

175 g /6 oz flour, plus extra
  for dusting
a pinch of salt
1.5 ml /¼ tsp ground cinnamon
100 g /4 oz butter, diced
75 g /3 oz ground hazelnuts
30 ml /2 tbls caster sugar
grated zest of 1 lemon

5 ml /1 tsp vanilla essence
15 ml /1 tbls rum or iced water
whipped cream, to serve
For the filling
450 g /1 lb raspberry jam, sieved
1.5 ml /¼ tsp ground cloves
lemon juice (optional)
For the glaze
1 egg yolk

1 Prepare the pastry. Sift together the flour, pinch of salt and cinnamon into a mixing bowl. Add the diced butter, cutting it in with a palette knife, then rub in with your fingertips until the mixture resembles fine breadcrumbs. Stir in the ground hazelnuts, caster sugar, grated lemon zest, vanilla essence and rum or iced water. Knead lightly to a smooth ball. Wrap in cling film and chill in the refrigerator for 1 hour.
2 Heat the oven to 190C /375F /gas 5.
3 In a heavy-based saucepan, melt the sieved raspberry jam. Add the ground cloves and a little lemon juice to sharpen the flavour, if the jam is very sweet. Bring it to the boil, then simmer it gently, until it is reduced by about one-third, stirring constantly with a wooden spoon. Remove it from the heat and put it aside until ready to use.
4 Press three-quarters of the pastry into the base of a 23 cm /9 in loose-bottomed, plain-edged tart tin. Push the pastry up the sides of the tin to make a neat border about 20 mm /¾ in thick. Using a fork, decorate the top of the border with a pattern.
5 Lightly beat the egg yolk with 15 ml /1 tbls water. Brush the pastry with the egg glaze and bake for 30 minutes, or until cooked and golden.
6 Pour the jam into the baked pastry case, spreading it evenly with a palette knife.
7 On a lightly-floured board, roll out the remaining pastry. Cut it into thin strips, about 15 mm /½ in wide. Lay the strips across the tart to make a lattice, trimming the ends neatly and sealing them to the border with egg glaze. Now brush the lattice with the remaining egg glaze.
8 Return the tart to the oven for 10 minutes, or until the lattice is golden. Allow it to cool before serving. Serve with whipped cream.

 1½ hours,
plus chilling and cooling

Tarte Tatin

Serves 6–8

75 g /3 oz butter
225 g /8 oz caster sugar
1.4–1.8 kg /3–4 lb dessert apples (Golden Delicious keep their
  appearance the best)
1 × Shortcrust pastry base (see page 58)
whipped cream, to serve

1 Heat the oven to 190C /375F /gas 5.
2 Slice the butter thinly and arrange the slices evenly to cover the base of a flameproof *tarte Tatin* mould (see note below) or a 23 cm / 9 in frying-pan with ovenproof handle(s). Sprinkle the sugar evenly over the butter.
3 Peel the apples, halve and core them. Arrange the halves, standing upright in overlapping circles, to fill the mould.
4 Place the mould over a moderate heat for 10–15 minutes, until a light caramel forms in the base of the mould. Transfer the mould to the oven and bake for 20 minutes, until the apples begin to soften. Remove them from the oven and leave them to cool a little.
5 Meanwhile, roll out the pastry and cut a circle large enough to cover the mould. Lay the circle on a baking sheet and then chill it for 15 minutes.
6 When the steam stops rising from the apples, cover them with the circle of chilled dough. Return the tarte to the oven and bake for 15 minutes, or until the pastry is golden.
7 Remove the tarte from the oven and leave it to cool until tepid, then turn it out, with the pastry underneath, onto a heatproof serving dish. If any apple sticks to the mould, remove it with a palette knife and return it to the tarte, so that the pattern is not spoiled.
8 Either serve immediately with whipped cream, or keep the tarte for up to 8 hours at room temperature and then reheat it lightly just before serving.

● A *tarte Tatin* mould is the same shape as a *moule à manqué*, with sides gently sloping outward, but it is made of a flameproof material so that it can be used on top of the stove as well as in the oven.
● This is a version of the famous upside-down French apple tart, baked with the pastry on top to keep it completely crisp, then reversed just before serving. The Tarte Tatin is named after the hotel proprietors who made it famous in the 19th century, *les demoiselles Tatin*, the Misses Tatin.

 making and chilling pastry,
then 1½ hours

Orange and almond tart

Serves 4

175 g /6 oz puff pastry
flour, for dusting
1 egg yolk
For the filling
275 g /10 oz caster sugar

3 seedless oranges
30 ml /2 tbls kirsch
50 g /2 oz butter, softened
2 egg yolks
100 g /4 oz ground almonds

1   On a lightly-floured board, roll out the pastry and cut out a circle, using a 20 cm /8 in flan ring. Place the circle inside the flan ring on a baking sheet.
2   Using a sharp knife, mark a circle inside the pastry, about 20 mm / ¾ in from the ring, without cutting right through it. Score the outside edge lightly in a lattice pattern.
3   In a small bowl, combine the egg yolk with 15 ml /1 tbls water, beating until well blended. Brush the lattice-patterned edge with the egg yolk glaze. Chill the pastry for 30 minutes.
4   Heat the oven to 220C /425F /gas 7. Dampen the baking sheet and bake the pastry for 20–25 minutes, or until risen and golden.
5   While the pastry is in the oven, prepare the filling. In a medium-sized, heavy-based saucepan, combine 275 ml /10 fl oz water with 200 g /7 oz caster sugar. Heat it gently, stirring with a wooden spoon, until the sugar is dissolved. Bring it to the boil and boil for 10 minutes until a light syrup forms.
6   Wash and dry the oranges, and slice them very thinly. Lay the slices in the syrup and simmer for 12–15 minutes, or until the skins are just tender. Remove the saucepan from the heat.
7   Remove the orange slices from the syrup with a slotted spoon and lay them on a wire rack over a tray to drain.
8   Return the syrup to the heat, adding any syrup drained from the orange slices, and boil it gently until reduced to one-third of the original quantity, and thick but still clear. Stir in the kirsch.
9   Put the remaining sugar in a bowl, then add the softened butter. Cream them together until light and fluffy, then beat in the egg yolks and ground almonds until well blended.
10   Remove the pastry from the oven, leaving the oven on. Remove the top of the centre circle from the pastry, taking out and discarding any soft and uncooked pastry.
11   Spread the almond filling in the pastry case. Arrange the orange slices in overlapping circles on top and pour the syrup over them.
12   Return the tart to the oven for 2–3 minutes to glaze the surface. Allow it to cool slightly before removing the flan ring. Transfer it to a flat serving plate and serve warm.

 1¾ hours,
including chilling the pastry

Old English Bakewell tart

Serves 4–6

200 g /7 oz puff pastry, defrosted if frozen
flour, for dusting
30 ml /2 tbls raspberry jam, sieved
15 ml /1 tbls lemon curd
75 g /3 oz butter
75 g /3 oz caster sugar
grated zest of 1 lemon
2 eggs, beaten
75 g /3 oz cake crumbs
150 g /5 oz ground almonds
10 ml /2 tsp lemon juice
50 g /2 oz flaked almonds
300 ml /10 fl oz whipped cream, to serve

1   Heat the oven to 220C /425F /gas 7.
2   Roll out the puff pastry on a lightly-floured board and use it to line a 1.1 L /2 pt oval pie dish. Prick the base with a fork and spread it with the sieved raspberry jam and the lemon curd. Chill it in the refrigerator for about 30 minutes.
3   In a bowl, cream together the butter and caster sugar until light and fluffy. Gradually add the grated lemon zest and the beaten eggs to the mixture, beating constantly. Fold in the cake crumbs, ground almonds and lemon juice.
4   Spread the mixture evenly over the sieved jam and lemon curd. Sprinkle it with the flaked almonds.
5   Bake the tart for 5 minutes in the hot oven. Reduce the heat to 180C / 350F /gas 4 and continue to bake for a further 25–30 minutes, or until the filling has set and the pastry is puffed and golden. Serve immediately accompanied by a bowl of whipped cream.

 1 hour,
including chilling

Chocolate and walnut tart

Serves 4

15 ml /1 tbls instant coffee
75 g /3 oz plain chocolate
7.5 g /1½ tsp gelatine
3 eggs, separated
120 g /8 tbls caster sugar
125 ml /4 fl oz thick cream
60 ml /4 tbls coarsely chopped walnuts
20 cm /8 in fully-baked shortcrust pastry case (using the recipe on
* page 58), 5 cm /2 in deep (made in a deep cake tin with removable base)*
30 ml /2 tbls icing sugar
8 walnut halves

1   Dissolve the coffee in 45 ml /3 tbls boiling water in a small bowl.
Break the chocolate into pieces and add it to the coffee. Place the
bowl over a saucepan of simmering water and stir with a wooden
spoon until the chocolate is melted and well blended with the coffee.
Leave it to cool.
2   Put 30 ml /2 tbls cold water into another small bowl, sprinkle the
gelatine on top and leave it to soften. Place the bowl in a saucepan of
hot water and stir until the gelatine is completely dissolved. Remove
it from the heat and leave it to cool.
3   Put the egg yolks and the sugar in the top pan of a double boiler.
Place them over simmering water and whisk until light and fluffy,
and the whisk leaves a trail when lifted. Remove it from the heat.
4   Stir the cooled coffee and chocolate mixture into the whisked egg
yolk mixture and then stir in the cooled gelatine; all three mixtures
should be at approximately the same temperature.
5   Place the pan in a bowl of crushed ice and stir until the mixture
starts to set.
6   Lightly whip the cream, then fold this into the chocolate mixture.
7   Whisk the egg whites until soft peaks form and fold them lightly
into the chocolate mixture with the coarsely chopped walnuts.
8   Pour the mixture into the pastry case and chill until set.
9   Before serving, sift the icing sugar over the top of the tart and
decorate with walnut halves. Remove the tart from the tin and place
on a flat serving platter.

 making the pastry,
then 1 hour, plus chilling

Creamy pear pie

Serves 4–6

900 g /2 lb firm pears
100 g /4 oz caster sugar
425 ml /15 fl oz thick cream
1 × sweet Shortcrust pastry base (see page 58)
flour, for dusting
1 egg yolk, beaten

1   Peel, quarter and core the pears and slice them thinly into a deep
bowl. Sprinkle with the caster sugar. Pour 225 ml /8 fl oz thick cream
over the fruit, stir to mix and cover with cling film. Refrigerate for
24 hours.
2   Heat the oven to 180C /350F /gas 4.
3   Roll out two-thirds of the pastry on a lightly-floured board to
3 mm /⅛ in thick and line a 20 cm /8 in loose-bottomed fluted flan
tin. Take care not to stretch the pastry or it will shrink back later.
Press it gently into the flutes with your index finger. Leave a border
of pastry around the edge of the tin about 5 mm /¼ in wide and
dampen it with a little of the beaten egg. Prick the base all over with
a fork.
4   Spoon the pear and cream mixture into the pastry-lined tin and
level off the filling with a palette knife.
5   Roll out the remaining pastry and cover the pie, pressing the
edges together. Cut away the excess pastry with scissors or a sharp
knife. Pinch the edges together to seal them, slanting them towards
the centre so that the pie can be released from the tin when cooked.
Use the remaining pastry to decorate the pie with pastry leaves.
Brush the whole surface lightly with beaten egg yolk to glaze and
make a round hole in the centre of the pastry large enough to take a
small funnel.
6   Bake for 40–45 minutes, or until golden brown.
7   Remove the pie carefully from the tin and transfer it to a serving
dish. Using a funnel, pour in the remaining cream through the hole
in the top. Tilt the pie gently so that the cream is evenly distributed.
Serve immediately.

 20 minutes, chilling,
making the pastry, then 1 hour

Black bottom pie

Serves 8
425 ml /15 fl oz milk
4 egg yolks
15 ml /1 tbls cornflour
100 g /4 oz caster sugar
15 ml /1 tbls gelatine
75 g /3 oz plain chocolate, broken
 into pieces
22 cm /8½ in pastry case,

*fully baked in a deep sandwich
tin (using the recipe on page 58)*
5 ml /1 tsp vanilla essence
3 egg whites
a pinch of cream of tartar
2 large bananas, just ripe
lemon juice
50 g /2 oz chocolate caraque or
 chocolate curls (see page 87)

1 In a saucepan, bring the milk to scalding point.
2 In the top pan of a double boiler, combine the egg yolks, cornflour
and 75 g /3 oz caster sugar. Whisk the mixture until it is light and
fluffy and then pour in the scalded milk. Whisk to blend.
3 Cook over simmering water for 15–20 minutes, or until the
custard coats the back of a wooden spoon, stirring occasionally. Leave
it to cool.
4 Meanwhile, in a small bowl, sprinkle the gelatine over 45 ml /
3 tbls cold water and leave it to soften. Place it over the pan of
simmering water and leave it until the gelatine is dissolved. Remove
the bowl and let the gelatine cool, but keep the water in the double
boiler simmering.
5 Place the chocolate pieces on a plate and melt them over the pan
of simmering water. Work it with a spatula until it is melted and
smooth. Leave it to cool.
6 Meanwhile, mix the cooled, dissolved gelatine into the cooled
custard.
7 Pour two-thirds of the custard into a bowl and stir in the cooled
melted chocolate. Set it over a bowl of crushed ice and stir until it is
on the point of setting. Pour it into the prepared pastry case and chill
until it is set. Flavour the remaining custard with the vanilla essence
and pour it into a large bowl.
8 In a clean bowl, whisk the egg whites with the cream of tartar
until stiff. Whisk in the remaining sugar and carry on whisking until
the mixture is stiff and glossy. With a large metal spoon, fold it into
the vanilla custard.
9 Peel one of the bananas and slice it thinly. Arrange overlapping
slices of banana on the set chocolate custard and pour the vanilla
custard mixture over. Return the pie to the refrigerator until set.
10 Just before serving, peel the remaining banana and slice it
thinly. Brush the slices with lemon juice and overlap them in a circle
around the edge of the pie. Decorate with chocolate caraque or curls.

 making the pastry, 1¾ hours,
plus chilling and setting

Orange and lemon chiffon pie

Serves 6–8
For the flan pastry
175 g /6 oz flour, plus extra
 for dusting
2.5 ml /½ tsp icing sugar
a pinch of salt
75 g /3 oz butter
1 medium-sized egg yolk
2.5 ml /½ tsp lemon juice
iced water

For the filling
15 ml /1 tbls gelatine
3 medium-sized eggs, separated
100 g /4 oz caster sugar
grated zest of 1 orange
grated zest of 1 lemon
juice of 2 oranges
juice of 2 lemons
segments from 1–2 oranges,
 to decorate

1 Make the flan pastry following the method on page 58 but using
the quantities given above. Put it in a 23 cm /9 in flan ring with a
removable base.
2 Heat the oven to 375F /190C /gas 5 and bake the pastry case
blind. Cool and leave the prepared pastry case in its tin on a baking
sheet.
3 To make the filling, sprinkle the gelatine over 30 ml /2 tbls cold
water in a small bowl and leave it to stand. In the top pan of a
double boiler, beat the egg yolks lightly with half the sugar, and all
the grated orange and lemon zest and orange and lemon juice. Put
the pan over simmering water and stir until the mixture thickens.
Remove from the heat.
4 Place the bowl containing the gelatine in the hot water
remaining in the bottom of the double boiler and stir until the
gelatine has completely dissolved and the liquid is clear. Beat this
into the custard mixture and put it aside until it has cooled, but do
not let it set.
5 Beat the egg whites until they are stiff but not dry. Gradually
beat in the remaining caster sugar and continue to beat to a stiff,
glossy meringue. Fold it into the cooled custard mixture.
6 Turn the custard mixture into the baked pastry case, smooth the
top with a knife, and decorate with orange segments cut from
between the membranes and arranged in fans of three. Return the
pie to the refrigerator until it is firmly set.

● This famous type of American chiffon pie can be flavoured with
limes or any other sharp-tasting fruit.

 making and baking the flan case,
then 1 hour, plus cooling and setting

Basque apple tart

Serves 6–8

*23 cm /9 in fully-baked shortcrust pastry case (using the recipe
  on page 58)*
6–8 crisp dessert apples
juice of 1 lemon
75 g /3 oz butter
100 g /4 oz caster sugar
15 ml /1 tbls ground cinnamon
thick cream, to serve

1 Place the fully-baked pastry case, still in its tin, on a baking sheet.
2 Peel, core and quarter the apples, then slice them fairly thickly.
Toss the slices in the lemon juice to prevent discoloration.
3 Melt 50 g /2 oz of the butter in a large, heavy-based saucepan.
Add the apple slices and lemon juice and sprinkle 75 g /3 oz of the
sugar and the cinnamon over them. Set the pan over a low heat and
cook the apples gently, carefully turning the slices with a wooden
spatula, until they are soft but not disintegrating. Remove the pan
from the heat.
4 Using a slotted spoon, remove the apple slices from the pan and
leave them to cool. Arrange the slices decoratively in overlapping
circles in the pastry case. Sprinkle with the remaining sugar and dot
it with the remaining butter.
5 Heat the grill to high.
6 Bring the apple juice left in the pan rapidly to the boil. Boil
briskly until thick and syrupy, then spoon it over the apples. Place
the tart under the grill until the apples are caramelized and golden.
(If necessary, protect the edges of the pastry case from over-browning
with crumpled foil.)
7 Serve the tart while still warm, cut into wedges and accompanied
by a jug of thick cream.

 making and baking the pastry case,
then 30–40 minutes

Apricot and almond tart

Serves 8

225 g /8 oz dried apricots
25 cm /10 in fully-baked shortcrust pastry case (using the recipe on page 58)
75 g /3 oz caster sugar
juice of 1 lemon
juice of 1 orange
1 blade of mace
1 stick of cinnamon
15 ml /1 tbls gelatine
1.5 ml /¼ tsp almond essence
225 ml /10 fl oz thick cream
2 egg whites
whipped cream, to garnish
25 g /1 oz toasted, slivered almonds, to garnish
sprigs of fresh mint, to garnish

1 Soak the apricots in cold water overnight.
2 Leave the pre-baked pastry case in its tin on a baking sheet. Drain
the soaked apricots, reserving 275 ml /10 fl oz of the soaking liquid,
adding water to the soaking liquid if necessary to make up the
volume. Place the apricots in a large pan with the reserved liquid,
50 g /2 oz caster sugar, the lemon and orange juice, mace and cinnamon.
Simmer for about 20–30 minutes until the apricots are tender and the
cooking liquid is the consistency of syrup. Stir the apricots
occasionally.
3 In a small bowl, sprinkle the gelatine over 45 ml /3 tbls cold water
and leave it to soften. Place the bowl in a pan of simmering water
until the gelatine has dissolved.
4 Remove the whole spices from the apricots and purée the fruit and
syrup in a blender or food processor. Pass the purée through a sieve if
necessary. Stir the dissolved gelatine and the almond essence into the
apricot purée, then chill it until the mixture is just beginning to set.
5 Whip the thick cream to soft peaks and fold it into the apricot
purée. Whisk the egg whites to soft peaks, add 25 g /1 oz caster sugar
and beat for 1–2 minutes. Fold it into the apricot mixture.
6 Pour the purée into the baked pastry case and chill it until firm.
Garnish with swirls of whipped cream, the toasted, slivered almonds
and sprigs of fresh mint.

 overnight soaking, making the pastry,
then 1 hour, plus chilling

Apricot bourdaloue tart

Serves 6

175 g /6 oz flour
2.5 ml /½ tsp icing sugar
a pinch of salt
75 g /3 oz cold butter
1 egg yolk
2.5 ml /½ tsp lemon juice
iced water

For the bourdaloue cream
200 ml /7 fl oz milk
5 cm /2 in vanilla pod, split

2 egg yolks
25 g /1 oz caster sugar
15 ml /1 tbls flour
7.5 ml /1½ tsp cornflour
15 g /½ oz butter
7.5 ml /1½ tsp kirsch
grated zest of 1 orange

For the decoration
900 g /1 lb 14 oz canned apricot
 halves, juice reserved

1 Heat the oven to 200C /400F /gas 6. Make the shortcrust pastry following the method given on page 58 but using the quantities above. Chill the pastry for 30 minutes.
2 Roll out the pastry to 3 mm /⅛ in thick and use it to line a greased 20 cm /8 in flan ring with a removable base. Line with greaseproof paper and beans and bake for 10 minutes, then reduce the heat to 180C /350F /gas 4. Remove the paper and beans. Bake for a further 10–15 minutes to cook fully.
3 To make the bourdaloue cream, pour the milk into a medium-sized pan and add the split vanilla pod. Bring to boiling point over a low heat. Cover the pan and put aside to infuse until needed.
4 In a bowl, whisk the egg yolks and the sugar with a wire whisk until thick and light. Gradually whisk in the flour and cornflour.
5 Remove the vanilla pod from the milk and gradually pour the milk onto the egg yolk mixture, whisking until it is well blended.
6 Pour the mixture back into the pan. Bring it to the boil over a moderate heat, stirring constantly. Now simmer it for 3 minutes longer, beating vigorously so it thickens smoothly.
7 Remove the pan from the heat. Beat in the butter and continue to beat for a minute or two longer to cool the bourdaloue cream slightly before adding the kirsch.
8 Pass the cream through a sieve if it is still lumpy. Transfer it to a bowl and stir in the grated orange zest. Cover the surface with a sheet of lightly-buttered greaseproof paper to prevent a skin forming on top. Allow the cream to become cold, then chill it until required.
9 Fill the cooled pastry shell with the chilled pastry cream and decorate the top with the strained apricot halves. Pour the apricot juice into a saucepan and cook it until it is reduced to a glaze. Spoon the glaze over the apricots and leave it to set.

 making the pastry, 35 minutes,
then chilling and assembling

Open apple cream tart

Serves 4

21 cm /8½ half-baked shortcrust pastry case (using the recipe on page 58)
1 egg white, beaten
juice of ½ lemon
6 tart, dessert apples
150 g /5 oz caster sugar
10 ml /2 tsp flour
5 ml /1 tsp cinnamon
275 ml /10 fl oz thick cream

1 Heat the oven to 180C /350F /gas 4. Brush the inside of the pastry case with beaten egg white and place it on a baking tray.
2 Prepare a bowl of acidulated water by adding water to the lemon juice. With a vegetable peeler, remove the skin from the apples. Core, quarter and thinly slice them. Toss the apple slices in the lemon juice to stop discoloration.
3 In a large bowl, combine the sugar, flour and cinnamon. Drain the sliced apples and add them to the sugar mixture, tossing them lightly to coat. Spoon them into the prepared pastry case and bake it in the oven for 20 minutes.
4 Pour 150 ml /5 fl oz thick cream over the tart filling and bake the tart for a further 10 minutes, or until the apples are tender and the cream is slightly caramelized. Serve the tart warm with the remaining thick cream.

 making the pastry case,
then 40 minutes

Cool &
Sophisticated

MOUSSES

These chilled, deliciously light and fluffy desserts are not difficult to make. It is best if they are prepared the day before they are due to be eaten to ensure that they set satisfactorily. Try this selection of tempting recipes.

Mousses can be a delicate combination of fruit purée, egg yolks and whites or a rich blend of whipped cream, flavouring and eggs. The word mousse comes from the French and means frothy or foamy and that is how the mousse should be — light enough to melt in the mouth.

In this chapter you will find a gorgeous collection of recipes to suit all tastes and menus, from an unusual Melon lime mousse to rich Kirsch mousses. The delicate Maple syrup and orange mousse is made with yoghurt instead of cream and the result is a refreshing dessert to follow any heavy main course as a marvellous finish to a meal.

Try my Crystallized fruit mousse, made with cottage cheese, as a change from the fresh fruit mousse recipes (Plum and honey, Apple or Blackcurrant mousses). For an unusual serving suggestion make the Iced orange mousses which are presented to each guest in the hollowed-out shell of an orange. Decorated with a swirl of cream, a sprinkle of grated chocolate and a pretty, shiny leaf, they are irresistible.

The Chocolate mousse recipe has a difference — a centre filled with chestnut Chantilly cream. Made with glacé chestnuts (marrons glacés), the Chantilly cream is a luxurious filling for this dessert. For a real treat you can make the Rum surprise, which has a layer of biscuit crumbs and a layer of pineapple purée and is topped by a rich, rum-flavoured chocolate mousse.

7 Stir the remaining purée into the egg mixture, then stir in the cooled gelatine.
8 Place the blackcurrant mixture over a bowl of crushed ice and stir until the mousse just begins to set. Now quickly but lightly fold in the whisked thick cream.
9 Divide between two 150 ml /5 fl oz ramekins. Cover with cling film and chill to set. To serve, pour half the liqueur mixture over each mousse.

Maple syrup and orange mousse

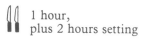 1 hour,
plus 2 hours setting

Serves 4
3 medium-sized eggs, separated
1 large orange
175 g /6 oz maple syrup
15 g /½ oz gelatine
575 ml /1 pt natural yoghurt

1 Put the egg yolks into the top half of a double boiler and whisk in the grated zest of half the orange. Stir over gently simmering water until they thicken, then take the pan off the heat. Stir in the maple syrup.
2 Squeeze the juice from the orange, then melt the gelatine in the juice in a small pan over a low heat — do not let it boil.
3 Stir this mixture into the egg yolks and leave it until it is on the point of setting. Use it when it is syrupy — the consistency of unbeaten egg whites.
4 Whisk the egg whites until they are stiff. Stir the yoghurt into the yolks and maple syrup, then fold in the egg whites. Pour the mousse into a serving dish and leave it in a cool place to set for 2 hours.

Crystallized fruit mousse

1 hour 15 minutes,
then chilling

Serves 6–8
225 g /8 oz mixed crystallized fruit
30 ml /2 tbls Cointreau or other orange liqueur
700 g /1½ lb cottage cheese
275 ml /10 fl oz thin cream
30 ml /2 tbls caster sugar, or to taste
a few drops of vanilla essence
candied angelica, to decorate

1 Using a knife dipped in hot water, chop up the crystallized fruit. Place it in a small bowl and pour the Cointreau or liqueur over the fruit and leave it to stand for 1 hour.
2 Sieve the cottage cheese into a large bowl. Stir in the cream with a fork, and beat until it is light and very smooth, adding the sugar and vanilla essence while beating.
3 Fold in the chopped fruit and liqueur. Taste and add more sugar if necessary. Turn the mousse into a glass serving bowl and chill it for several hours or overnight.
4 Just before serving, decorate with pieces of angelica cut into leaf shapes.

Blackcurrant mousses

 40 minutes,
plus setting

Serves 2
175 g /6 oz fresh or frozen blackcurrants
1 egg
1 egg yolk
30 ml /2 tbls caster sugar
15 ml /1 tbls crème de cassis
5 ml /1 tsp gelatine
45 ml /3 tbls thick cream

1 Put the blackcurrants in a saucepan with 50 ml /2 fl oz water. Bring to the boil, then

Blackcurrant mousses

lower the heat, cover and simmer for 5 minutes, or until tender.
2 Drain, reserving the liquid. Sieve, then mix the purée with the liquid.
3 Put the whole egg and the yolk in the top pan of a double boiler with the sugar. Whisk over simmering water until pale and frothy. Remove from the heat.
4 Mix 30 ml /2 tbls blackcurrant purée with the crème de cassis and reserve.
5 Put 15 ml /1 tbls blackcurrant purée in a small bowl and sprinkle the gelatine over it. Leave the gelatine to soften. Place the bowl in a pan of simmering water and leave until the gelatine is completely dissolved. Allow it to cool slightly.
6 Whisk the cream to soft peaks.

Plum and honey mousses

These light, fluffy mousses combine all the sharpness of cooking plums with the mellow sweetness of honey.

1½ hours,
plus 1½ hours setting

Serves 4
juice of 1 lemon
15 g /½ oz gelatine
400 g /14 oz cooking plums
75 ml /3 fl oz unsweetened apple juice or water
5 cm /2 in piece of cinnamon stick
a blade of mace
45 ml /3 tbls clear honey
2 eggs, separated
150 ml /5 fl oz thick cream
30 ml /2 tbls chopped nuts, to garnish

1 Put the lemon juice in a saucepan and sprinkle the gelatine on top. Leave to soak.
2 Halve and stone the plums. Put them in a large saucepan with the apple juice or water and the cinnamon and mace. Cover and cook over a low heat for 20 minutes, until the plums are very soft. Rub them through a nylon sieve. Discard the spices.
3 Return the plum purée to the rinsed saucepan and set it over a low heat. Add the honey and stir until it has dissolved. Remove the pan from the heat.
4 Gently melt the gelatine, without letting it boil, and then stir it into the plum purée. Beat in the egg yolks.
5 Return the pan to a very low heat and stir with a wooden spoon, without letting the mixture boil, until it will coat the back of the spoon.
6 Remove the pan from the heat. Allow the mixture to cool, then chill it in the refrigerator for about 30 minutes, until it is on the point of setting.
7 Lightly whip the cream and whisk up the egg whites until they are stiff. Fold first the cream and then the egg whites into the plum mixture.
8 Pour the mixture into individual glasses and chill for about 1 hour in the refrigerator until set. Just before serving, decorate the mousses with a sprinkling of chopped nuts.

Rum surprise

1 hour,
plus setting and chilling

Serves 6
150 g /5 oz digestive biscuits, finely crushed
65 g /2½ oz butter, melted
225 g /8 oz canned pineapple chunks, drained
125 ml /4 fl oz dark rum
175 g /6 oz plain chocolate
275 ml /10 fl oz thick cream
30 ml /2 tbls soft, dark brown sugar
30 ml /2 tbls strong coffee
3 eggs
7.5 ml /½ tbls gelatine

Melon lime mousse

1 Put the crushed biscuits into a bowl. Add the melted butter and mix well. Line an 850 ml /1½ pt sandwich tin with the crumbs, pressing them down and making an even layer. Chill for 2 hours in the refrigerator.
2 Put the pineapple chunks in a blender and purée with 30 ml /2 tbls rum. Spread the purée evenly over the crumbs.
3 Break the chocolate into small squares and melt it in a small pan with 45 ml /3 tbls of the cream over a low heat, stirring until the chocolate is quite smooth.
4 In a cup, dissolve the sugar in the coffee and then add this to the melted chocolate.
5 Separate the eggs and add the yolks, one by one, to the chocolate mixture.
6 Sprinkle the gelatine over 30 ml /2 tbls cold water in a small bowl, then place the bowl over a pan of simmering water, stirring until the gelatine dissolves. Add it to the chocolate mixture, then stir in the remaining rum.
7 In a large bowl, whisk the egg whites until they are stiff and then fold them very gently, but thoroughly, into the chocolate mixture. Next, pour the mousse on top of the pineapple purée and chill to set.
8 Just before serving, whip the rest of the cream until thick but not buttery and spread it over the mousse. With the back of a spoon, flick the cream into little peaks all over and serve immediately.

● Use a dark rum to enhance the flavour of this exotic chocolate mousse.

Melon lime mousse

Ogen, honeydew, Galia or Lavan melons are all suitable for this pale, delicately-flavoured dessert, which can also be served in small, individual bowls.

30 minutes,
plus 3 hours setting

Serves 4–6
½ medium-sized, very ripe melon, about 700 g /1½ lb
a large pinch of ground ginger
grated zest and juice of 1 lime
30 ml /2 tbls natural yoghurt
2 eggs, separated
50 g /2 oz caster sugar
15 g /½ oz gelatine
slices of lime, to decorate

1 Remove and discard the melon seeds and seed membrane. Scoop out the flesh, drain it, and reduce it to a purée in a blender or in a bowl, using a fork.
2 Turn the melon purée into a bowl. Add the ground ginger, grated lime zest, all but 5–10 ml /1–2 tsp of the juice and the natural yoghurt, stirring well. Set aside.
3 In a medium-sized mixing bowl, whisk together the egg yolks and the caster sugar. Set the bowl over a pan of hot (but not boiling) water and whisk until the mixture is pale in colour and thick enough to retain the impression of the whisk for 3 seconds. Remove the bowl from the heat.
4 Pour the melon purée into the whisked egg mixture, stirring constantly with a wooden spoon to blend. Dissolve the gelatine in 30 ml /2 tbls hot water. Blend a little of the melon mixture with the dissolved gelatine, then pour the mixture back into the bowl, stirring constantly.
5 Lightly cover the bowl and leave it in a cool place for 45–60 minutes until the mixture has thickened to a syrupy consistency but not set. In a clean, dry bowl, whisk the egg whites until stiff. Fold the whisked whites into the melon mixture.
6 Pour the mousse into a serving bowl, cover lightly and leave it in a cool place for about 2 hours until it is completely set. Just before serving, decorate the mousse with slices of lime and sprinkle these with the remaining lime juice.

Chocolate mousse

Serves 6

*350 g /12 oz dark, bitter
   chocolate*
75 g /3 oz butter
*30–60 ml /2–4 tbls rum or
   cognac*
2 oranges
6 eggs, separated

15 g /½ oz gelatine
150 ml /5 fl oz thick cream
*6 glacé chestnuts (marrons glacés),
   chopped, to garnish*
For the Chantilly cream
300 ml /10 fl oz thick cream
15–30 ml /1–2 tbls iced water
8 glacé chestnuts, chopped

1 Break the chocolate into a bowl which will fit over a saucepan.
Add the butter and heat over simmering water, stirring occasionally,
until the chocolate and butter have melted. Remove the pan from the
heat and stir in 30 ml /2 tbls rum or cognac.
2 Cut the oranges into slices and purée the oranges slices (rind, pips
and all) in a blender. Add the purée to the chocolate mixture. In a
bowl, beat the egg yolks thoroughly. Stir in the warm chocolate and
orange mixture, beating constantly, so it is thoroughly blended.
3 Soak the gelatine in 60 ml /4 tbls cold water. When it has
softened, heat it gently until it is dissolved, then beat it into the
chocolate mixture. Strain the chocolate mixture through a fine sieve
into a clean bowl and allow it to cool to the point of setting.
4 Beat the egg whites until stiff but not dry. Whip the cream and
gently but thoroughly fold it into the chocolate orange mixture. Taste
the mixture, adding a little more rum or cognac, if wished. Very
gently fold in the beaten egg whites.
5 To assemble the dessert, put a collar of greaseproof paper or foil
tightly around a 1 L /1½ pt soufflé dish. The collar must extend
5 cm /2 in above the rim. Rinse a 200 ml /8 fl oz tumbler in cold
water and place the tumbler, open end up, in the centre of the soufflé
dish; pour the mousse mixture around it. (It is best to weight down
the glass to prevent it from moving.) Chill the mousse until set.
6 To make the Chantilly cream, whip the cream, add 15–30 ml /1–2
tbls of iced water and whip it again until smooth. Fold in the
chopped glacé chestnuts.
7 Just before serving, cut around the glass with a wet knife; pour a
little warm water into the glass and gently remove it from the centre
of the mousse. Remove the greaseproof paper or foil collar from
around the edge. Fill the cavity with Chantilly cream. Garnish with
the chopped glacé chestnuts and serve with any extra Chantilly cream
handed separately.

 2¾ hours,
including setting

Kirsch mousses

Serves 6–8

15 g /½ oz gelatine
4 eggs
75 g /2½ oz caster sugar
90 ml /6 tbls kirsch
275 ml /10 fl oz thick cream, whipped
For the decoration
non-toxic green leaves
fresh flowers

1 Sprinkle the gelatine over 75 ml /5 tbls cold water in a small bowl
and leave it to soften for a few minutes. Place the bowl in a saucepan
of simmering water and leave it until the gelatine is dissolved.
Remove it from the heat and leave it to cool slightly.
2 Select a large bowl in which to whisk up the mousse and a large
saucepan over which it will fit firmly. Pour 5 cm /2 in water into the
saucepan and bring it to the boil. Reduce the heat.
3 Place the eggs, caster sugar and kirsch into the bowl. Set the bowl
over the barely simmering water and whisk for 10 minutes, or until
the egg and sugar mixture is thick and mousse-like. Remove it from
the heat and whisk until cool.
4 Stir the dissolved gelatine into the mousse mixture and place the
bowl in a bowl of cracked ice. Stir until it is on the point of setting.
5 Fold in the whipped cream, then pour the mousse into individual
glass dishes. Leave it to set in the refrigerator.
6 To serve, decorate with non-toxic green leaves and fresh flowers.

 40 minutes,
plus setting

Iced orange mousses

Serves 6
6 large oranges
6 medium-sized egg yolks
75 g /2½ oz caster sugar
90 ml /6 tbls Grand Marnier or Marsala
225 ml /8 fl oz thick cream, whipped
For the decoration and serving
125 ml /4 fl oz thick cream, whipped
a pinch of cocoa powder or 10 ml /2 tsp grated chocolate
6 bay leaves or any other non-toxic, glossy leaves
petits fours or macaroons

1   Using a sharp knife, slice off the top of each orange. Using a grapefruit knife and small metal spoon, carefully scoop out all the orange flesh and enough of the pith to leave a firm shell. Save the flesh and juice for another recipe. Place the orange shells on a small baking sheet or in a small, metal tin. Arrange them so that they support each other and do not topple over. Set aside.
2   Combine the egg yolks, caster sugar and Grand Marnier or Marsala in a mixing bowl and beat until smooth and creamy. Fold in the whipped cream — the mixture will be fairly liquid.
3   Fill the orange shells with the egg yolk and cream mixture. Place them in the freezing compartment of the refrigerator and leave for at least 8 hours or overnight until the mixture is firm.
4   Twenty minutes before serving, transfer the oranges to the refrigerator to soften a little. Just before serving, decorate the tops with piped whipped cream and dust with cocoa or grated chocolate. Spike each orange with a bay leaf or any other non-toxic, glossy green leaf. Serve with petits fours or macaroons.

Apple mousse

Serves 4
1.4 kg /3 lb cooking apples
25 g /1 oz butter
50 g /2 oz caster sugar
grated zest of 1 lemon
150 ml /5 fl oz thick cream, whipped

1   Wipe the apples and without peeling or removing the cores, chop them into pieces.
2   Butter the bottom of a large heavy-based saucepan. Spread the apple pieces evenly over the base and sprinkle with caster sugar. Cover the saucepan with a lid and sweat the apples over a low heat for 15 minutes, shaking the pan occasionally.
3   Remove the lid. Over a moderate heat, cook the apples for a further 20 minutes, stirring and mashing with a wooden spoon until the apple mixture is soft and thick.
4   Using the back of a wooden spoon, rub the apple pulp through a sieve into a bowl. Discard the pips and skins. Leave the purée to become cold.
5   Stir the grated lemon zest into the purée and fold in the whipped cream. Pour the mousse into a serving dish and chill it for at least 1 hour or until it is needed.

● This mousse can be attractively garnished with slices of red-skinned dessert apple which have been dipped in lemon juice to prevent them turning brown. Arrange the slices in a fan design in the centre of the mousse.
● Serve with sponge fingers and a jug of thick cream, if wished.

 45 minutes,
plus freezing

 1 hour, then cooling
and chilling

PARTY ICE CREAMS

Bombes, ice-cream gateaux and truffles are just a few of the delicious desserts that are made easy in this chapter. Use your ice-cream moulding skills to the full by creating these party show-pieces.

Once you have mastered the techniques of making ice creams, you can experiment further with a whole new realm of iced desserts that are spectacular for parties. They are not too difficult to make, they look impressive and, of course, because they are prepared well in advance, they leave you more time for the rest of the meal and your guests.

Bombes
A bombe is an ice cream moulded into a rounded, pudding-bowl shape. It can be a combination of two or more ice creams frozen together. In most cases the outer layer is a plain ice cream and the inner layer, or layers, a wonderful contrast of colour and flavour — made with nuts, glacé fruit, cream and egg.

Cassata is another bombe variation, well known for its three different-coloured layers. It may have a vanilla ice cream outer layer, then a pink layer — usually strawberry or raspberry ice cream — and finally a centre of creamy pistachio ice cream with glacé cherries, angelica and nuts folded in (see recipe).

A bombe makes a wonderfully, elegant ending to a meal. As it can be prepared the day before, or even several days ahead, it provides a perfect end to a small dinner party.

My Italian chestnut chocolate bombe (see recipe) makes a super dessert for a buffet party and if there is any ice cream bombe left over, it can go straight back into the freezer for serving on another day.

The best bombes will, of course, be those made with home-made ice cream. But for speed, you can cheat a little if you prefer. Buy a really good commercial ice cream for the outer layer and then fill the centre with your own special mixture to complement any dessert wine you choose to serve.

Equipment
The question of a special mould for making bombes can be postponed for a while until you decide whether you are going to use it enough to justify the expense. A proper bombe mould is made of metal, so that the mixture freezes as quickly as possible, and it has a lid that fits tightly over it. The most attractive ones are tall with a domed top, made of copper and lined with tin. A little flat disc attached to the rounded end allows it to stand steady while you pour in the filling.

However, a pudding bowl or tall measuring jug will do just as well, although the shape will not be as rounded. Use a double thickness of foil to cover the surface of the ice cream tightly. The bombe will take longer to freeze in an earthenware or ovenproof bowl than in a metal mould, but the finished result will be quite satisfactory. A plastic bowl is a good choice, as the slight flexing of the plastic makes the bombe easier to turn out. (However, initially it is slightly more difficult to line.) If you do not have a mould or bowl of the correct capacity, use a larger one. It does not matter if the mould is not full.

Lining a bombe mould
Before you start, chill the empty mould thoroughly in the freezer to help the ice cream adhere to the sides. At the same time, the ice cream needs to be softened so that you can work it, so transfer it from the freezer to the main part of the refrigerator about 30 minutes before you start.

Turn the ice cream for the outer layer into a bowl and work it with a spatula until it is soft enough to spread. Spoon it into the chilled mould and press it all around the bottom and sides in a layer about 15–25 mm / ½–1 in thick, using a large metal spoon to smooth it. Make sure that the layer over the bottom is not too thick and that it does not get too thin towards the rim.

Put the lid on the mould, or cover the bowl with foil, and put it in the freezer until the ice cream is completely hard again. If you have accidentally let the ice cream soften too much, line half the mould only and return it to the freezer until the ice cream is hard before you line the remaining half.

If you are making a cassata with three layers, go through the same procedure again, leaving a hollow in the centre for the final filling. The centre filling is usually a soft one that can be spooned straight in. Cover the mould and freeze again until it is firm.

Unmoulding a bombe
A bombe is best unmoulded while it is still frozen hard — before the softening-up period in the main part of the refrigerator. Remove the lid or foil covering and invert the mould onto a flat serving plate. Wrap a cloth wrung out in hot water around the mould for 30 seconds, or a little longer for an earthenware bowl, re-dipping the cloth in hot water and wringing it out again as it cools.

Carefully lift off the mould. If you find you have overdone it and melted the surface of the bombe too much, smooth it over with the blade of a palette knife and return it to the freezer. (If quite a lot of the surface has melted away, you will have to repeat this reshaping process several times at 15-minute intervals.)

Finally, for a perfect surface, heat the blade of the palette knife thoroughly in a jug of hot water, dry it and draw it, with a few rapid strokes, over the surface of the bombe so that it is completely smooth.

Softening time: the amount of time required for the bombe to soften will depend not only on the type of ice cream used and the size of the bombe, but also on the efficiency of your refrigerator and freezer. In individual recipes mentioned in this chapter I have given softening times, but it is advisable to keep checking the bombe as it softens

Lining a bombe mould

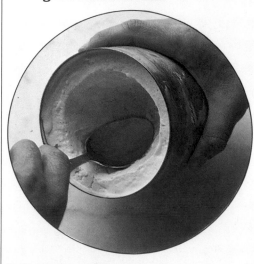

Smooth the softened ice cream in an even layer inside the chilled mould.

to see that it is not melting too quickly. **Storing:** if you have a deep freeze you can make a variety of bombes, using the same mould. As each bombe is prepared, unmould it as above, return it to the freezer until it is rock-hard again, then store it in a sealed polythene bag. They will keep well for up to 3 months. Before serving, unwrap the ice cream, put it on a serving dish and leave it in the main part of your refrigerator for the recommended softening time. What could be more convenient?

Ice-cream cakes and gateaux
Ice cream layered with a sponge or meringue becomes an ice-cream cake or gateau. Be liberal with the alcohol used to soak the sponge, and decorate it with cream and nuts.

For another variation, try setting the ice-cream mixture in a ring mould and filling the centre, when it is turned out, with diced fresh fruit in syrup, whipped cream or a combination of the two. Here are some delicious ideas: a strawberry or raspberry ice-cream border with whipped cream in the centre and a few crystallized rose petals to decorate it; a lemon-coloured ice cream with small pieces of pineapple and whipped cream in the centre; or a vanilla ice-cream ring with strawberries or raspberries in the centre.

Iced souffles and other desserts
As well as bombes and ice-cream cakes and gateaux, there are other delicious frozen desserts that can be made. In this chapter I have chosen a variety of ice cream desserts — Melba medley, Champagne ice with brandy strawberries, Refrigerated rich lime pudding, Vanilla charlotte glacé with rich apricot sauce, Iced chocolate truffles and Iced soufflés au Grand Marnier (see recipes).

Iced soufflés are lighter and fluffier than ice cream, with a lovely texture, instead of being completely smooth. This texture is achieved by using gelatine instead of beating the mixture while it is freezing. As it chills, the mixture gels and the gelatine then prevents ice crystals forming while the soufflé freezes. Prolonged freezing then breaks down the gelatine and, as a result, the frozen dessert is too soft to unmould. Nor could you defrost it — the soufflé would simply collapse.

Presentation is all-important with an iced soufflé because it has to be served in the dish in which it is made. The most usual way is to mould it by tying a paper collar around the dish so that the finished look is like a risen hot soufflé. The top can be decorated while the paper collar is still in place. The sides will have to wait until the collar is removed; whipped cream, finely chopped nuts or crushed macaroons are the usual choice of decorations.

Other desserts in this chapter feature the aptly named Ice-cream surprise — crispy, deep-fried balls filled with vanilla or chocolate ice cream. Alternatively, try the exotic Spanish pineapple. This dish is made using a whole fresh pineapple. The flesh is puréed and sieved, then combined with milk, sugar syrup and lemon juice, and frozen. The ice is formed into a pineapple shape, scored to resemble a pineapple skin, and then almonds are pressed into the surface.

Presentation
Because party ice creams are moulded and solid, the scope for decoration is much greater than with ice creams which are scooped or sliced. Whipped cream is often piped around the top or bottom of the bombe or gateau, and this can be dotted with crystallized fruit. If there are fruit or nuts in the ice cream, use some more for the decoration.

Melba medley

Slightly tart and brilliantly coloured, this Melba sauce is a classic fruit sauce.

10 minutes,
plus 1–2 hours chilling

Serves 4
For the Melba sauce
225 g /8 oz raspberries
45–60 ml /3–4 tbls icing sugar, sifted
For Peach Melba
425 ml /15 fl oz vanilla ice cream
2 peaches, skinned, halved and stoned
toasted almond slices, to decorate
For Strawberries cardinal
450–700 g /1–1½ lb strawberries, hulled
caster sugar
15 ml /1 tbls kirsch
ratafias, to decorate

1 First make the sauce. Crush the raspberries through a sieve into a heatproof bowl.
2 Set the bowl over a very low heat until the purée is just warm, then remove it from the heat and beat in the sifted icing sugar to taste. Turn the Melba sauce into a container, cover it tightly and chill it for 1–2 hours.
3 For Peach Melba, divide the ice cream among 4 chilled glass serving dishes and add a peach half. Spoon a quarter of the chilled Melba sauce over each portion and spike with toasted almonds slices.
4 For Strawberries cardinal, divide the strawberries among 4 chilled serving dishes and sprinkle them lightly with caster sugar and the kirsch. Decorate with Melba sauce and ratafias.

Melba medley

Iced soufflés au Grand Marnier

🍴 1 hour, then
3–5 hours freezing

Serves 6
2.5 ml /½ tsp gelatine
4 eggs, separated
125 g /4 oz sugar
300 ml /10 fl oz milk
45 ml /3 tbls Grand Marnier
a few drops of vanilla essence
300 ml /10 fl oz thick cream
6 small Italian macaroons (amaretti), crushed

1 Turn the freezing compartment of your refrigerator to its coldest setting about 1 hour before you start. Select 6 individual soufflé dishes about 6.5 cm /2½ in wide across the base. Tie double-thickness collars of grease-proof paper around them to come 25 mm / 1 in above the top.
2 In a small cup, sprinkle the gelatine over 15 ml /1 tbls cold water and leave to soften.
3 In a bowl, beat the egg yolks with the sugar until the mixture is thick and light.
4 Pour the milk into the top pan of a double boiler and bring to the boil over direct heat. Then whisk it into the egg mixture in a steady stream.
5 Return the mixture to the double boiler and stir it over simmering water until it coats the back of a spoon, taking care not to let the custard boil or the egg yolks will curdle. Cool it slightly.
6 Dissolve the softened gelatine by standing the cup in hot water until the liquid is clear. Blend it into the cooling custard, with the Grand Marnier and vanilla essence.
7 Whip the thick cream until it forms soft

Iced soufflés au Grand Marnier

peaks and then fold it into the custard.
8 Whisk the egg whites to soft peaks and fold them into the custard. Divide the soufflé mixture among the prepared soufflé dishes. It should come well above the rim of each dish.
9 Freeze until they are firm. Transfer them to the main part of the refrigerator 30 minutes before serving to soften slightly.
10 To serve, sprinkle the top of each iced soufflé with crushed macaroons, patting the crumbs in lightly to make them stick. Then carefully peel away the paper collars.

Champagne ice with brandy strawberries

It really *is* worth opening a bottle of champagne to accompany this delicious and luxurious dessert.

🍴 5½–7 hours, including
freezing and steeping

Serves 6–8
350 g /12 oz sugar
190 ml /¼ bottle dry champange
60 ml /4 tbls brandy
45 ml /3 tbls lemon juice
300 ml /10 fl oz thick cream, chilled
For the brandy strawberries
500 g /1 lb ripe strawberries, hulled
30–45 ml /2–3 tbls brandy
7.5–15 ml /½–1 tbls caster sugar

1 Turn the freezing compartment of your refrigerator to its lowest temperature (the highest setting) 1 hour before you start.
2 Put the sugar in a heavy-based saucepan with 300 ml /10 fl oz water and stir it over a low heat until the sugar is dissolved. Raise the heat and bring it to the boil, then simmer it slowly for 15 minutes. Remove it from the heat and leave the syrup to cool.

3 Stir the champagne, brandy and lemon juice into the cooled syrup. Pour it into a shallow, freezerproof container, cover and freeze for about 2 hours, or until the mixture has the consistency of wet snow.
4 Whip the chilled thick cream until it forms soft peaks. Turn the half-frozen champagne ice into a bowl and fold in the whipped cream. Return the mixture to the freezer container and freeze again until firm.
5 To make the brandy strawberries, put the strawberries into a bowl, add the brandy and sugar to taste and leave them to steep for at least 2 hours.
6 About 30 minutes before serving, transfer the ice cream to the main part of the refrigerator to soften slightly.
7 To serve, scoop the ice cream into champagne glasses and top each serving with the brandy strawberries.

Ice-cream surprise

🕐🍴 making the ice cream,
2½ hours, plus 1½ hours chilling

Serves 4
225 g /8 oz butter, chilled
150 ml /5 fl oz vanilla or chocolate ice-cream
flour, for coating
3 eggs, beaten
100 g /4 oz cake crumbs
oil, for deep frying
sifted icing sugar
non-toxic green leaves, to garnish

1 Cut the chilled butter into 24 equal-sized cubes. Squeeze the cubes gently to round the corners, without trying to make them into complete ball shapes. Place them on a baking tray and chill them for 1 hour, or until firm.
2 Roll the butter balls to perfect rounded shapes and return them to the refrigerator to firm again.

Ice-cream surprise

3 Transfer the ice cream to the main part of the refrigerator to allow it to soften.
4 Coat the butter balls lightly with flour. Roll them in the beaten egg and then in the cake crumbs. Return them to the refrigerator to set.
5 Roll the butter balls in egg again, then in the cake crumbs, pressing them on with a palette knife. Chill once more.
6 Heat the oil in a deep-fat frier to 190C / 375F; at this temperature a 15 mm /½ in cube of day-old bread will turn golden brown in 50 seconds.
7 Deep-fry the crumbed butter balls, a few at a time, until they are browned. Remove them from the oil with a slotted spoon, then make a little hole with the point of a very sharp knife to release the melted butter from inside the crust, holding the slotted spoon over a bowl. (Reserve the melted butter for use in another recipe.)
8 Place the fried crumb balls on absorbent paper, hole side down. Leave them to get cold.
9 Fit a large piping bag with a 5 mm /¼ in plain nozzle and spoon in the softened ice cream. Carefully pipe the ice cream into the cold crumb balls. Transfer them to the freezing compartment of the refrigerator for about 30 minutes, or until they are firm.
10 About 5–10 minutes before serving, transfer them to the main part of the refrigerator to soften slightly.
11 To serve, roll the ice cream balls in sifted icing sugar and pile them up in a chilled glass serving dish. Garnish them with green leaves and serve at once.

Spanish pineapple

⏱ 45 minutes, plus 3½ hours freezing, then 45 minutes

Serves 6–8
1 large pineapple, about 1.5 kg /3¼ lb
225 ml /8 fl oz milk
350 g /12 oz sugar
45 ml /3 tbls lemon juice
15–30 ml /1–2 tbls apricot jam
toasted almonds, to decorate

1 Cut a thin slice from the top of the pineapple, to include the leaves, and reserve. Remove the skin from the pineapple and discard it.
2 Remove the hard core from the centre of the pineapple. Dice the pineapple flesh, purée it in an electric blender and press it through a sieve. There should be 1 L /1¾ pt of purée. Add the milk and mix well.
3 Put the sugar and 250 ml /9 fl oz water in a pan and heat gently, stirring, until the sugar is dissolved; bring it to the boil. Simmer, covered, for 5 minutes. Remove the pan from the heat and allow the sugar syrup to cool.
4 Combine the pineapple purée, the cooled syrup and lemon juice. Divide this mixture equally between two 600 ml /1 pt pudding bowls. Put them in the freezer until the mixture freezes to 25 mm /1 in thick around the sides of the bowls. Whisk the sorbet with a fork to break up the ice particles and return the bowls to the freezer for 30 minutes. Repeat this process twice more.

5 In a small saucepan, heat the apricot jam until it is runny. Remove it from the heat and allow it to cool.
6 To re-form the pineapple, turn the sorbet out of the pudding bowls by either dipping them for a few seconds in hot water or by wrapping the base and sides of the bowls in cloths wrung out in hot water. Place one half of the sorbet, right side up, on a serving plate and brush the large, flat surface area with apricot jam. Invert the other half of the sorbet onto the apricot jam and position. Smooth the join with a palette knife and return the sorbet to the freezer.
7 Half an hour before serving, transfer the sorbet to the refrigerator to soften slightly. To serve, replace the pineapple leaves on top of the sorbet. Score the sorbet diagonally and place a toasted almond in each diamond to resemble the pineapple skin. Place the 'pineapple' on non-toxic leaves on a serving plate.

● If you do not have a freezer you may be able to use the freezing compartment of your refrigerator. Check before you begin that it is high enough to accommodate the sorbets when they are combined in step 6; remember to turn the refrigerator to its lowest temperature (the highest setting) about 1 hour before starting.

Spanish pineapple

the ice-cream cake, transfer the coffee walnut and vanilla ice creams to the refrigerator to soften slightly.

9 Line the base of a 1.7 L /3 pt charlotte mould with buttered greaseproof paper.

10 Cut the sponge cake in half horizontally and cut 2 strips to line the sides of the mould. Place them cut sides to the middle. Cut the remaining sponge into about 11 fingers, 15 mm /½ in wide and 3 cm / 1¼ in long. Trim one end of each finger to a point. Lay them, cut side up, in the base of the mould, cartwheel fashion. Brush the inside of the sponge with the rum.

11 Spoon half the coffee walnut ice cream into the mould and press it firmly into a flat layer using a spoon. Spoon the vanilla ice cream on top, flatten it into a layer and finish with a layer of the remaining coffee walnut ice cream. Cover and freeze.

12 Thirty minutes before serving, unmould the ice cream cake onto a flat serving dish and place it in the main part of the refrigerator to soften slightly.

13 Just before serving, pipe whipped cream around the base and the top of the cake and decorate it with the walnut halves.

Italian chestnut chocolate bombe

🔪🔪 6–7 hours, including freezing

Serves 12
850 ml /1½ pt Chocolate ice cream (see Iced chocolate truffles, page 79)
225 g /8 oz canned whole chestnuts in syrup, drained
225 g /8 oz canned sweetened chestnut purée
15–30 ml /1–2 tbls brandy
350 ml /12 fl oz thick cream
1 egg white
For the decoration
whipped cream
glacé cherries
marrons glacés
holly or marzipan leaves

1 If you are using the freezing compartment of your refrigerator, turn it down to its lowest temperature (the highest setting) about an hour before you start. At the same time, put a 1.7 L /3 pt bombe mould to chill and transfer the chocolate ice cream to the refrigerator to soften.

2 Spoon the chocolate ice cream into the bombe mould. Smooth it into an even layer over the bottom and up the sides of the mould, about 20 mm /¾ in thick. Cover with foil and freeze until firm.

3 Coarsely chop the canned chestnuts, spoon them into the chocolate-lined mould and press them gently into the ice cream. Cover and freeze again.

4 Put the chestnut purée in a bowl with the brandy and whisk them together until well blended. In another bowl, whisk the thick cream until soft peaks form. Fold the whipped cream into the chestnut purée.

5 In another clean, dry bowl, whisk the egg white until it is stiff but not dry, then fold it

Ice-cream cake

🕐🔪 making the cake and ice cream, then 7–10 hours, including freezing

Serves 8
1 × Fatless sponge mixture (see page 30)
5–10 ml /1–2 tsp instant coffee
300 ml /10 fl oz vanilla ice cream
butter, for greasing
45 ml /3 tbls rum
thick cream, whipped, to decorate
5 walnut halves, to decorate
For the coffee walnut ice cream
7 egg yolks
50 g /2 oz caster sugar
a pinch of salt
700 ml /1¼ pt whipping cream
30 ml /2 tbls instant coffee
vanilla essence
125 g /4 oz chopped walnuts

1 Heat the oven to 180C /350F /gas 4. Flavour the cake mixture with instant coffee, then bake it in a 30 × 22 cm /12 × 8½ in Swiss roll tin for 20 minutes. Turn out the cake and allow it to cool. If using the freezing compartment of your refrigerator, turn it to its coldest setting 1 hour before you start.

Ice-cream cake

2 For the coffee walnut ice cream: put the egg yolks, the sugar and the salt in a large bowl and whisk until the mixture is light and lemon-coloured.

3 Put the cream and the instant coffee in the top pan of a double boiler and stir to blend. Bring to just below boiling point over direct heat. Pour the scalded coffee cream onto the whisked egg mixture in a thin stream, whisking constantly.

4 Pour the mixture back into the top pan of the double boiler. Place it over simmering water and cook, stirring constantly, until it thickens and coats the back of a spoon. Do not let it boil or the egg yolks will curdle.

5 Remove the pan from the heat, strain the custard through a fine sieve into a bowl and leave it until it is cold. Flavour the custard with a few drops of vanilla essence to taste, and fold in the chopped walnuts.

6 Pour the custard into a shallow freezer-proof container and freeze it for 1 hour, or until it is firm to a depth of 25 mm /1 in round the edges of the container.

7 Remove the ice cream from the freezer and beat it to break down the ice crystals. Cover and freeze again until firm.

8 About 1 hour before you start to mould

gently into the chestnut mixture. Spoon this into the centre of the mould, cover and freeze the bombe until it is set.

6 About 30 minutes before serving, turn out the bombe onto a flat serving dish and place it in the main part of the refrigerator to soften slightly.

7 Just before serving, decorate the bombe with piped whipped cream, the glacé cherries, the sliced marrons glacés and the holly or marzipan leaves.

Coffee ice-cream gateau

🍴 6–7 hours, including freezing time

Serves 6
oil, for greasing
4 egg whites
225 g /8 oz caster sugar
425 ml /15 fl oz thick cream
15 ml /1 tbls instant coffee
30 ml /2 tbls Tia Maria
150 ml /5 fl oz chocolate ice cream

1 If you are using the freezing compartment of your refrigerator, turn it to its lowest temperature (the highest setting). Heat the oven to 150C /300F /gas 2. Lightly oil 2 baking sheets.

2 Make the meringue: whisk the egg whites in a large bowl until they form stiff peaks. Whisk in 50 g /2 oz of the sugar and continue whisking for 1 minute, or until the mixture is very stiff. Using a large metal spoon, fold in the remaining sugar.

3 Using a teaspoon, place nuggets of the

meringue mixture on the baking sheets, spacing them well apart. Bake the meringues for 1 hour. Turn off the heat and leave the meringues in the oven for a further 10–15 minutes, or until they are crisp on the outside but still soft in the centre. Leave them to cool in the oven.

4 In a bowl, whisk the thick cream to soft peaks. In a small bowl, dilute the coffee with 25 ml /1 fl oz boiling water and leave it to cool. Fold the coffee, the Tia Maria and the meringues, reserving 4, into the cream, trying not to break the meringues.

6 Line the base of an 18 cm /7 in round, loose-bottomed cake tin with a disc of greaseproof paper and spoon in the cream mixture; cover and freeze. Transfer the ice cream to the main part of the refrigerator to soften it.

7 When the cream gateau is hard, remove it from the freezer. Run a sharp knife around the edge of the gateau and turn it out of the tin onto a flat plate or a baking sheet. Carefully remove the base of the tin and peel off the greaseproof paper.

8 Fit a piping bag with a 15 mm /½ in star nozzle. Beat the chocolate ice cream to soften it a little, then spoon it into the piping bag. Pipe rosettes around the top of the gateau to decorate it. Return the gateau to the freezer to harden it completely.

9 Transfer the gateau to a serving dish, decorate with reserved meringues and place in the main part of the refrigerator for 10–15 minutes to soften slightly, then serve.

Refrigerated rich lime pudding

🍴 40 minutes, plus at least 8 hours freezing

Serves 10
3 eggs, separated
100 g /4 oz caster sugar
grated zest of 2 limes
juice of 3 limes
425 ml /15 fl oz thick cream
225 g /8 oz plain digestive biscuits, crushed
For the decoration
fresh lime slices
3 red cherries
5 wafer biscuits

1 Line the base of a 1.7 L /3 pt loaf tin with greaseproof paper.

2 Put the egg yolks in the top half of a double boiler. Add the caster sugar and whisk over gently simmering water until the mixture is pale and thick. Remove it from the heat and stir in the lime zest and juice.

3 Whip the cream until soft peaks form, and then fold it into the lime mixture.

4 In a clean, dry bowl, whisk the egg whites until soft peaks form. Using a large metal spoon, fold the egg whites into the lime mixture.

5 Sprinkle a thin layer of biscuit crumbs over the base of the tin. Carefully pour in the lime mixture and top it with a layer of the remaining biscuit crumbs. Cover it with foil, then place it in the freezer for at least 8 hours, until firm.

6 To serve, run a palette knife around the edge of the pudding to loosen it. Turn it out onto a flat serving plate and remove the greaseproof paper. Decorate the pudding with slices of fresh lime, cherries and wafer biscuits, and then serve.

● Undecorated, this pudding can be kept in the freezer for up to 1 month.

Refrigerated rich lime pudding

Cherry cream bombe

Serves 8
1.4 L /2½ pt vanilla ice cream
75 ml /5 tbls glacé cherries
75 ml /5 tbls kirsch
150 ml /5 fl oz thick cream, to decorate
crystallized violets, to decorate

1 If you are using the freezing compartment of your refrigerator, turn it down to its lowest temperature (the highest setting), about 1 hour before you start. At the same time, put a 1.4 L /2½ pt bombe mould to chill, and transfer the vanilla ice cream to the main part of the refrigerator to soften.
2 In a small bowl, combine the glacé cherries and the kirsch. Leave them to steep for 1 hour.
3 In a large bowl, beat the softened vanilla ice cream with a wooden spoon. Stir in the steeped fruit and kirsch. Spoon the mixture into the chilled bombe mould and press it down well. Cover and freeze until it is very firm.
4 About 45 minutes before serving, remove the bombe from the freezer. Dip the mould briefly into a bowl of hot water, then turn the bombe out onto a flat serving platter.
5 Return to the freezer for 10–15 minutes, to harden the surface again, then transfer it to the main part of the refrigerator for at least 10 minutes.
6 Meanwhile, whip the cream. Spoon the whipped cream into a piping bag fitted with a 15 mm /½ in star nozzle and pipe scrolls around the base of the bombe. Decorate it with crystallized violets and serve immediately.

1½ hours,
plus freezing

Vanilla charlotte glacé with rich apricot sauce

Serves 4
about 24 sponge fingers or boudoir fingers
60–75 ml /4–5 tbls kirsch
500 ml /18 fl oz vanilla ice cream, softened
For the rich apricot sauce
415 g /14½ oz canned apricot halves in syrup
15 ml /1 tbls caster sugar
5 ml /1 tsp arrowroot
15 ml /1 tbls lemon juice
5–10 ml /1–2 tsp kirsch
For the decoration
thick cream, whipped
8 whole blanched almonds

1 Cut the sponge fingers or boudoir fingers in half, then cut the pieces to fit the base and sides of 4 individual 150 ml /5 fl oz ramekins or soufflé dishes. Mix the kirsch with 60–75 ml /4–5 tbls water. Dip each piece of sponge or boudoir finger in the kirsch and water mixture for a few seconds to moisten them all over. Lay them carefully in the ramekins, cut sides against the dish.
2 Fill the sponge finger-lined moulds carefully with the vanilla ice cream. Cover and put them in the freezer for about 4 hours.
3 Meanwhile, make the rich apricot sauce. Drain the apricot halves, reserving the syrup, and purée the halves through a fine sieve, or purée them in an electric blender and then sieve them. Add the caster sugar to the purée and mix thoroughly.
4 Measure out 45 ml /3 tbls of the apricot syrup and gradually blend this into the arrowroot until smooth. Stir the apricot and arrowroot mixture into the apricot purée, together with the lemon juice.
5 Put the apricot mixture in a pan and stir it over a medium heat until the sauce reaches boiling point. Reduce the heat and simmer it, stirring occasionally, for 5–6 minutes or until the sauce has thickened.
6 Allow the sauce to cool slightly and then flavour it with the kirsch to taste.
7 Just before serving, unmould each charlotte glacé onto a dessert plate and cover the tops with apricot sauce. Pipe whipped cream onto each charlotte glacé and top each with 2 whole almonds. Serve immediately with the remaining sauce served separately.

45 minutes, plus 4 hours freezing,
then 10 minutes decorating

Iced chocolate truffles

Serves 6

90 g /3½ oz quartered glacé
 cherries, plus extra to garnish
60 ml /4 tbls cherry liqueur
450 g /1 lb plain dessert chocolate
275 ml /10 fl oz thick cream,
 for whipping

1.5 ml /¼ tsp vanilla essence
For the chocolate ice cream
575 ml /1 pt thick cream
100 g /4 oz dark dessert chocolate
175 g /6 oz sugar
5 medium-sized egg yolks

1 Begin the truffles 2 days ahead of serving. Place the quartered cherries in a bowl, and pour the cherry liqueur over them. Cover and refrigerate for 24 hours. Finely grate the chocolate (or chop it in a food processor), place it in an airtight container and refrigerate.
2 Make the chocolate ice cream: first turn the refrigerator to its lowest temperature and chill a bowl and a metal container. Place the cream, the chocolate and half the sugar in a small, heavy-based saucepan. Bring to scalding point over a low heat and mix well.
3 In the top of a double boiler, whisk together the egg yolks and the remaining sugar. Pour the hot chocolate cream onto the egg yolk mixture in a thin stream, whisking constantly. Place over hot, not boiling, water and cook over a low heat, stirring constantly. To test when the custard is cooked, draw your finger across the back of the spoon — it should leave a clean line. Turn the custard mixture into the chilled bowl and leave it until it is cold.
4 Turn the mixture into the chilled metal container; cover with foil. Freeze, stirring vigorously every 30 minutes, until the ice cream is half-frozen. Now, freeze it undisturbed for 2–3 hours or overnight, until it is completely firm.
5 On the day before serving, soften the ice cream in the refrigerator for 15–20 minutes, then make 6 ice-cream balls using a large ice cream scoop. Put these on a chilled baking tray, and press 15 ml /1 tbls macerated cherries into the centre of each one, then smooth over.
6 Place the ice-cream balls in the freezing compartment for 10 minutes, or until they are very firm. With your hands, form the ice-cream balls into smooth, perfectly round shapes. Roll each ball in the finely grated or chopped chocolate until evenly coated, then return to the freezing compartment.
7 Just before serving, whisk the cream with the vanilla essence until it holds its shape. Spoon some of the cream into a piping bag fitted with a star nozzle, and pipe a swirl of cream onto 6 chilled dessert plates. Place an iced chocolate truffle on each swirl of cream. Decorate with extra cherries and serve at once with the remaining whipped cream handed round separately.

start 2 days ahead, then 1 hour,
plus 4–5 hours chilling and freezing

Cassata

Serves 4–6

850 ml /1½ pt vanilla ice cream
275 ml /10 fl oz strawberry or raspberry ice cream
275 ml /10 fl oz pistachio ice cream
25 g /1 oz glacé cherries, chopped
25 g /1 oz angelica, chopped
25 g /1 oz almonds, blanched and chopped
crystallized fruit, to decorate

1 Place a 1.1 L /2 pt bombe mould or pudding bowl and a 600 ml / 1 pt bombe mould or pudding bowl in the freezer to chill for at least 15 minutes. Take the vanilla ice cream out of the freezer to soften it slightly.
2 When the larger bombe mould is quite cold, smooth the vanilla ice cream around the inside of it, using the back of a tablespoon. Make sure the ice cream is not too thick across the bottom, and that you have a good thickness inside the rim of the mould. Smooth horizontally across the top. Place the smaller mould in the centre to hold the ice cream in position and then return it to the freezer for 30 minutes. Take the strawberry or raspberry ice cream out of the freezer to soften it slightly.
3 Carefully remove the inner mould from the vanilla ice cream by wiping the inside quickly with a cloth wrung out in very hot water. With the back of a tablespoon, work the strawberry or raspberry ice cream into an even layer on top of the vanilla ice cream. Return the mould to the freezer for a further 30 minutes. Take the pistachio ice cream out of the freezer to soften it slightly.
4 In a bowl, combine the chopped cherries, the angelica and the nuts with the pistachio ice cream and mix well. Fill the centre of the mould with this mixture and return it to the freezer for at least 6 hours. About 30 minutes before serving, remove the mould from the freezer and put it in the main part of the refrigerator to soften.
5 To serve, unmould the cassata by placing the mould in hot water for a few seconds to loosen the ice cream, then turn it out onto a chilled plate, and decorate with the crystallized fruit.

● If using the freezing compartment of the refrigerator, turn it to the lowest temperature (the highest setting) well before you start. Remember to turn the refrigerator back to its normal setting when you have finished.

1½ hours, then
at least 6 hours freezing

SORBETS & WATER-ICES

Refreshing, tangy, delicious and attractive, my selection of sorbets and water-ices will tempt and please everyone. Try a plain Apple sorbet or an elaborate Grapefruit mint ice served in a grapefruit basket.

The beauty of serving a sorbet or water-ice as a dessert is that any preparation can be done in advance and the dessert kept in the freezer until just before you are ready to serve it.

Whether you decide to make a simple Blackberry sorbet (see recipe) or a more involved Peach and white wine sorbet (see recipe) you will find that they are really not too difficult to prepare. If you have the time, present your ice in a fruit container — see the instructions for making pretty grapefruit baskets in Grapefruit mint ice (page 84). You can also use oranges, lemons or limes depending on how you wish to complement the flavour and look of the ice you are serving.

Try offering your dinner party guests a choice of two gorgeous desserts — a rich Grape water-ice made from Muscat grapes with Marsala as an added flavouring, or a portion of Prune sorbet (see recipe) made with armagnac-soaked prunes — I am sure that both will impress and please them.

Peach and white wine sorbet

The peach skins are cooked in the syrup to give this sorbet a delicate pink blush.

45 minutes, plus cooling the syrup, then 6–7 hours freezing

Serves 6–8
550 g /1¼ lb ripe peaches
juice of 1 lemon
For the syrup
225 g /8 oz caster sugar
zest and juice of ½ lemon
275 ml /10 fl oz Graves, Chablis or similar
  full-bodied, dry white wine

1 If using the freezing compartment of your refrigerator, turn it down to its lowest temperature (the highest setting) about 1 hour before you start.
2 Cut the peaches in half and stone them. Submerge the peach halves in boiling water for 30 seconds, then plunge them into cold water. Peel them and reserve the skins.
3 Chop the fruit coarsely and quickly (or it will discolour) and put it in a blender with the lemon juice. Purée the mixture, cover it with cling film and reserve.
4 To make the syrup, put the sugar, peach skins, lemon zest and 225 ml /8 fl oz water in a heavy-based saucepan. Gently dissolve the sugar, stirring. Boil rapidly for 1 minute. Plunge the base of the pan into cold water.
5 Strain, discarding the skins and zest. Stir in the lemon juice, wine and peach purée.
6 Pour the mixture into a shallow, freezer-proof container, cover and freeze for 2 hours or until the sorbet is frozen to a depth of about 25 mm /1 in all around the sides. Stir

vigorously, cover and freeze. Repeat the stirring every 30 minutes until the sorbet is half frozen.
7 Cover the sorbet and freeze for at least 3 hours or overnight. Transfer the sorbet to the main part of the refrigerator about 1 hour before serving to allow it to soften.

Blackberry sorbet

For a lovely dessert, serve a scoop of this sorbet with a scoop of the Peach and white wine sorbet. Garnish them with a sprig of mint, a couple of peach slices and some blackberries (see picture opposite).

45 minutes, plus cooling the syrup, then 6–7 hours freezing

Serves 10
350 g /12 oz caster sugar
550 g /1¼ lb blackberries
a pinch of salt
juice of 1 large orange
juice of 1 large lemon
2 medium-sized egg whites

1 If using the freezing compartment of your refrigerator, turn it down to its lowest temperature (the highest setting) about 1 hour before you start.
2 Put the sugar and 200 ml /7 fl oz of water over a low heat and stir it until the sugar has dissolved, then boil the syrup rapidly for 1 minute. Plunge the base of the pan into cold water and leave the syrup to cool.
3 Purée the blackberries in a blender. Press the pulp through a nylon sieve to remove the pips. (You should have 600 ml /1 pt of purée.) Stir in the salt, the orange and lemon juices and the cold syrup.
4 Pour the mixture into a shallow, freezer-proof container, cover and freeze for 2 hours or until it is frozen to a depth of about 25 mm /1 in all around the sides.
5 Stir up the mixture vigorously with a fork or wire whisk, then freeze it again. Repeat the stirring every 20 minutes until the sorbet is half frozen.
6 Whisk the egg whites until they are stiff but not dry. Put the sorbet into a large bowl and beat it with a fork or whisk it until smooth. Whisk in the beaten egg whites.
7 Turn the mixture into a freezer-proof container, cover and freeze it for at least 3 hours or overnight, until it is hard.
8 About 30 minutes before serving, transfer the sorbet to the main part of the refrigerator to allow it to soften.

Claret granita

10 minutes, cooling the syrup, then 3½ hours freezing

Serves 6
200 g /7 oz sugar
75 cl bottle of red wine, preferably St Emilion
juice of 1 orange
juice of 1 lemon
6 fresh mint leaves, to garnish

1 If using the freezing compartment of your refrigerator, turn it down to its lowest temperature (the highest setting) about 1 hour before you start.
2 Put the sugar and 200 ml /7 fl oz water in a heavy-based saucepan and stir it over a gentle heat until the sugar is dissolved. Boil it for 1 minute and then allow it to cool.
3 When the syrup is cold, add the wine, the orange and lemon juices and mix together with a small whisk.
4 Strain the mixture through a muslin-lined sieve into a shallow, freezer-proof container and freeze for 1½ hours or until frozen to a depth of 25 mm /1 in all around the sides.
5 Turn the claret ice into a large bowl and whisk it until it is smooth — use an electric mixer, if you have one. Pour it back into the freezer-proof container and freeze it again until it is lightly set and a mass of small, light crystals.
6 Stir the granita and spoon it into 6 claret glasses, shaping it into a dome with a spoon. Garnish each one with a mint leaf and serve it immediately with long spoons.

Apple sorbet

35 minutes, cooling the syrup, then 6–7 hours including freezing

Serves 2–3
125 g /4 oz sugar
500 g /1 lb cooking apples
30 ml /2 tbls lemon juice
1 egg white

1 If using the freezing compartment of your refrigerator, turn it down to its lowest temperature (the highest setting) about 1 hour before you start.
2 Put the sugar and 225 ml /8 fl oz water in a heavy-based saucepan and stir it over a gentle heat until the sugar is dissolved. Then boil it for 5 minutes. Cool until tepid.
3 Core the apples and dice them, but do not bother to peel them. Place them in a blender with the sugar syrup and lemon juice and blend until smooth. Pass the purée through a sieve. The purée should measure 600 ml /1 pt, so add water if necessary. Cool the mixture completely.
4 Pour the apple mixture into a shallow, freezer-proof container, cover and freeze for 1 hour or until it is frozen to a depth of 25 mm / 1 in all around the sides.
5 Whisk the apple sorbet with a fork or a wire whisk until smooth (you can use a food processor). Whisk the egg white until stiff peaks form, then whisk it into the purée. Return it to the freezer-proof container and freeze it again until the sorbet is firm.
6 Transfer the apple sorbet to the refrigerator 1 hour before serving to soften.

Two refreshing sorbets: Peach and white wine sorbet and Blackberry sorbet

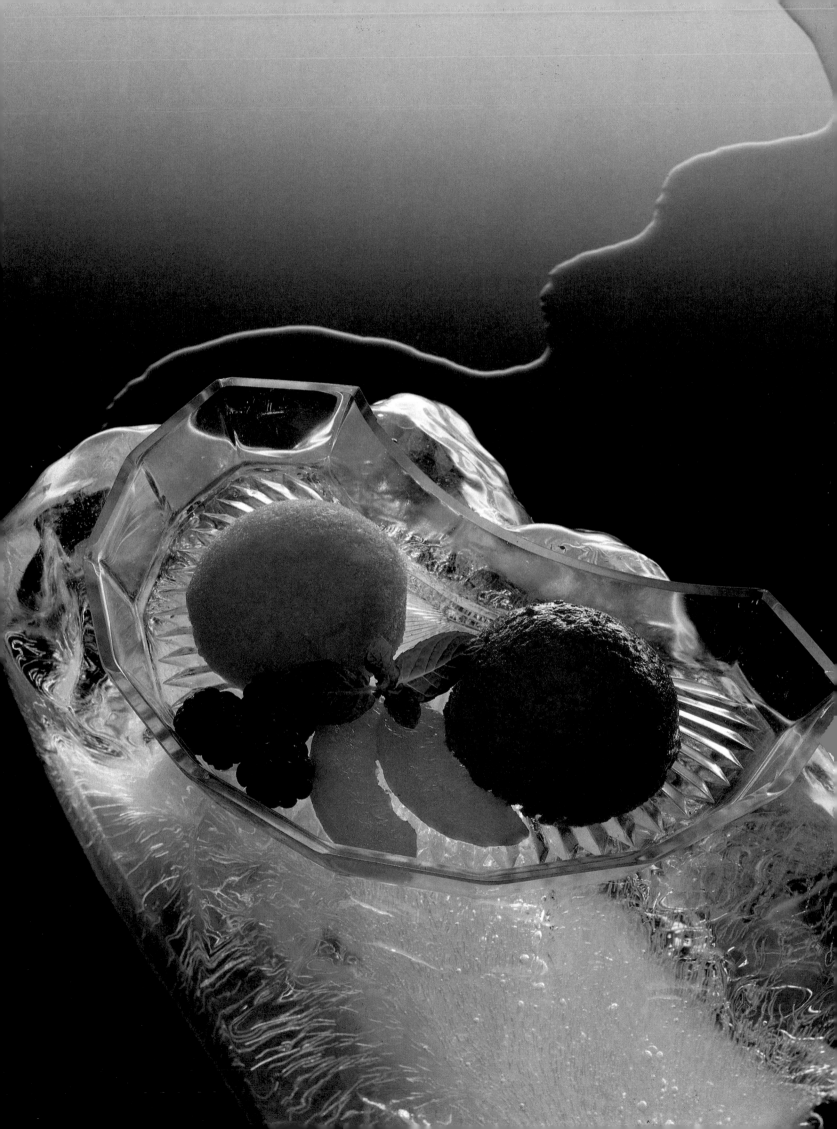

Honeyed fig sorbet

Serves 4
800 g /1 lb 12 oz canned green figs in syrup, with
60 ml /4 tbls fig syrup reserved and 4 figs
reserved for the garnish
150 ml /5 fl oz clear honey
60 ml /4 tbls lemon juice
60 ml /4 tbls white rum
whipped cream, to garnish
20 ml /4 tsp white rum, to serve

1   If using the freezing compartment of your refrigerator, turn it down to its lowest temperature (the highest setting) about 1 hour before you start.
2   Drain the figs. Reserve 60 ml /4 tbls of the syrup and keep 4 figs for the garnish.
3   Blend the figs, half at a time, to a purée in a blender. Transfer the purée to a bowl and add the honey, reserved fig syrup and lemon juice to taste. Stir in the white rum.
4   Pour the purée into an ice-cube tray (with the dividers removed) or a loaf tin and freeze it until the mixture is solid to a depth of 25 mm /1 in around the edge of the tray or tin. This will take about 3 hours.
5   Spoon the fig mixture into a large bowl and beat it hard until it is just mushy, but not melted.
6   Pile the sorbet into individual glass sorbet dishes. Return them to the freezer for 10 minutes.
7   When ready to serve, pipe a swirl of whipped cream on top of each sorbet, add a reserved fig, then pour 5 ml /1 tsp of white rum over each portion.

● This is an easy pudding to make as the main ingredient is canned. The timing is quite important, though, as this sorbet should be eaten when it is a soft purée. Remember that if you leave your glass dishes in the freezer for too long, they could shatter. If you wish to freeze and then soften the sorbet, allow it at least 1 hour to soften in the refrigerator before spooning it into individual glasses.

20 minutes, plus 3 hours freezing,
then 20 minutes

Grape water-ice

Serves 6
225 g /8 oz sugar
juice of 2 lemons
500 g /1 lb Muscat grapes
15 ml /1 tbls orange-flower water
60 ml /4 tbls Marsala
For the garnish
pistachio nuts, finely chopped

1   If using the freezing compartment of your refrigerator, turn it down to its lowest temperature (the highest setting) about 1 hour before you start.
2   Put the sugar and 575 ml /1 pt water in a heavy-based saucepan and heat gently, stirring with a wooden spoon, until the sugar is dissolved. Then boil it for 10 minutes. Add the lemon juice and strain the syrup through a muslin-lined sieve into a bowl. Leave it to cool until it is lukewarm.
3   Purée the grapes in a blender and rub them through a fine nylon sieve to remove the skin and pips.
4   Add the lukewarm syrup to the grape purée with the orange-flower water and the Marsala. Pour the syrup into a shallow, freezer-proof container and freeze it for 1 hour or until it is frozen to a depth of 25 mm /1 in all around the sides of the container.
5   Whisk the mixture vigorously with a fork until it is smooth, then freeze it again. Repeat the whisking every 30 minutes until the ice is half frozen.
6   Cover the ice and freeze it for a further 2–3 hours or until it is frozen hard. Transfer the ice to the main part of the refrigerator about 30 minutes before serving.
7   To serve, arrange 3 scoops of ice on each plate. Garnish each serving with finely chopped pistachio nuts and serve immediately.

20 minutes, cooling the syrup,
then 6–7 hours freezing

Apricot brandy sorbet

Serves 4
175 g /6 oz sugar
grated zest and juice of 1 lemon
75 ml /5 tbls apricot brandy
1 egg white
non-toxic green leaves, to decorate

1   If using the freezing compartment of the refrigerator, turn it down to its lowest temperature (the highest setting) about 1 hour before you start.
2   Bring the sugar and 365 ml /12½ fl oz water slowly to the boil in a medium-sized saucepan, stirring until it is dissolved. Then boil it for 5 minutes without stirring. Remove it from the heat, add the grated lemon zest and leave the syrup to stand until it is lukewarm.
3   Add the lemon juice and the apricot brandy to the lukewarm syrup, stir it once and leave it to cool completely.
4   When it is cold, strain it through a fine sieve into a shallow freezer-proof container. Cover it and freeze until the sorbet mixture is frozen to a depth of 25 mm /1 in all around the sides of the container. This will take about 2½ hours.
5   Whisk the apricot sorbet with a fork or wire whisk to break up the ice particles and return it, covered, to the freezer for 30 minutes.
6   Remove the sorbet from the freezer and whisk it with a fork or wire whisk (in the freezer container, if it is not too shallow) until smooth. Whisk the egg white until stiff peaks form, then fold into the sorbet. Return the sorbet to the freezer, covered, until it is firm.
7   About 30 minutes before serving, transfer the sorbet to the main part of the refrigerator to soften it slightly.
8   To serve, scoop out the sorbet and form it into 8 balls. Pile the balls into glass dishes. Decorate with non-toxic shiny green leaves and serve immediately.

Prune sorbet

Serves 4
250 g /8 oz prunes
90 ml /6 tbls armagnac
100 g /4 oz sugar
juice of 1 lemon
1 egg white
julienne strips of lemon zest, to garnish

1   If using the freezing compartment of your refrigerator, turn it down to its lowest temperature (the highest setting) about 1 hour before you start.
2   Soak 4 prunes in 60 ml /4 tbls armagnac overnight. Soak the remaining prunes in 150 ml /5 fl oz water overnight.
3   Put the sugar and 300 ml /10 fl oz water in a small pan and dissolve it over a gentle heat, stirring. Then bring it to the boil and boil for 10 minutes, removing any scum that rises. Add the lemon juice and strain the syrup through a muslin-lined sieve into a bowl.
4   Drain and stone the water-soaked prunes and purée them in a blender or food processor. Rub the purée through a fine sieve into the sugar syrup; stir it once and allow it to cool completely.
5   Pour the cold prune mixture into a shallow, freezer-proof container and put it in the freezer until the sorbet mixture freezes to a depth of 25 mm /1 in all around the sides of the container. Now whisk the sorbet with a fork or wire whisk to break up the ice particles and return it to the freezer for another 30 minutes.
6   In a bowl, beat the egg white until it is frothy. Whisk the sorbet again with a fork or wire whisk until it is smooth; then whisk in the beaten egg white. (You can do this in a food processor.) Return the sorbet to the freezer until it is firm.
7   An hour before serving, transfer the sorbet to the main part of the refrigerator to soften it slightly.
8   To serve, pile the sorbet into 4 tall-stemmed glasses. Garnish each sorbet with a prune soaked in armagnac and julienne strips of lemon zest and pour the rest of the armagnac over the servings.

 15 minutes, cooling,
plus beating and freezing

 overnight soaking,
then 3½ hours, including freezing

Lemon and lime sorbet

Serves 6
8 lemons
150 g /5 oz granulated sugar
1 egg white
25 g /1 oz caster sugar
juice of 2 limes
30 ml /2 tbls white rum
6 sprigs of mint, to garnish
12 maraschino cherries, to garnish

1 If using the freezing compartment of your refrigerator, turn it down to its lowest temperature (the highest setting) about 1 hour before you start.
2 Carefully slice the tops from 6 lemons and scoop out the pulp, taking care not to pierce the skins. Reserve the pulp. Trim a small slice off the bottom of each lemon so that it stands firmly upright.
3 Heat the granulated sugar and 850 ml /1½ pt water in a heavy-based saucepan, stirring all the time, until the syrup boils. Boil, without stirring, for 5 minutes.
4 Meanwhile, strain the reserved lemon pulp and grate the zest from the 2 remaining lemons. Add the lemon juice and zest to the syrup, and bring the pan back to the boil. Remove the pan from the heat and allow it to cool completely.
5 Pour the cold syrup into an ice-cube tray (with the dividers removed). Freeze for about 1½ hours or until the mixture is frozen at the sides but is still liquid in the centre. Transfer it to a large bowl.
6 Whisk the egg white until it is stiff. Fold in the caster sugar and whisk it again. Fold the egg white into the sorbet mixture and stir the lime juice and rum into the mixture.
7 Spoon the sorbet into the hollowed-out lemons, and return them to the freezer. Freeze them for at least 2 hours before serving. Stick 1 sprig of mint in the top of each of 6 maraschino cherries and garnish each lemon with 1 mint-filled cherry and 1 plain cherry.

 4¼ hours,
including freezing

Grapefruit mint ice

Serves 6
6 large grapefruit
about 250 ml /9 fl oz grapefruit juice
15 g /½ oz gelatine
150 g /5 oz caster sugar
peppermint essence
2 medium-sized egg whites
12 glacé cherries, to garnish
6 sprigs of mint, to garnish

1 If using the freezing compartment of your refrigerator, turn it down to its lowest temperature (the highest setting) 1 hour before you start.
2 Make the grapefruit baskets. With a pen, draw a line around each grapefruit two-thirds of the way up. Next, draw in the handle over the top. With a small, sharp knife, carefully cut out the wedges on either side of the handle and reserve them. Run the knife close to the handle of the basket to remove the grapefruit flesh from underneath it. Scoop out all the remaining flesh with a spoon and clean out any membranes that are left. Repeat with the other grapefruit.
3 Using the flesh from 2 grapefruit only, purée it in a blender and make it up to 700 ml /1¼ pt with the grapefruit juice.
4 Stir the gelatine into one-third of the grapefruit purée and allow it to soften for 5 minutes.
5 Put the rest of the grapefruit mixture into a saucepan and heat it gently, adding the sugar gradually, until it is just below boiling point. Pour the hot liquid onto the gelatine mixture and stir. Let it cool.
6 Stir in a few drops of peppermint essence. Freeze the mixture until it starts to set — about 1 hour.
7 Whisk the egg whites until they form stiff peaks. Remove the ice from the freezer and whisk in the egg whites. Return it to the freezer until it is set.
8 About 30 minutes before serving, transfer the ice to the refrigerator to soften it slightly.
9 Using 6 of the reserved grapefruit wedges, cut 5 thin slices for each grapefruit basket; next make the decorative bows. Peel a long, thin strip of grapefruit skin from each of the remaining reserved wedges, tie into bows and attach them to the handles of the grapefruit baskets with a small piece of wooden cocktail stick.
10 To assemble the dessert, scoop the Grapefruit mint ice into the baskets and place the thinly-sliced wedges around each basket between the ice and the sides of the basket. Garnish each with 2 glacé cherries and a sprig of mint. Serve as soon as possible.

● Use the reserved grapefruit flesh for a refreshing breakfast dish, or for marmalade.

3 hours,
including freezing

That Special Touch

DECORATING DESSERTS

The presentation of desserts and puddings allows tremendous scope for the imaginative cook. Cream, fruit, chocolate, nuts and biscuits can all be used to transform plain desserts into spectacular and glamorous ones.

Always choose a decoration appropriate for the flavour and texture of your dessert. Plan the appearance of the sweet, remembering that the colour of the plate will be part of the pattern and that this should complement the overall colour of the contents. For a grand effect use a plate on a stand.

Bear in mind that you do not have to spend a long time making intricate designs; simple ones are often the best.

Whipped cream

Whipped cream is the most useful form of decoration, though not often the cheapest. Apart from giving a sophisticated finish to most desserts, whipped cream may also be used to hide defects, such as a crack in a sponge cake. If the sponge or meringue breaks up while it is being assembled, it can be masked with cream and then decorated. For piping cream, whisk the cream until it is fairly stiff and holds its shape. For masking, the cream should be a little softer in consistency so that it will spread easily.

To pipe, spoon the cream into a cold piping bag, fitted with a 5–10 mm /¼–½ in fluted nozzle. Only half-fill the bag and make sure that your hand is cool (hold it under a cold, running tap for a few moments), or the cream may curdle as you pipe it.

Cream is effective when piped as a border around the top edge of a dessert. If the dessert is unmoulded, then cream can be piped onto the plate to neaten the edges. In this case the centre is best decorated with different ingredients.

There are many designs you can use for piping cream. Rosettes are particularly suitable for borders around the edges of a dessert and they look pretty with a decoration on top of every alternate one. Shells and scrolls also make attractive borders.

Fruit

Use different fruits to make really refreshing and colourful decorations.

Fresh fruit: small summer fruits, in season, are good when used whole; individual fruit can be placed on top of rosettes of cream; non-toxic leaves can be used for extra colour — try strawberry, raspberry or blackcurrant leaves. Mint leaves are good for decorating sorbets and creams.

Use sliced fruit to cover the top of a gateau or a cheesecake. Remember that sliced apples, pears, peaches and bananas will have to be dipped in lemon juice to prevent discoloration. Fresh fruits can also be covered with a jam glaze of an appropriate colour and flavour. Sieve your jam (apricot, strawberry

or raspberry), into a pan, add one-third as much water and heat the mixture gently. When the jam has melted, allow the glaze to cool before you use it.

Frosted fruit makes an eye-catching edging or a dramatic central decoration. To frost the fruit, lightly whisk the white of an egg, then brush it onto the fruit, dip the fruit in caster sugar and leave it to dry for 24 hours.

Julienne strips of orange, lemon or lime zest add colour if sprinkled on desserts.

Glacé and crystallized fruits are useful in the winter months. Marrons glacés, glacé pineapple and cherries and crystallized angelica and pineapple are all lovely.

Chocolate

Chocolate is probably the most versatile decoration of all. Try these variations:

Caraque: melt chocolate in a bowl over simmering water, then pour it onto a cold, hard surface (a marble slab or the bottom of a solid baking tin) and leave it to set. Use a sharp knife to shave the chocolate into long curls. Pile the caraque on top of desserts or around the sides of gateaux.

Curls: either freeze the chocolate and grate it firmly on a coarse grater to make fine curls or, using chocolate at room temperature, peel off thick curls with a potato peeler.

Leaves: paint the underside of clean rose leaves with melted chocolate. Leave them to dry, then peel away the leaf.

Shapes: melt the chocolate, spread it on a flat surface to cool, then cut out any shape you wish and spike them into cream borders.

Flakes, vermicelli or drinking chocolate: these can easily be used to sprinkle over the top of a dessert for an elegant finish.

Grated chocolate: this can be used to make a lattice or chess-board design on the top of a flat surface, such as a cheesecake or a mousse. It is also pretty sprinkled in between lines of piped cream.

Drizzled: melt the chocolate, and when it has cooled slightly, drizzle it over a surface of masking cream, leaving a thin trail.

Nuts

Nuts make excellent decorations; you can arrange whole hazelnuts, split almonds, pistachio nuts or walnut halves on the top of desserts with or without piped cream. A sprinkling of finely chopped nuts makes a very pretty pattern.

Biscuits

A delicious accompaniment to complement many desserts is a biscuit. Instead of ice cream wafers, try serving Cigarettes russes (see recipe) with water-ices and sorbets; try German pepper cookies (see recipe) with an apple- or strawberry-based dessert, or Almond butter biscuits (see recipe) with a dessert such as Peaches with fresh raspberry sauce (see page 33). Alternatively, they can be handed round separately with the after-dinner coffee.

Sweet Chinese rice cakes (see recipe), however, can be served as a dessert on their own.

From the left, back row: cream and chocolate complement a coffee dessert; chopped nuts, cream and angelica make a decorative top to a trifle; sugared orange and lemon slices and cream brighten up a pale mousse. At the front, strawberries and their leaves match the dessert's flavour.

Sweet Chinese rice cakes

Makes 18
100 g /4 oz flour
a pinch of salt
25 g /1 oz ground rice
30 ml /2 tbls cornflour
90 ml /6 tbls caster sugar
2.5 ml /½ tsp baking powder
75 g /3 oz lard
1 egg, beaten
2.5 ml /½ tsp almond essence
butter, for greasing
18 blanched almonds

1 Sift the flour, salt, ground rice, cornflour, caster sugar and baking powder into a mixing bowl. Add the lard in tiny pieces and rub it in with the fingertips until the mixture resembles fine breadcrumbs. Add half of the beaten egg, 15 ml /1 tbls cold water and the almond essence and mix well to make dough.
2 Knead the dough until it is smooth, then shape it into a ball and wrap it in greaseproof paper. Chill for 30 minutes.
3 Heat the oven to 190C /375F /gas 5. Grease 2 baking trays with plenty of butter. Form the dough into 18 small balls and place them on the baking trays, 5 cm /2 in apart. Press a blanched almond in the top of each cake and then brush them all over with the rest of the beaten egg.
4 Bake the cakes in the oven for 15 minutes, or until they are golden.

10 minutes, chilling,
then 25 minutes

German pepper cookies

Makes 30
225 g /8 oz flour, sifted
25 g /1 oz cornflour
5 ml /1 tsp baking powder
5 ml /1 tsp ground cinnamon
2.5 ml /½ tsp ground cloves
2.5 ml /½ tsp ground white pepper
2.5 ml /½ tsp ground mace
2 eggs
225 g /8 oz caster sugar
grated zest of 1 lemon
60 ml /4 tbls candied peel, finely chopped
butter, for greasing
sifted icing sugar, for coating

1 Into a bowl, sift together the flour, cornflour, baking powder, ground cinnamon, cloves, white pepper and mace. Set it aside.
2 In a clean bowl, whisk the eggs and caster sugar until the mixture is light and fluffy. Stir this into the dry ingredients, with the grated lemon zest and candied peel. Chill for 1 hour, or until the dough is stiff enough to roll.
3 Heat the oven to 180C /350F /gas 4 and lightly grease 3 baking trays with butter.
4 Roll the dough into thirty 25 mm /1 in balls and place the balls 25 mm /1 in apart on the prepared baking trays.
5 Bake each tray in turn in the oven for 20 minutes, or until the cookies are puffed and slightly golden. Transfer the cookies to a wire rack with a palette knife and leave them to get cold.
6 Roll the cold cookies in sifted icing sugar to coat them and store them in an airtight container for at least 1 week, to allow the spicy flavour to develop.

20 minutes, plus chilling, then 1¼ hours,
plus cooling and 1 week storing

Almond butter biscuits

Makes 36 biscuits
softened butter, for greasing
50 g /2 oz ground almonds
100 g /4 oz caster sugar
50 g /2 oz flour, sifted
5 ml /1 tsp vanilla essence
2 medium-sized egg whites
100 g /4 oz butter
flaked almonds, to garnish

1 Heat the oven to 180C /350F /gas 4 and grease 3 large baking
trays with softened butter.
2 Combine the ground almonds, sugar, flour and vanilla essence in a
bowl. Beat the egg whites lightly with a fork to break them up, then
add them to the ground almond mixture and mix them together
thoroughly.
3 Melt the butter over a low heat, taking care not to let it bubble.
Gradually pour it into the almond mixture, beating vigorously with a
spoon as you pour, so that it is well blended.
4 Spoon the mixture into a piping bag fitted with a plain 10 mm /
½ in nozzle. Pipe out 5 cm /2 in lengths onto the prepared baking
trays, spacing them well apart as the biscuits will spread quite
considerably as they cook.
5 Place the baking trays in the oven for 5 minutes. Remove the trays
from the oven and sprinkle the biscuits with flaked almonds.
Continue to bake them for a further 5–10 minutes, or until they are
firm and tinged golden brown around the edges.
6 Transfer the biscuits to a wire rack, lifting them on a spatula or
fish slice. Allow them to become quite cold and crisp before storing
them in an airtight container until they are needed.

 35 minutes,
plus cooling

Cigarettes russes

Makes 15–20
butter and flour, for greasing
2 egg whites
100 g /4 oz icing sugar, sifted
40 g /1½ oz flour
65 g /2½ oz butter, melted
a few drops of vanilla essence
25 g /1 oz dark chocolate

1 Heat the oven to 200C /400F /gas 6 and then grease and flour 2
baking trays.
2 In a bowl, whisk the egg whites until they are stiff. Sift the icing
sugar onto them and gently beat it in with a wooden spoon.
3 Sift the flour onto the mixture. Beat it in carefully, making sure
the mixture is well combined, then beat in the melted butter and the
vanilla essence.
4 Drop 15 ml /1 tbls of the mixture on one of the trays. Smooth it
out thinly and evenly with a knife. Bake it for 5–6 minutes until the
biscuit is set and golden brown. Repeat the procedure using the other
tray when the first biscuit is half cooked.
5 Run a palette knife or fish slice under the first cooked biscuit and
turn it upside down. Quickly roll it up around a pencil. After a few
seconds, when the biscuit has hardened, remove the pencil and cool
the biscuit on a wire rack.
6 Cook the remaining mixture in pairs in the same way.
7 Melt the chocolate in a bowl over a saucepan of hot water. Dip
one end of each biscuit into it. Use the end of a wooden spoon to
clear the chocolate from the centre of the biscuits. Put the biscuits
back on the wire rack until the chocolate has cooled. Store the biscuits
in an airtight container in a cool place.

● The secret of success with these elegant 'Russian cigarettes' is to
cook one at a time to ensure that they are soft for rolling.

 1¼ hours

MERINGUES

There can be few more glamorous culinary transformations than that from unbeaten egg white to meringue. From simple beginnings comes a crisp, white confection — the basis for many wonderful desserts.

The simplest meringue is known as *meringue suisse* and is the usual type made at home. For this the egg whites are beaten and caster sugar is folded in. The mixture can then be spooned or piped into shape. Variations of meringues containing chopped or ground nuts are very popular.

Professional bakers generally use *meringue cuite*, which involves whisking icing sugar into the egg whites over a low heat. It produces a good-looking meringue, but one which is less tasty.

Meringues store beautifully in an airtight container (2–3 weeks), so make ideal dinner party desserts when it is helpful to do as much preparation as possible in advance. Try my delicious Chocolate-hazelnut meringue baskets which can be assembled in minutes.

I have included three vacherins in this chapter — they do take time and patience to produce, but once you have succeeded you will be able to impress your family and guests with the spectacular results.

Chocolate-hazelnut meringue baskets

Almond-topped meringue cake

🔪🔪 1½ hours, plus cooling

Serves 8
50 g /2 oz butter, plus extra for greasing
125 g /4 oz flour, plus extra for dusting
125 g /4 oz caster sugar
4 egg yolks
5 ml /1 tsp baking powder
75 ml /5 tbls milk
a few drops of vanilla essence
icing sugar, to serve
For the meringue
4 medium-sized egg whites
a pinch of salt
225 g /8 oz caster sugar
30 ml /2 tbls flaked almonds
For the filling
225 ml /8 fl oz thick cream, whipped
125 g /4 oz strawberries, sliced

1 Heat the oven to 150C /300F /gas 2. Grease two 23 cm /9 in layer tins and line them with greaseproof paper. Brush the paper with melted butter and dust with flour.
2 In a large bowl, whisk the butter and sugar together until light and creamy. Beat in the egg yolks one at a time. Sift together the flour and baking powder and add it to the butter mixture alternately with the milk and vanilla essence. Divide this mixture evenly between the prepared tins.
3 Make the meringue. In a large bowl, whisk the egg whites with a pinch of salt until they are stiff but not dry. Gradually whisk in the sugar 15 ml /1 tbls at a time until the meringue is stiff and glossy. Divide the mixture between the 2 tins containing the cake mixture. Sprinkle them with the flaked almonds. Bake them in the oven for 45 minutes. Now turn them out onto a wire rack, remove the paper and allow them to cool.
4 Place one layer of the cake, meringue side down, on a serving platter. Spread it with the whipped cream and sliced strawberries. Place the other layer on top, meringue-side-up, sprinkle it with icing sugar and serve.

Chocolate-hazelnut meringue baskets

⏱🔪🔪🔪 making the ice cream, then 5 hours, plus cooling

Serves 6
melted butter and flour, for the baking sheet
5 medium-sized egg whites
a pinch of salt
275 g /10 oz caster sugar
For the hazelnut ice cream
120 ml /8 tbls caster sugar
300 ml /10 fl oz milk
600 ml /1 pt thick cream
8 egg yolks
150 g /5 oz ground hazelnuts
150 g /5 oz peeled, toasted hazelnuts, chopped
For the chocolate sauce
175 g /6 oz plain chocolate
50 g /2 oz butter
90 ml /6 tbls thick cream
90 ml /6 tbls thin cream
a few drops of vanilla essence

1 Heat the oven to 70C /150F /gas low.
2 Brush a baking sheet with melted butter and dust it with sifted flour.
3 In a large mixing bowl, whisk the egg whites with a pinch of salt until stiff but not dry. Whisk in half the sugar, 15 ml /1 tbls at a time. Continue whisking for 1 minute or until it is very smooth and glossy. Fold in the remaining sugar.
4 Fit a piping bag with a 15 mm /½ in plain nozzle, fill it with meringue and pipe the meringue baskets. Pipe the bases 7.5 cm / 3 in in diameter, starting in the centre and working outwards in a spiral. To form the sides, pipe the meringue around the edge of the base in 3 layers. Make 6 baskets.
5 Bake the baskets in the oven for 4½ hours, until crisp on the outside but still soft in the centre. Cool on a wire rack. In the meantime, about one hour before starting to make the ice cream, if using the freezing

compartment of your refrigerator, turn it down to its lowest temperature (the highest setting).

6 To make the hazelnut ice cream, combine the caster sugar, milk and thick cream in a pan and bring it to the boil. Remove it from the heat. In a bowl, beat the egg yolks lightly. Pour the scalded cream mixture onto the egg yolks in a thin stream, beating until the custard is light and foamy. Transfer the custard to the top pan of a double boiler and cook it over simmering water, stirring, until the custard coats the back of a spoon. Pour the custard into a bowl set in another bowl filled with ice and let the custard cool. Chill it, covered, for 2 hours.

7 Fold all the hazelnuts into the custard and pour it into a shallow, freezer-proof container. Freeze, covered, until the mixture begins to harden to a depth of about 25 mm / 1 in around the edges, about 1–2 hours.

8 Remove the ice cream from the freezer and beat it with a fork to amalgamate it. Cover it, return it to the freezer and leave it until it is firmly frozen, at least 5 hours.

9 Make the chocolate sauce: break the chocolate into the top of a double boiler, add the butter and stir over hot water until they melt. Beat in the creams. Place the top of the double boiler directly over the heat, bring it gently to the boil and simmer for 2–3 minutes, stirring. Flavour with vanilla essence.

10 Before serving, arrange the baskets on plates and place some ice cream in each. Pour sauce over them and serve immediately.

Rose petal and blackberry vacherin

6 hours for the basket and the ice cream, plus 20 minutes decorating

Serves 10
oil, for greasing
3 egg whites
175 g /6 oz vanilla caster sugar (see page 10)
For the meringue cuite
6 egg whites
350 g /12 oz icing sugar, sifted
3 drops of vanilla essence
For the blackberry-rose ice cream
250 g /9 oz sugar
700 g /1½ lb blackberries, fresh or frozen
30 ml /2 tbls crème de cassis
30 ml /2 tbls rose-flower water
5 ml /1 tsp lemon juice
425 ml /15 fl oz thick cream
For the filling and decoration
12 pink rose petals
1 egg white, lightly beaten
caster sugar
150 ml /5 fl oz thick cream
15 ml /1 tbls maraschino liqueur or brandy

1 Line 3 baking trays with oiled grease-proof paper. Draw an oval 27 cm /10½ in long in the middle of each one. Draw a second line about 20 mm /¾ in outside the first.

2 Fit a piping bag with a 15 mm /½ in plain nozzle. Stand the bag in a tall glass and fold back the cuff. Heat the oven to 110C / 225F /gas ¼.

3 For the basket, whisk the whites until peaks form. Still whisking, add 15 ml /1 tbls vanilla caster sugar, and then a second; whisk until smooth and glossy. Gently sift and fold in the remaining sugar, a little at a time.

4 Spoon some of the meringue into the bag and pipe around the oval on each sheet, between the 2 lines. Pile the remaining meringue onto one oval and smooth it out with the back of a spoon to make the base. With the basket base at the bottom, bake the 3 trays in the oven for 2 hours or until they are crisp but not dry.

5 Remove the top 2 from the oven and move the bottom tray to the top shelf for an extra 10 minutes baking. Let the meringues cool on the trays. Remove the paper from the 2 ovals and pile them, one on top of the other, on the base on the tray. Wrap tightly and store in an airtight container.

6 Heat the oven to 110C /225F /gas ¼. Fit a piping bag with a 15 mm /½ in plain nozzle. Stand it in a tall glass and fold back the cuff of the bag.

7 To make the meringue cuite, select a bowl no smaller than 2 L /3½ pt and a saucepan over which it will fit comfortably.

8 Using a hand-held electric whisk, whisk the whites in the bowl until they are foamy but not white. Sprinkle the icing sugar over the surface, 5 ml /1 tsp at a time, and whisk it in, until all the sugar has been absorbed and the mixture is white, glossy and lump-free. Whisk in the vanilla essence.

9 Set the bowl over a pan of gently simmering water and whisk continuously, until the meringue doubles in volume and is thick and stiff, about 10–12 minutes.

10 Remove it from the heat and whisk for a further minute. Spoon some meringue cuite into the piping bag.

11 Working on the basket base on the tray, pipe a ring around the top edge. Place one of the ovals on top. Sandwich the third oval on top in the same way.

12 With a steady hand, pipe meringue cuite from the inside top of the rim diagonally over it and down the outside to the base, continue along the base for about 25 mm /1 in, then release the pressure. Pipe a second shape about 25 mm /1 in away and parallel to it. Continue around the basket.

13 Pipe a rosette in each of the spaces on top of the rim, and a second rosette beneath the upper ones. Bake in the oven for 2 hours or until it is still white but dried through. In the meantime, one hour before starting to make the ice cream, if using the freezing compartment of your refrigerator, turn it down to its lowest temperature (the highest setting).

14 For the ice cream, put the sugar and 425 ml /15 fl oz water into a pan and bring to the boil, stirring until the sugar has dissolved. Boil rapidly for 2 minutes, then remove the pan from the heat. Leave the syrup until it is cold.

15 Meanwhile, put the blackberries in a blender, purée them until smooth and then sieve them to remove the pips.

16 Stir together the cold syrup and the purée, then add the crème de cassis, rose-flower water and lemon juice. Turn the purée into a 2 L /3½ pt freezer container, cover and freeze until frozen to a depth of 25 mm /1 in around the edge, about 2 hours.

17 Remove it from the freezer and gently stir through with a fork. Return to the freezer until a frozen slush is formed.

18 Whip the cream until soft peaks form. Beat the semi-frozen blackberry purée, then gently but thoroughly fold in the cream. Cover it and freeze until it is firm.

19 On the day of serving, paint the rose petals on either side with lightly beaten egg white and dust them with caster sugar. Shake off the excess and leave them to dry.

20 About 1½ hours before serving, carefully transfer the basket to a serving platter or foil-covered board. Move the ice cream to the refrigerator to soften for 45 minutes.

21 Fork through the ice cream, then spoon it gently into the basket. Whip the cream and fold in the maraschino or brandy. Spoon it into a piping bag fitted with a star nozzle and pipe rosettes around the basket. Return the vacherin to the freezer for 20–30 minutes to stop it softening further. Transfer it to the refrigerator 30 minutes before serving.

22 Before serving the vacherin, scatter the sugared rose petals over the ice cream.

Rose petal and blackberry vacherin

Raspberry meringue tower

⏱🍴🍴🍴 2 batches of meringue — 3½ hours each, plus 20 minutes

Serves 8
oil, for greasing
8 egg whites
2 pinches of salt or cream of tartar
450 g /1 lb caster sugar
600 ml /1 pt thick cream
350 g /12 oz fresh raspberries
angelica 'leaves', to garnish

1   The meringue is made in two batches. Start by preparing 2 baking sheets: cover them with foil or greaseproof paper and grease well. Draw a circle 23 cm /9 in in diameter on one sheet and two circles, one 12 cm /5 in and one 7.5 cm /3 in on the other sheet. Put a large plain nozzle into a piping bag, stand it upright in a tumbler and turn back the top of the bag, like a cuff, ready for filling. Heat the oven to 110C /225F /gas ¼.
2   Prepare the first batch of meringue:

Raspberry meringue tower

whisk 4 egg whites with 1 pinch of salt or cream of tartar until stiff peaks are formed. Whisk in 100 g /4 oz caster sugar, then gently fold in 100 g /4 oz more.
3   Fill the piping bag with half the meringue and pipe it around the 23 cm /9 in circle, just inside the guideline. Work inwards in circles until the bag is empty. Refill the bag with the remaining meringue, complete the first meringue circle, then pipe in the other 2 circles in the same way.
4   Place the meringue circles in the oven and bake for 2½–3 hours (the bottom sheet will need a little longer). Set aside to cool.
5   For the second batch, line and grease 2 baking sheets (as before). Draw an 18 cm / 7 in circle on one sheet. Put a large plain nozzle into a piping bag. Make up more meringue with the remaining egg whites and sugar, in the same way as the first batch. Put half of it in the bag; pipe the 18 cm /7 in circle.
6   Clean the piping bag and fit a medium star nozzle. Fill the bag with the remaining meringue and pipe 24 rosettes 25 mm /1 in across onto the baking sheets. Bake for 2½–3 hours.
7   Assemble the gateau not more than 1 hour before eating. Whip the cream and mix half of it with half of the raspberries.

8   Put the 23 cm /9 in meringue layer on a flat serving plate. Arrange 10 meringue rosettes around the edge, 25 mm /1 in from the rim. Spread some raspberry cream in the centre.
9   Gently place the 18 cm /7 in meringue layer on top and spread some raspberry cream in the centre. Place 8 meringue rosettes around the inside edge.
10   Position the 12 cm /5 in layer on top, fill the centre and place 6 rosettes around the edge. Top with the smallest layer.
11   Fit a piping bag with a medium star nozzle and fill it with the remaining whipped cream. Pipe rosettes of cream, one on the top layer then one in between each meringue rosette. Place a raspberry and two angelica 'leaves' on each cream rosette.

Classic pavlova

⏱🍴🍴 2 hours, plus cooling, then filling

Serves 10
oil, for greasing
5 egg whites
400 g /14 oz caster sugar
25 ml /5 tsp cornflour
5 ml /1 tsp lemon juice
For the filling
300 ml /10 fl oz thick cream
15 g /½ oz icing sugar
30 ml /2 tbls kirsch
2 fresh peaches, peeled, stoned, sliced and
*   tossed in lemon juice*
1 small pineapple, peeled, cored and diced
100 g /4 oz strawberries, hulled
10 grapes, peeled and seeded
2 kiwi fruit, peeled and sliced
2 passion fruit

1   Heat the oven to 90C /195F /gas low. Line a baking sheet, at least 28 cm /11 in wide, with silicone paper or greaseproof paper. Using a 23 cm /9 in plate as a template, draw a circle on the paper. Oil the greaseproof paper, if using.
2   In a large bowl, whisk the egg whites with an electric beater or a balloon whisk until stiff peaks are formed. Combine the caster sugar and the cornflour. Sift half of this mixture over the egg whites, a spoonful at a time, whisking in each addition. When the mixture is smooth and glossy, fold in the remaining sugar with a large metal spoon. Fold in the lemon juice.
3   Spoon the meringue mixture into the centre of the drawn circle and use the spoon to push and mould the mixture into a round with a slightly hollowed centre (it should resemble a nest).
4   Bake for 1½–2 hours or until the meringue is firm on the outside and dry underneath. Turn off the oven and leave the meringue to become cold.
5   Remove the meringue from the oven and carefully peel away the paper. It can now be stored in an airtight container until required.
6   To assemble, about 30 minutes before serving, whip the cream to soft peaks, fold in the icing sugar and the kirsch. Put the meringue on a serving dish and spoon the cream into it; put all the fruit, except the

passion fruit, on top. Halve the passion fruit, scoop the pulp over the top and serve.

Meringue basket

🍴🍴 2 hours,
plus assembly

Makes 4
175 g /6 oz icing sugar
3 egg whites
300 ml /10 fl oz thick cream, whipped
30 ml /2 tbls caster sugar
350–500 g /12 oz–1 lb strawberries, hulled

1 Heat the oven to 140C /275F /gas 1. Line 2 baking sheets with non-stick baking paper. Draw a circle on each one using a 22 cm /9 in plate as a guide.
2 Sift the icing sugar into a bowl. In a separate bowl, whisk the egg whites lightly, then add the icing sugar 15 ml /1 tbls at a time, whisking all the time.
3 When all the sugar has been added, place the bowl over a saucepan of simmering water (the bowl must not touch the water) and continue to whisk until the meringue is very thick and stiff. It must hold its shape firmly when the whisk is lifted. Be careful to whisk continually round the sides and bottom so the meringue does not overcook.
4 Spoon one-third of the meringue into a

piping bag fitted with a 25 mm /1 in star nozzle and pipe a ring around one circle. Spoon the remaining meringue into the piping bag and pipe around the second circle and then fill it in to make a disc.
5 Bake the ring on the centre shelf of the oven, with the disc above it, for about 1½ hours, then allow them to cool.
6 To serve, sweeten the whipped cream with the caster sugar and use a little to stick the ring to the disc. Put the remaining cream in the case, reserving some to pipe a decorative border around the edge of the meringue and arrange the fruit on top.

Coffee meringues with nut cream

🥄 3 hours, plus cooling,
then 10 minutes

Makes 16 shells
3 egg whites
a pinch of salt or cream of tartar
10 ml /2 tsp instant coffee powder
175 g /6 oz caster sugar
oil, for greasing
For the hazelnut cream
100 g /4 oz ground hazelnuts
225 ml /8 fl oz thick cream
30 ml /2 tbls icing sugar, sifted

Meringue basket

1 Heat the oven to 110C /225F /gas ¼. Place the egg whites in a large bowl with the salt or cream of tartar. Whisk the whites until they stand in stiff peaks.
2 Place 60 ml /4 tbls of the whites in another bowl and stir in the coffee powder until it is well mixed. Add the coffee mixture and half the sugar to the whites and whisk until they regain their stiffness. Gently fold in the remaining sugar, with a metal spoon.
3 Line a baking tray with oiled greaseproof paper. Fit a piping bag with a plain 12 mm /½ in nozzle, fill the bag with the mixture and pipe 16×5 cm /2 in whirls on the tray.
4 Place the tray on the lowest shelf of the oven with the door slightly ajar for 2–3 hours, until the meringues are firm and dry. Cool the meringue shells on the baking tray for 10–15 minutes and store them immediately in an airtight container until needed.
5 For the filling, heat the grill to medium. Place the ground hazelnuts on a tray under the grill for 2–3 minutes until they are lightly browned, then allow them to cool.
6 Lightly whip the cream and gently fold two-thirds of the ground nuts and the icing sugar into it. Sandwich the meringue shells with a generous spoonful of the hazelnut cream and spread a little cream around the edges. Press the remaining ground nuts into the cream at the sides of the meringues.

Orange vacherin

Serves 8
5 egg whites
275 g /10 oz caster sugar
grated zest of 1 orange
For the filling
50 g /2 oz unsalted butter
275 g /10 oz icing sugar
2 egg yolks

4 drops of orange food colouring
30 ml /2 tbls lemon juice
grated zest of 1 orange
30 ml /2 tbls orange-flavoured
   liqueur
30 ml /2 tbls thick cream
4 oranges, peeled, white pith
   removed and thinly sliced

1 Heat the oven to 150C /300F /gas 2. With a pencil and using a plate as a guide, draw a 23 cm /9 in circle on a piece of non-stick silicone paper. Place the paper on a baking sheet. Set aside.
2 In a large mixing bowl, whisk the egg whites until they form stiff peaks. Whisk in 50 g /2 oz of the sugar and continue working for 1 minute or until the mixture is very stiff and glossy.
3 Using a metal spoon, fold in the remaining sugar and the grated orange zest.
4 Spread one-third of the mixture onto the circle of paper to make a layer about 5 mm /¼ in thick. Fit a large piping bag with a 25 mm / 1 in star nozzle and fill it with the remaining mixture. Pipe decorative swirls around the edge of the circle to form a case.
5 Place the baking sheet in the oven and bake the meringue for 1 hour. Turn off the oven, leaving the meringue inside for a further 10–15 minutes, or until it is crisp on the outside but still soft in the centre.
6 Remove the meringue from the oven and cool it completely. When it is cold, lift it off the baking sheet and carefully remove and discard the paper from the bottom.
7 Not more than 1 hour before serving make the filling. In a medium-sized bowl, beat the butter until it is soft and creamy. Gradually sift in the icing sugar and beat it until the mixture is thoroughly blended. Add the egg yolks and beat well.
8 Combine the orange food colouring with the lemon juice, grated orange zest and liqueur. Add this to egg yolk mixture. Beat until the mixture is well blended, then beat in the thick cream.
9 Spoon the mixture into the meringue case, smoothing it with the back of the spoon. Arrange thin orange slices on top and serve the vacherin immediately.

 1½ hours, plus cooling,
then 10 minutes

German nut torte

Serves 4–6
butter and flour, for the tin
2 egg whites
125 g /4½ oz caster sugar
100 g /4 oz hazelnuts, toasted and then ground
To decorate
100 ml /4 fl oz thick cream, whipped
powdered cinnamon
16 whole hazelnuts

1 Heat the oven to 190C /375F /gas 5. Line the base of a 20 cm / 8 in sandwich tin with non-stick silicone paper, then lightly butter and flour the tin.
2 In a large mixing bowl, whisk the egg whites until they form stiff peaks. Gradually whisk in the caster sugar until the peaks are very stiff and glossy.
3 Using a metal spoon, carefully fold the ground hazelnuts into the beaten egg whites, cutting down with the side of the spoon to the bottom of the bowl and gently turning the whites over.
4 Pour the mixture into the prepared cake tin and smooth over the top. Place the tin in the oven and bake for 30–40 minutes or until the meringue is light golden and firm to the touch. Do not let the torte become too crisp.
5 Remove the tin from the oven and allow the mixture to cool in the tin for 5 minutes. Turn out the meringue onto a wire rack and carefully peel away the paper. Leave it to become cold.
6 Spread the cold torte with the cream and sprinkle it with cinnamon. Decorate with the whole hazelnuts.

 1 hour

Strawberry vacherin

Serves 4
4 egg whites
225 g /8 oz caster sugar
For the filling
1 L /1¾ pt strawberry ice cream, softened slightly
175 g /6 oz strawberries, sliced
For the decoration
75 ml /3 fl oz thick cream, whipped
225 g /8 oz strawberries, halved
sifted icing sugar

1 Heat the oven to 150C /300F /gas 2. Draw two 23 cm /9 in circles on 2 pieces of non-stick silicone paper. Put each paper circle on a baking sheet. Set aside.
2 In a large mixing bowl, beat the egg whites with an electric or rotary beater until they form stiff peaks. Whisk in the sugar, 30 ml / 2 tbls at a time, until the mixture is very stiff and glossy.
3 Pipe or spoon the meringues onto the silicone paper circles. Bake them in the oven for 1 hour. Turn off the oven but leave the meringues in it overnight.
4 The next day, remove the meringues from the oven. Peel away and discard the paper from the bottom of each meringue. Make the filling by combining the softened ice cream and the strawberry slices.
5 Sandwich the meringue layers with the ice cream mixture and place them on a serving plate. Place in the freezer immediately and leave until the ice cream has reset, or until required.
6 Before serving the vacherin, use a palette knife to spread the whipped cream around the sides of the meringue. Decorate the sides with strawberry halves and sprinkle the vacherin with icing sugar. Serve immediately.

 1¼ hours, plus drying,
then 20 minutes, plus freezing

Rich meringue gateau

Serves 6–8
6 egg whites
350 g /12 oz caster sugar
175 g /6 oz hazelnuts, chopped
For the chocolate sauce
350 g /12 oz good-quality, plain chocolate, broken into small pieces
350 ml /12 fl oz thick cream

1 Heat the oven to 180C /350F /gas 4. Line the bases of three 20 cm /8 in sandwich tins with non-stick silicone.
2 Whisk the egg whites until stiff, then whisk in the sugar, one-third at a time, until the mixture is thick and glossy. Fold in the hazelnuts, reserving a few tablespoonfuls for decoration.
3 Divide the mixture equally among the 3 tins and smooth over the surfaces. Bake in the oven for 30–35 minutes until the meringue is crisp on top. Alter the position of the tins in the oven during the baking time to ensure all 3 cook to the same degree of crispness.
4 Leave the meringues in the tins for 1 minute after baking, then very carefully turn them out onto a wire rack and peel away the lining paper. The meringue underneath should be soft and squashy in texture. Leave all 3 until cold.
5 Meanwhile, make the chocolate sauce. Reserve a few pieces of chocolate for decoration. Put the rest of the chocolate pieces in a heavy-bottomed pan. Add 150 ml /5 fl oz of the cream and heat gently, stirring occasionally, until the chocolate has melted and the mixture is smooth. Leave the chocolate until it is cold. Stir it occasionally.
6 Place 1 meringue on a serving plate. Whip the remaining cream and spread one-third of it over the meringue. Spread half the chocolate over the top of the cream, then cover it with another round of meringue. Spread half the remaining cream over the meringue, then spread the remaining chocolate over the top of that. Top it with the last round of meringue, then pipe the remaining cream on the top of the gateau.
7 Sprinkle the reserved nuts in the centre; grate the reserved chocolate, then sprinkle it around the edge. Chill the gateau in the refrigerator. Before serving, allow it to come to room temperature for about 30 minutes.

● Chopped hazelnuts give the meringue a crunchy texture. If you prefer a smoother meringue, you can grind the hazelnuts, reserving a few tablespoonfuls of chopped ones for decoration.

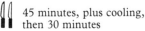 45 minutes, plus cooling,
then 30 minutes

MERINGUE AS A TOPPING

Sweet, soft, airy and crisp all at once. These are the pleasures of meringue. A thick topping of meringue can quickly and easily transform an ordinary pudding into a delectable dessert. Try it and see.

Meringue is probably one of the most versatile ingredients for desserts: its texture and taste complement a wide range of other sweet foods. Its crisp texture contrasts well with ingredients like custard, rice pudding and tapioca. Its sweetness complements the sharpness of stewed fruit — apples, pears, rhubarb and apricots, for example.

A snowy topping of meringue not only tastes good but it looks decorative, too. The uncooked mixture can be smoothed onto the dessert with a round-bladed knife, or 'peaked' with the flat side of the knife, if you wish; or it can be piped on in a lattice pattern. Another pretty idea for decoration is to pipe large 'stars' of meringue over the top of the dessert (see my popular Lemon meringue pudding recipe on page 100, for example.)

A meringue covering for individual cooked fruits looks particularly inviting. Try my recipes for Chocolate pear meringue and for Apple snowballs on pages 100 and 101.

Perhaps best of all is the combination of a hot meringue shell and an ice-cold ice cream filling in my Meringue glacé surprise recipe. This cake-like dessert consists of a layer of chocolate cake, a layer of sliced pears, a layer of chocolate ice cream and finally a hot, crisp covering of sweet meringue. This dessert is not difficult to prepare provided you work quickly and carefully. To make it more spectacular, you can flame the sweet with a liqueur of your choice!

Apricot and rice meringue

overnight soaking,
then 1 hour 20 minutes

Serves 6
450 g /1 lb fresh, ripe apricots or
350 g /12 oz dried apricots soaked
overnight in water to cover
25 g /1 oz butter
125 g /4 oz short-grain rice
500 ml /18 fl oz milk
1 vanilla pod
325 g /11½ oz sugar
2 medium-sized eggs, separated
15 ml /1 tbls icing sugar

1 If using dried apricots, put them with the soaking liquid into a large pan with the butter and bring them to the boil over a medium heat. Turn the heat to low and simmer them, covered, for 1 hour until the apricots are very tender, and all the liquid has been absorbed. If using fresh apricots, just cover them with water, bring them to the boil with the butter and simmer until they are tender, about 10 minutes. Drain the fresh apricots and reserve them.
2 Wash the short-grain rice thoroughly in a

sieve under hot, running water. Bring a large pan of cold water to the boil and drop in the rice. Boil it for 3 minutes, then drain.
3 Bring the milk to the boil in a large saucepan with the vanilla pod, add the rice, reduce the heat and simmer, very gently, for 20 minutes. Remove the vanilla pod.
4 Add 100 g /4 oz of the sugar to the rice and simmer for another 25 minutes, stirring occasionally to prevent the rice from sticking to the pan.
5 Turn the rice into a shallow, oval ovenproof serving dish, let it cool for 2 minutes, then beat in the 2 egg yolks. Heat the oven to 180C /350F /gas 4.
6 Put the apricots in a layer on top of the cooked rice.
7 Whisk the egg whites in a large bowl until stiff peaks form. Carefully fold in the remaining sugar with a metal spoon, then spoon the meringue mixture into a piping bag fitted with a 15 mm /½ in plain nozzle.
8 Pipe the meringue in a lattice pattern over the apricots, sprinkle it with the icing sugar and bake it in the oven for 15 minutes.
9 Turn the oven up to 220C /425F /gas 7 and bake the meringue for a further 5 minutes. Remove it from the oven and serve hot, warm or cold.

Coconut and lemon cream pie

This lemon-flavoured pie with its creamy filling is a delicious variation of the American favourite, coconut cream pie.

2 hours 40 minutes,
including resting the pastry

Serves 6–8
1 × Shortcrust pastry (see page 58)
1 fresh coconut
butter, for greasing
For the filling
45 ml /3 tbls cornflour
700 ml /1¼ pt milk
125 g /4 oz caster sugar
4 medium-sized egg yolks
grated zest and juice of 1 lemon
For the topping
4 medium-sized egg whites
30 ml /2 tbls caster sugar

1 Make the pastry and let it rest for 1 hour in the refrigerator, while you shell, peel and grate the coconut. Heat the oven to 200C /400F /gas 6.
2 Roll out the pastry and use it to line a 25 cm /10 in greased tart tin. Bake, lined with foil and beans, for 10 minutes and then remove the foil and beans and bake for a further 5 minutes. Remove the pastry case from the oven and set it to one side.

Now lower the heat to 170C /325F /gas 3.
3 Meanwhile, mix the cornflour in a bowl with 150 ml /5 fl oz milk. Bring the remaining milk to simmering point in a saucepan. Add it to the cornflour mixture and mix well.
4 Return the mixture to the pan and bring it to the boil, stirring. Stir constantly, for 4 minutes, until you have a smooth, thick sauce.
5 Remove the pan from the heat. Stir in the sugar, then beat in the egg yolks, one at a time. Stir in the lemon zest and juice and three-quarters of the grated coconut.
6 Pour the mixture into the pastry case and bake it for 10 minutes, until it is set. Remove it from the oven and lower the heat to 140C / 275F /gas 1.
7 Whisk the egg whites until stiff peaks form. Whisk in the sugar, 15 ml /1 tbls at a time. Fold in the remaining coconut.
8 Cover the coconut filling with the meringue and put the pie into the oven for 15 minutes, until the meringue goes crisp and colours slightly. Serve the Coconut and lemon cream pie warm.

Colchester pudding

making the fruit purée,
then 50 minutes, plus cooling

Serves 4–6
600 ml /1 pt milk
20 g /¾ oz tapioca
150 g /5 oz caster sugar
a few drops of vanilla essence
75 ml /3 fl oz thick cream
4 medium-sized eggs, separated
425 ml /15 fl oz sweetened rhubarb or
apple purée
butter, for greasing

1 Heat 300 ml /10 fl oz milk in a small saucepan over a moderate heat. Sprinkle in the tapioca and stir briskly until it is boiling. Turn the heat down and simmer for 10 minutes, stirring occasionally. Sweeten with 25 g /1 oz sugar and add the vanilla essence.
2 In a small saucepan, bring the remaining milk and the cream almost to boiling point.
3 Prepare a double boiler. In the top pan, off the heat, whisk together the egg yolks and 2 of the egg whites with 25 g /1 oz sugar.
4 Pour the hot milk onto the eggs and cook over simmering water, stirring constantly with a wooden spoon, until the custard thickens and will coat the back of the spoon.
5 Heat the oven to 200C /400F /gas 6. Put the fruit purée in the bottom of a greased 1.4 L /2½ pt ovenproof dish. Spoon the tapioca mixture over the top and smooth it. Carefully pour the custard over the tapioca.
6 Whisk the remaining 2 egg whites in a large bowl until they are stiff and add the rest of the sugar, 15 ml /1 tbls at a time, whisking vigorously after each addition, until the meringue is firm and glossy.
7 Fit a piping bag with a 20 mm /¾ in star nozzle and spoon in the meringue mixture. Pipe a basket-weave pattern over the top.
8 Bake in the oven for 12 minutes, or until the meringue is pale golden brown. Cool and then chill before serving.

Apricot and rice meringue

Meringue glacé surprise

Serves 6

250 g /8 oz very ripe pears, sliced
23 cm /9 in layer of chocolate cake
  (see note below)
45–60 ml /3–4 tbls orange juice
15 ml /1 tbls Grand Marnier,
  brandy, or other liqueur
1 L /1¾ pt chocolate ice cream
sifted icing sugar
For the meringue
1.5 ml /¼ tsp cream of tartar
4 egg whites
75 g /3 oz caster sugar

1   Heat the oven to 220C /425F /gas 7. Peel and slice the pears, saving any juices which drip from the fruit.
2   Place the chocolate cake on a baking tray. Prick the base and sides of the cake with a fork. Sprinkle it with 60 ml /4 tbls orange juice (or 45 ml /3 tbls orange juice and 15 ml /1 tbls Grand Marnier, brandy or other liqueur), plus any juices from the fruit.
3   Cover the cake with the sliced fruit, to within 12 mm /½ in of the edge of the cake. Slice the ice cream, then arrange it on top of the fruit. Place the cake in the freezer compartment of the refrigerator while you make the meringue. Do not leave the cake there too long, or the fruit will freeze and be unpleasantly icy to eat.
4   Add the cream of tartar to the egg whites and whisk until stiff. Gradually add the sugar and continue whisking until stiff and glossy.
5   Remove the cake from the refrigerator. Spread the meringue over the top and sides of the cake, covering it completely. Peak the meringue with the flat side of a knife. Dust it with icing sugar.
6   Bake immediately for about 3–6 minutes, or until the meringue is lightly coloured and the tips are lightly browned. Serve immediately.

● To make the chocolate cake, follow the recipe for the Fatless sponge on page 30 and replace 30 ml /2 tbls of flour with 30 ml / 2 tbls cocoa powder. Use a 23 cm /9 in Victoria sandwich cake tin.
● The pears may be replaced with whatever fruit is available: soft fruit, peaches, pineapple or fruit salad are all good, fresh or canned.
● To make a softer meringue for this dessert, whisk the egg whites until they form peaks, beat in 15 ml /1 tbls caster sugar and then fold in the remaining sugar with a metal spoon. Do not dust it with icing sugar and the meringue will be glossier.

making the chocolate layer,
plus 1 hour

Floating island

Serves 6

melted butter and caster sugar, for the mould
4 medium-sized egg whites
salt
225 g /8 oz caster sugar
2.5 ml /½ tsp vanilla essence
1 × English custard (see page 38)
For the caramel
125 g /4 oz sugar

1   Brush a 1.5 L /2¾ pt charlotte mould with melted butter and dust it lightly with caster sugar. Heat the oven to 180C /350F /gas 4.
2   In a large bowl, whisk the egg whites with a pinch of salt until stiff but not dry. Sprinkle in 30 ml /2 tbls caster sugar and continue beating for 15 seconds, or until the whites are slightly glossy. Fold in the remaining caster sugar and the vanilla essence.
3   Spoon the meringue mixture into the prepared charlotte mould and cover it with foil. Place it in a roasting tin. Add hot water to come halfway up the sides of the mould and bake it for 30 minutes, or until the meringue has puffed and is firm.
4   Allow the meringue to cool in the mould. It will shrink to its original size. One hour before serving, turn the meringue out into a shallow serving bowl. Pour the English custard around the meringue.
5   Make the caramel. In a small, heavy-based saucepan, heat the sugar and 50 ml /2 fl oz water over a moderate heat, stirring with a wooden spoon to dissolve the sugar.
6   Bring it to the boil and boil it for 5 minutes, or until the syrup turns a pale-gold colour. Plunge the saucepan into cold water to stop the cooking process.
7   Pour the caramel, while still warm and liquid, over the meringue, allowing it to drip down the sides into the custard. Chill until ready to serve.

● The original French name of this dish, *Ile flottante*, and its English translation are very appropriate as the meringue really looks like an island 'floating' in a sea of custard. A traditional French version has an 'island' made of layers of dried sponge cake, soaked in rum, sandwiched together with apricot jam and coated with crème chantilly. The 'sea' can also be a purée of red fruit.
● Do not confuse this recipe with another well-known French dessert, *Oeufs à la neige* — small, soft meringues poached in milk and served with custard.

making the English custard,
then about 1 hour, plus cooling

Chocolate meringue pie

Serves 6
18.5 cm /7½ in Shortcrust pastry case, half baked (see page 58)
1 egg white
425 ml /15 fl oz milk
100 g /4 oz plain chocolate, broken into small pieces
40 g /1½ oz cornflour
50 g /2 oz sugar
2.5 ml /½ tsp vanilla essence
15 ml /1 tbls brandy
grated zest of 1 orange
2 egg yolks, beaten
For the meringue topping
3 egg whites
75 ml /5 tbls caster sugar

1 Brush the half-baked pastry case inside with egg white to seal the surface.
2 In a medium-sized saucepan, combine the milk and pieces of chocolate. Place it over a low heat, stirring constantly with a wooden spoon, until the chocolate is melted.
3 In a small bowl, combine the cornflour with 45 ml /3 tbls cold water. Stir in a little of the chocolate milk and blend until smooth. Pour into the pan and bring it to the boil, whisking constantly to prevent lumps forming.
4 Reduce the heat and simmer for 2–3 minutes, stirring, until the chocolate cream mixture has thickened and no longer tastes of cornflour. Remove it from the heat.
5 Beat in the sugar until it is dissolved. Stir in the vanilla essence, brandy, grated orange zest and egg yolks until they are well blended. Leave the mixture to cool slightly.
6 Heat the oven to 220C /425F /gas 7.
7 Prepare the meringue topping. In a clean bowl, whisk the egg whites to stiff peaks. Whisk in the caster sugar, 15 ml /1 tbls at a time, and continue whisking until the mixture is stiff and glossy.
8 Spread the slightly cooled chocolate cream over the prepared pastry case, using a palette knife to level off the top.
9 Spoon the meringue mixture over the chocolate layer, spreading it evenly to touch the sides of the pastry case. Form small peaks all over the meringue surface, using a palette knife.
10 Cook in the oven for 15 minutes, or until the meringue is golden brown. Serve hot or cold.

 making the pastry case,
then 1 hour

Apple amber

Serves 4–6
1 kg /2 lb cooking apples
150 g /5 oz caster sugar
2 medium-sized eggs, separated
7 slices stale, white bread
100 g /4 oz butter, melted
1 medium-sized egg white
a pinch of salt

1 Heat the oven to 200C /400F /gas 6. Peel, quarter and core the apples and simmer in 60 ml /4 tbls water until soft, 3–5 minutes. Sieve the apples or purée them in a blender and sweeten them with 40 g /1½ oz sugar. Beat in the 2 egg yolks.
2 Use a biscuit cutter about 4 cm /1½ in in diameter to cut the white bread into rounds. Check that you have enough to line the sides of a 1.4–1.7 L /2½–3 pt pie dish.
3 Dip the rounds in melted butter and then place them around the sides of the pie dish. Fill the centre with the apple and egg mixture and bake for 15 minutes. Remove the pie dish from the oven and reduce the heat to 170C /375F /gas 3.
4 Whisk the 3 egg whites with the salt until they are stiff. Carefully fold in 75 g /3 oz sugar with a metal spoon and then pile the meringue on top of the apples. Sprinkle it with the remaining 15 g /½ oz sugar. Bake until the meringue is crisp on the outside and lightly coloured, about 4 minutes.

● An amber is an old-fashioned English fruit pudding. The yolks of the eggs are added to the fruit inside the pie and the whites are used for a splendid meringue on the top.

 1 hour

Chocolate pear meringue

Serves 4
4 pears
150 ml /5 fl oz lemon juice
165 g /5½ oz caster sugar
30 ml /2 tbls redcurrant jelly
butter, for greasing
2 egg whites

For the sauce
75 g /3 oz plain chocolate
60 ml /4 tbls sugar
10 ml /2 tsp cocoa powder
1.5 ml /¼ tsp vanilla essence
2 egg yolks

1 Before you peel the pears, select a saucepan in which they will fit tightly in a single layer. Pour in 600 ml /1 pt water, add 30 ml /2 tbls lemon juice and bring it to the boil. Reduce the heat and simmer.
2 With a vegetable peeler, remove the skin from the pears, then core them with an apple corer, leaving them whole. Place them in the saucepan and simmer them gently for 15–20 minutes, according to the ripeness of the pears, until they are tender. Remove with a slotted spoon and leave them to cool.
3 Put the remaining lemon juice, 45 ml /3 tbls caster sugar and the redcurrant jelly in a small saucepan. Bring it slowly to the boil, stirring with a wooden spoon, until the mixture becomes a syrup. Keep the syrup warm. Heat the oven to 150C /300F /gas 2.
4 To make the sauce, break the chocolate into a saucepan, add the sugar, the cocoa powder and 275 ml /10 fl oz water and bring to the boil, stirring with a wooden spoon until it is well blended. Boil for 15 minutes until the sauce is syrupy. Remove it from the heat and leave it to cool slightly. Whisk in the vanilla essence and egg yolks. Leave the sauce to become cold, then chill.
5 Butter a large ovenproof dish. Stand the pears upright in the dish 5 cm /2 in apart. Pour the redcurrant syrup over them.
6 In a bowl, whisk the egg whites until stiff. Fold in the remaining caster sugar with a metal spoon. Fit a piping bag with a star nozzle and spoon in the meringue mixture. Pipe lines of meringue from the base upwards to cover each pear, leaving the core cavity open. Finish with a circle of rosettes around the top, again leaving the core cavity open. Bake the pears in the oven for 20 minutes, or until the meringue is lightly browned. Leave to cool.
7 When ready to serve, transfer the pears to individual serving plates. Pour redcurrant syrup around the base of each pear. Carefully fill the centres with the chocolate sauce. Serve the remaining chocolate sauce separately.

 1½ hours, plus cooling

Lemon meringue pudding

Serves 4
3 lemons
75 g /3 oz butter, softened
125 g /4 oz caster sugar
2 egg yolks
150 g /5 oz fresh, white breadcrumbs
butter, for greasing
For the meringue topping
2 egg whites
50 g /2 oz caster sugar

1 Heat the oven to 200C /400F /gas 6.
2 Grate the zest from two of the lemons and then squeeze the juice from all of them. Combine the grated zest and juice with 150 ml / 5 fl oz cold water.
3 In a bowl, cream the butter and gradually beat in the sugar until light and fluffy. Beat in the egg yolks one at a time. Stir in the breadcrumbs and the lemon and water mixture. Beat the ingredients until well blended.
4 Butter a 575 ml /1 pt soufflé dish and spoon in the breadcrumb mixture. Cover it with foil and place it in a roasting tin. Add hot water to come halfway up the sides of the dish. Cook it in the oven for 45 minutes or until it is set.
5 To make the meringue topping, place the egg whites in a bowl and whisk to stiff peaks. Gradually whisk in the sugar, then continue whisking until the meringue is stiff and glossy. Using a piping bag fitted with a star nozzle, pipe the meringue on top of the set lemon pudding and return it to the oven for 10–15 minutes or until the meringue is golden. Serve immediately.

 1½ hours

French meringue cake

Serves 6
butter and oil, for greasing
flour, for dusting
6 eggs, separated
175 g /6 oz sugar
grated zest of 1 lemon
75 g /3 oz flour
30 ml /2 tbls cornflour
a pinch of salt

440 g /15½ oz canned, halved
   apricots, drained
For the filling
440 g /15½ oz canned, halved
   apricots, drained
60 ml /4 tbls marmalade
For the meringue
4 egg whites
120 l /8 tbls caster sugar

1 Heat the oven to 180C /350F /gas 4. Grease two 23 cm /9 in layer cake tins with butter. Line the bases with buttered greaseproof paper and dust with flour, shaking out the excess.
2 Choose a large bowl which will fit over a saucepan. Put the egg yolks and sugar, 30 ml /2 tbls water and the lemon zest in the bowl. Set it over barely simmering water and whisk with a hand-held electric mixer until it is pale, light and fluffy. The mixture should leave a trail when the beaters are lifted.
3 Off the heat, sift the flour, cornflour and salt over the whisked mixture. Fold them in with a large metal spoon.
4 Whisk the egg whites until they are stiff but not dry and fold them gently into the cake mixture. Divide the mixture between the two tins and bake for 30–35 minutes or until golden. When pressed lightly with a finger, the cake should spring back. Turn out the cakes onto wire racks to cool. Cover with a clean cloth and leave for 1 day.
5 Heat the oven to 220C /425F /gas 7. For the filling, blend the well-drained apricots until smooth or purée them with a vegetable mill. Pour the purée into a bowl, add the marmalade and mix well.
6 Cut each cake horizontally into 2 thin layers. Sandwich 3 layers with apricot mixture and put the plain layer on top. Cover a baking sheet with foil, oil it lightly and place the cake on it.
7 In a bowl, whisk the egg whites until stiff. Gradually add the sugar and continue to whisk until the meringue stands in stiff peaks. Mask the cake with the meringue, using a palette knife to spread it evenly. Bake it in the oven for 10–15 minutes or until the meringue is lightly golden and set.
8 To garnish, thinly slice the remaining canned apricots. Arrange an overlapping circle of slices around the top edge of the cake. Serve the cake immediately, while the meringue is still warm.

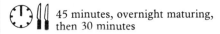 45 minutes, overnight maturing, then 30 minutes

Apple snowballs

Serves 4
4–6 large, firm eating apples
5 ml /1 tsp lemon juice
50 g /2 oz softened butter
2 egg yolks
100 g /4 oz caster sugar
65 g /2½ oz ground almonds

15 ml /1 tbls dark rum
20 ml /4 tsp redcurrant jelly
For the meringue mixture
3 egg whites
a pinch of salt
75 g /3 oz icing sugar, sifted

1 Peel the apples and carefully remove the cores without piercing the bases. Place the apples in a large bowl of water and add the lemon juice to prevent discoloration. Heat the oven to 190C /375F /gas 5.
2 In a bowl, cream half the butter with a fork. Add the egg yolks, half the caster sugar, the almonds and the rum and beat vigorously until well blended. Drain the apples and dry them thoroughly. Divide the almond filling among the apples, pressing it into each cavity.
3 With the remaining butter, generously grease a shallow overproof dish or roasting tin large enough to take all the apples in one layer. Arrange the apples in the dish and pour over 150 ml /5 fl oz water and sprinkle with the remaining caster sugar. Bake for 10 minutes. Now increase the oven temperature to 220C /425F /gas 7 and bake the apples for a further 8–10 minutes or until the apples are golden and soft but not disintegrating.
4 About 4 minutes before the end of cooking time, make the meringue. Whisk the egg whites and salt in a bowl until they just begin to hold the shape of the whisk. Next, whisk in the icing sugar, a spoonful at a time. Place the bowl over a pan half filled with simmering water and whisk the egg white mixture until it is thick.
5 Remove the apples from the oven and, using a round-bladed knife, cover each apple with meringue, leaving the central cavity free. Reduce the oven temperature to 150C /300F /gas 2 and bake for 10–15 minutes until the meringue is set and golden.
6 Cool the apples slightly. Put 5 ml /1 tsp redcurrant jelly into the centre of each apple. Serve the apple snowballs on individual plates with any syrup left in the dish spooned around them, if wished.

● This is an attractive dessert which will appeal to children. Take care not to overcook the apples, as they must remain whole.

 1 hour

TIPSY SWEETS

From a traditional Sherry trifle to an unusual substitute for a Christmas pudding, this chapter has some marvellous suggestions for ways to use a splash of alcohol to make your desserts extra exciting.

A dash of Madeira, a noggin of brandy, a glass of red wine or a measure of port — these are some of the alcoholic beverages that can be used to make the delectable desserts in the next few pages. Try the elegant Pansy jelly which has a small flower set in the jelly, or make the Coffee and brandy trifle which originally came from Treviso in Italy. Its name in Italian, *Tiramesu*, means 'pull me up', because the coffee and brandy are thought to have an invigorating effect.

On the other hand, why not treat yourself to Peaches in champagne as the ultimate in luxurious sweets?

Little blackcurrant and orange towers

30 minutes,
plus setting

Serves 6
225 g /8 oz redcurrant jelly
150 ml /5 fl oz red wine
150 ml /5 fl oz port
juice of 2 oranges
juice of 2 lemons
225 g /8 oz blackcurrants
45 ml /3 tbls sugar
grated zest of 1 orange
grated zest of 1 lemon
15 g /½ oz gelatine
orange and lemon twists, to garnish
angelica leaves, to garnish

1 In a saucepan, combine the redcurrant jelly, red wine, port, orange and lemon juice. Bring them slowly to the boil, stirring to dissolve the jelly. Boil the liquid rapidly for about 5 minutes, or until reduced to 425 ml / 15 fl oz. Leave it to cool.
2 Meanwhile, top and tail the blackcurrants. Place them in a small saucepan with the sugar. Bring to simmering point, and simmer gently for about 3 minutes, or until the blackcurrants are tender, shaking the pan occasionally.
3 Stir the cooked blackcurrants and grated orange and lemon zests into the reduced liquor.
4 In a small bowl, sprinkle the gelatine over 45 ml /3 tbls cold water and leave it to soften for a few minutes. Place the bowl in a saucepan of simmering water and allow it to dissolve. Leave it to cool a little.
5 Stir the cooled gelatine into the blackcurrant and orange jelly and then pour the mixture into six 125 ml /4 fl oz dariole moulds. Place them in the refrigerator to set.
6 To serve, dip each mould in hot water for a few seconds and turn it out onto a large serving platter or individual dishes. Garnish with orange and lemon twists and angelica leaves. Serve immediately.

Sherry trifle

15 minutes, plus soaking, then 45 minutes, plus cooling

Serves 6
6 trifle sponge cakes
100 g /4 oz raspberry jam
50 g /2 oz ratafias or macaroons
150 ml /5 fl oz sweet sherry
For the custard
4 medium-sized eggs
50 g /2 oz caster sugar
10 ml /2 tsp cornflour
600 ml /1 pt milk
1.5 ml /¼ tsp vanilla essence
6 large, fresh peaches
425 ml /15 fl oz thick cream
diamonds of angelica, to decorate

1 Split the trifle sponge cakes in half, spread the cut sides thinly with jam, then sandwich them back together again. Cut each sponge cake sandwich into 3 pieces and arrange them in a glass bowl.

2 Crumble the ratafias over the sponges, then sprinkle them with the sherry. Cover the bowl and leave it to stand overnight.

3 Make the custard. Place the eggs in a bowl with the sugar and cornflour and whisk lightly. Heat the milk to just below boiling point then pour it onto the egg mixture, stirring well. Return the mixture to the pan and cook it over a very gentle heat, stirring

constantly with a wooden spoon until the custard has thickened and coats the back of the spoon.

4 Strain the custard into a bowl and stir in the vanilla essence. Cover the custard with a piece of dampened greaseproof paper and leave until cold.

5 Skin, halve and stone the peaches. Cut each half into 3 slices and arrange them around the sides of the bowl and over the soaked sponge. Remove the paper from the custard and pour the custard over the fruit.

6 Lightly whip the cream. Spread two-thirds of it over the custard. Put the

remaining cream into a piping bag with a 15 mm /½ in star nozzle and pipe the cream in rosettes around the edge, with one in the middle. Decorate the rosettes with diamonds of angelica and serve as soon as possible.

● Medium-dry sherry can be used instead of sweet sherry for this dessert.

● Angelica is the dark green, candied stems of the angelica plant, and is used for flavouring as well as decoration. It is usually sold in short lengths in plastic containers.

Sherry trifle

Zabaione

Elegant but very simple, this dessert can be eaten hot or cold. The Sicilian version, which is much better known, is made with Marsala rather than white wine.

🍴 15 minutes

Serves 6
6 egg yolks
45 ml /3 tbls caster sugar
175 ml /6 fl oz dry white wine

1 Place the egg yolks in the top of a double boiler off the heat and whisk the yolks with a wire whisk or a rotary beater until they become pale yellow. Gradually add the sugar and beat until the mixture becomes foamy.
2 Place the mixture over simmering water and gradually beat in the wine. Continue whisking until the mixture is thick and triples in quantity. Serve warm.

● For cold zabaione, pour the hot dessert into a bowl and place that in a bowl of ice. Whisk the zabaione until it is thick and cold.

Zabaione

Pineapple and oranges in red wine

🍴 30 minutes,
plus chilling

Serves 4
225 g /8 oz sugar
325 ml /11 fl oz red burgundy
1 clove
1 stick of cinnamon, broken in half
2 strips of lemon zest
3 oranges
1 small pineapple

1 Place the sugar in a small pan with 150 ml /5 fl oz water and stir over a gentle heat until the sugar has dissolved. Bring it to the boil and boil for 2–3 minutes.
2 Add all but 30 ml /2 tbls of the red burgundy to the pan. Add the clove, cinnamon stick and the strips of lemon zest. Using a potato peeler or a small, sharp knife, cut 2 strips of zest from 1 of the oranges. Add them to the pan. Return the pan to the heat and bring to the boil, then boil until the syrup has reduced to 225 ml /8 fl oz. Add the remaining red wine.
3 Peel the oranges with a sharp, serrated knife, removing all the pith and membrane. Cut the oranges into 5 mm /¼ in slices. Cut the leafy top from the pineapple and reserve it for decoration. Skin the pineapple, remove any woody 'eyes' from the surface with the point of a knife, then cut the flesh into thin slices. Remove the central core from the slices with an apple corer or a small, plain biscuit cutter.
4 In a shallow glass serving dish, arrange the orange and pineapple slices, overlapping, in circles, alternating orange and pineapple slices. Leave a space in the centre for the pineapple top, but do not put it in position yet. Pour the hot, spicy wine syrup over the fruit slices and leave them to cool, then chill them.
5 Just before serving, spoon the syrup from around the fruit over the fruit again and place the leafy pineapple top in the centre of the dish.

Pansy jelly

🍴🍴 30 minutes,
then 4 hours setting

Serves 6
50 g /2 oz gelatine
225 g /8 oz sugar
thinly pared zest of 4 lemons
300 ml /10 fl oz lemon juice
1 stick of cinnamon
whites and finely crushed shells of 3 eggs
125 ml /4 fl oz medium-dry sherry or sweet white wine
6 pansy flowers, washed and dried
12 small meringues, to serve

1 Sprinkle the gelatine over 45 ml /3 tbls cold water in a small bowl. Leave it to soften and then dissolve by standing the bowl in another bowl of hot water.

Pansy jelly

For the decoration
275 ml /10 fl oz thick cream, whipped
coffee beans
30 ml /2 tbls finely ground coffee

1 Make the sponge cakes and then allow them to cool.
2 To make the custard, put the egg yolks and sugar in a heavy saucepan. Beat the mixture until it is pale and creamy and add the flour, 15 ml /1 tbls at a time.
3 In another saucepan, bring the milk to simmering point. Pour the milk onto the egg mixture, stirring all the time. Put the pan over a very low heat and cook for 3 minutes or until a bubble breaks the surface. Remove the pan from the heat, add the vanilla essence and stir well. Leave until cold.
4 Cut the cakes vertically into 15 mm /½ in thick slices and cover the bottom of a 15 × 20 cm /6 × 8 in deep cake tin with one layer of cake, trimming it for a good fit.
5 Mix together the coffee, coffee essence and brandy. Brush some of this mixture over the cake in the tin. Cover the cake with some custard, then place another layer of cake slices on top of the custard and repeat the operation until the ingredients are used up, finishing with a layer of cake.
6 Refrigerate the trifle for at least 6 hours. Turn it out onto a serving dish, pipe whipped cream around the base and decorate the swirls with coffee beans. Just before serving, sprinkle the top of the cake with the ground coffee, pipe the remaining cream in the centre and top with a coffee bean.

Coffee and brandy trifle

2 Pour 850 ml /1½ pt water into a large pan (do not use an aluminium one). Add the sugar, lemon zest and juice and cinnamon.
3 Stir it over a medium heat until the sugar has dissolved. Remove the cinnamon stick and leave the pan on the heat. Stir in the dissolved gelatine.
4 Beat together the egg whites and crushed shells until they are frothy. Pour them into the pan, add the sherry or wine and whisk until the mixture boils. Remove the pan from the heat and leave it until the froth sinks.
5 Bring it to the boil again and set it aside. Do this twice more. Leave the mixture to cool for about 15 minutes.
6 Line a sieve with a double thickness of scalded muslin or cheesecloth and place it over a bowl. Pour in the liquid jelly, leaving the frothy sediment in the bottom of the saucepan. Roll the sediment very gently into the sieve, then strain the liquid again by pouring it through the sediment.
7 Reserve 275 ml /10 fl oz of the jelly mixture. Divide the rest equally among 6 glasses. Float a pansy, face upwards on top of each jelly. Place them in the refrigerator to set.
8 Re-melt the remaining jelly, if it has begun to set, and pour a little jelly over each pansy. Place the jellies in the refrigerator again to set.
9 When ready to serve, stand each glass on a side plate with 2 small meringues.

● Before using any flowers for cooking or decorating and garnishing food, do check that they have not been sprayed with chemicals and that they are clean and insect-free.

Coffee and brandy trifle

11 making the sponge, then 30 minutes, plus 6 hours chilling

Serves 8
1 × Fatless sponge (see recipe, page 30)
200 ml /7 fl oz strong black coffee
10 ml /2 tsp coffee essence
100 ml /3½ fl oz brandy
For the custard
3 medium-sized egg yolks
100 g /4 oz caster sugar
45 ml /3 tbls flour
500 ml /18 fl oz milk
2.5 ml /½ tsp vanilla essence

Spicy brandied fruit

Serves 4–6
175 g /6 oz prunes
175 g /6 oz dried apricots
175 ml /6 fl oz brandy
75 g /3 oz Demerara sugar
10 cm /4 in cinnamon stick, broken in half
1 strip of dried orange peel
2 cloves
40 g /1½ oz glacé cherries

1 Place the prunes and the apricots in a bowl with the brandy and 375 ml /13 fl oz water. Stir and cover to prevent the brandy evaporating too quickly. Leave it to soak overnight.
2 The following day, in a saucepan, combine the fruit and the soaking liquid with the Demerara sugar, cinnamon stick, dried orange peel and cloves. Heat it all gently for a few minutes to dissolve the sugar. Cover them and simmer them for about 25 minutes until the fruit is tender when pierced with a fine skewer.
3 Strain the syrup from the fruit into a small saucepan and return the cinnamon stick, orange peel and cloves to the syrup and reserve. Place the cooked fruit in a shallow serving dish.
4 Wash the cherries in hot water to remove the sugar glaze. Dry them thoroughly, then sprinkle the cherries over the cooked fruit.
5 Bring the reserved syrup and flavourings to the boil and boil for 5 minutes, or until the syrup is reduced to 75 ml /3 fl oz. Discard the cinnamon stick, orange peel and cloves, and pour the syrup evenly over the fruit. Cool and chill.
6 When ready to serve, remove the chilled fruit from the refrigerator and serve it in individual bowls.

● Serve this dessert with 500 ml /18 fl oz vanilla ice cream or 150 ml / 5 fl oz thick cream which has been whipped and chilled.
● To make dried orange peel, cut the peel into 5 cm /2 in strips, 6 mm /¼ in wide. Dry it out in a 140C /275F /gas 1 oven for 30 minutes.

 soaking overnight,
then 45 minutes, plus chilling

Banana flambé

Serves 4
8 small bananas
juice of 2 lemons
75 g /3 oz butter
juice and grated zest of 2 oranges
25 g /1 oz caster sugar
60–90 ml /4–6 tbls rum
chilled thick cream, whipped, to serve

1 Peel 2 bananas for each guest; brush the bananas with lemon juice to avoid discoloration and leave them to steep in the lemon juice for a few minutes.
2 Melt the butter in a large, flameproof baking dish, into which the bananas will fit side by side and which is attractive enough to take to the table. Add the orange juice, grated orange zest and sugar. Stir over a low heat until the sugar has dissolved. Now stir in the lemon juice from the steeped bananas to taste.
3 Arrange the bananas side by side in the pan and brown them gently all over. Shake the pan and spoon orange-flavoured butter over the bananas from time to time, taking care not to burn the sauce or overcook the bananas.
4 Remove the pan from the heat; pour the rum over the bananas and immediately set a lighted taper to it.
5 Serve the dessert as soon as the flames have died down, accompanied by chilled, thick whipped cream.

● So simple, yet spectacular and rich in flavour, this dish is an easy way to make an impression, but take care that the bananas do not overcook and become mushy.

 25 minutes

Peaches in champagne

Serves 6

6 large, ripe peaches
90 ml /6 tbls brandy
30 ml /2 tbls caster sugar
12 blanched almond halves, cut into 3 spikes each
38 cl bottle champagne, or dry sparkling wine, chilled
mint sprigs, to decorate

1 Put the peaches in a large bowl, pour boiling water over them to cover and leave them for 30 seconds. Drain the peaches and peel them carefully.
2 Put the peaches in a shallow dish and sprinkle them with the brandy and sugar. Cover and refrigerate them for at least 2 hours, turning the peaches 2 or 3 times in the brandy and sugar mixture.
3 Just before serving, stick 6 almond spikes into each peach and then place it in a wide champagne or wine glass. Top up the glass with chilled champagne or dry, sparkling wine and decorate each peach with mint sprigs. Serve immediately.

2 hours steeping,
then 5 minutes

Melon with white port

Serves 4

1 ripe canteloupe or Charentais melon, weighing about 1.1 kg /2½ lb
caster sugar (optional)
150–275 ml /5–10 fl oz white port
cracked ice, to serve (see note below)

1 Using a very sharp knife with a thin point, cut a scalloped lid about 7.5–10 cm /3–4 in in diameter from the stem end of the melon. Reserve the lid. With a large spoon, scoop out all the seeds.
2 Taste a small piece of melon and, if necessary, sprinkle the inside with a little caster sugar. Pour the port into the melon and replace the lid.
3 Put a layer of cracked ice at the bottom of a large bowl. Set the melon on top, cover with foil or cling film and chill for several hours. (As the melon has a very strong aroma, the foil or cling film is used to prevent other food in the refrigerator from being tainted.)
4 Serve the melon on cracked ice. Remove the lid and scoop out the melon flesh and port with a large serving spoon, making sure that everyone has some of the port.

● If you do not own an ice crusher you can still make cracked ice. Freeze water in a shallow tray. Remove the ice from the tray, place it in a polythene bag or tea-towel and use a hammer to smash it into large lumps.

15 minutes,
plus chilling

Brandy bread pudding

Serves 6

butter, for greasing
100 g /4 oz stale French loaf,
  thinly sliced
75 ml /3 fl oz brandy
275 ml /10 fl oz milk
100 g /4 oz sugar

6 eggs, beaten
175 g /6 oz seedless raisins
50 g /2 oz candied orange peel, chopped
For the sauce
75 g /3 oz sugar
30 ml /2 tbls brandy

1 Lightly butter an 800 ml /1½ pt pudding bowl.
2 Place the sliced bread in a large bowl and pour the brandy over it. Leave it to soak.
3 In a medium-sized saucepan, combine the milk and sugar, then bring them to the boil. Remove them from the heat and pour onto the beaten eggs, stirring constantly, until the mixture becomes a thick custard.
4 In a bowl, mix together the raisins and chopped candied peel.
5 Fill the buttered pudding bowl with alternate layers of bread, fruit and custard. Leave it to soak for 15 minutes.
6 Cover the pudding bowl with buttered greaseproof paper, pleated across the middle to allow for expansion. Scald a tea-towel or plain cotton cloth and cover the paper with it. Tie both firmly around the rim of the bowl with string. Knot the corners of the cloth on top of the bowl so that they do not trail in the water.
7 Place the bowl in a large saucepan. Add boiling water to come one-third of the way up the bowl and steam for 1 hour, or until the pudding is set.
8 Meanwhile, prepare the sauce. In a small saucepan, combine the sugar with 150 ml /5 fl oz water and stir it over a low heat until the sugar has dissolved.
9 Bring it to the boil and boil it for about 5 minutes, or until the syrup is slightly thickened. Skim off any froth.
10 Leave the syrup to become nearly cold, then stir in the brandy until it is blended. Pour the sauce into a sauceboat.
11 Remove the cloth and greaseproof paper from the pudding. Turn it out onto a heated serving dish and serve it immediately, accompanied by the sauce.

● If you have not made a traditional Christmas pudding in time, try this festive version of a classic English pudding.

 1½ hours

Flaming apple mincemeat cups

Serves 6

6 large, even-sized cooking apples
500 g /1 lb mincemeat
50 g /2 oz butter, melted
175 ml /6 fl oz dry white wine
90 ml /6 tbls soft, dark brown sugar
15 ml /1 tbls caster sugar, to sprinkle
60 ml /4 tbls brandy, warmed
To serve
150 ml /5 fl oz thick cream, whipped and flavoured with
  30 ml /2 tbls rum

1 Heat the oven to 180C /350F /gas 4.
2 Wash the apples thoroughly and core them, taking care not to go right through the bottom. Using a grapefruit knife, hollow them out, leaving a shell about 15 mm /½ in thick and taking care not to pierce the skin.
3 Finely chop the flesh from the apples and put it in a bowl.
4 Reserving 60 ml /4 tbls mincemeat, add the remainder to the chopped apple, with the melted butter. Mix until it is well blended.
5 Carefully spoon the mixture into the apple cups.
6 Arrange the apples in an ovenproof dish just large enough to hold them side by side in a single layer. Pour in 150 ml /5 fl oz dry white wine and sprinkle each apple with 15 ml /1 tbls dark brown sugar. Bake the apples in the oven for 12–15 minutes, or until tender.
7 Transfer the cooked apples to a heated serving dish. Sprinkle each apple with 2.5 ml /½ tsp caster sugar.
8 Stir the remaining mincemeat and wine into the baking syrup.
9 Add the warmed brandy to the sauce and ignite it, using a taper and standing well back.
10 Pour the flaming sauce over the apples and serve them with a bowl of rum-flavoured whipped cream.

 35–40 minutes

Oranges in spiced wine

Serves 4
4 large oranges
150 ml /5 fl oz red wine
60 ml /4 tbls caster sugar
1.5 ml /¼ tsp ground cinnamon
1.5 ml /¼ tsp ground cloves

1 With a sharp knife, peel the oranges, removing the membrane and all the pith. Thinly slice across each orange and remove the pips from each slice with the point of the knife. Arrange the oranges in overlapping slices on a large dish or individual serving dishes.
2 In a saucepan, combine the wine, sugar, cinnamon and cloves, bring to a simmer and stir constantly until the sugar dissolves. Pour the hot liquid over the oranges. Leave them to cool, then chill them for 2–3 hours.
3 Serve very cold.

🕐 20 minutes, cooling,
then 2–3 hours chilling

Little port jellies

Serves 6
15 g /½ oz gelatine
30 ml /2 tbls sugar
15 ml /1 tbls blackcurrant jelly
25 mm /1 in cinnamon stick
3 cloves
pared zest and juice of 1 lemon
300 ml /10 fl oz port
2–3 drops red food colouring (optional)
1 orange, cut into thin half-slices

1 In a small bowl, sprinkle the gelatine over 45 ml /3 tbls cold water and leave it to soften for a few minutes. Place the bowl in a pan of simmering water until the gelatine has dissolved.
2 Combine 300 ml /10 fl oz water, the sugar, blackcurrant jelly, cinnamon stick, cloves and pared lemon zest in another pan. Heat it through until the sugar and blackcurrant jelly have dissolved. Add the lemon juice, port and dissolved gelatine.
3 Strain the liquid through a sieve and, if wished, add a few drops of red food colouring.
4 Pour the liquid into 6 individual ramekins or glass bowls and set them aside to cool, then chill the jellies in the refrigerator until they are firm.
5 Just before serving, arrange overlapping orange half-slices in an upright position around the edge of each ramekin or glass bowl.

🕐 20 minutes,
then chilling and decorating

Prune and red wine purée

Serves 4
500 g /1 lb dried prunes
275 ml /10 fl oz red wine
50 g /2 oz caster sugar
15 mm /½ in vanilla pod, split
cream cheese or yoghurt, to serve

1 Rinse the prunes, then place them in a saucepan and cover them with boiling water. Leave them to stand for 1 hour.
2 Bring to the boil, then reduce the heat and simmer the prunes gently for 20 minutes. Drain the prunes, reserving 275 ml /10 fl oz of the cooking liquid.
3 Return the prunes to the pan. Add the reserved cooking liquid, the red wine, caster sugar and vanilla pod. Simmer gently for about 35 minutes, or until the prunes are tender.
4 Remove and discard the vanilla pod. Drain the prunes and reserve the syrup. Stone the prunes and press them through a sieve into a bowl, using the back of a wooden spoon. Stir in enough of the syrup to give the purée the consistency of thick cream. (Reserve the remaining syrup for use in another recipe or for making a fruit sauce.)
5 Chill the prune purée for 2 hours.
6 When ready to serve, if using cream cheese beat it until it is light and soft. Spoon the chilled purée into a serving bowl, or individual glass dishes, and top each with cream cheese or yoghurt. Serve immediately.

 1¾ hours,
plus standing and chilling

Apricot whip with Madeira

Serves 6
225 g /8 oz dried apricots, soaked overnight in cold water
175 g /6 oz caster sugar
125 ml /4 fl oz Madeira
2 egg whites
125 ml /4 fl oz thick cream, whipped
For the decoration
125 ml /4 fl oz thick cream
50 ml /2 fl oz Madeira
50 g /2 oz blanched, slivered almonds, toasted

1 Drain the soaked apricots, put them in a saucepan and cover them with fresh water. Add half the caster sugar, cover and bring the apricots to the boil. Simmer them gently for 20 minutes or until they are tender. Drain and leave the apricots until cold.
2 Put the apricots and Madeira in a blender and blend them until smooth, or press them through a vegetable mill. Transfer the purée to a large bowl.
3 In a clean, dry bowl, whisk the egg whites to stiff peaks. Whisk in the remaining sugar, a little at a time, then whisk until the whites are stiff and glossy.
4 With a large metal spoon, fold the meringue mixture into the apricot purée. Fold in the whipped cream. Pour the mixture into a serving dish and chill.
5 To serve, in a bowl, whisk together the thick cream and Madeira until stiff. Fit a piping bag with a 15 mm /½ in star nozzle and spoon in the Madeira-flavoured cream. Pipe a continuous scroll around the edge of the apricot whip. Sprinkle the top with toasted, slivered almonds. Serve it as soon as possible.

 overnight soaking,
then 50 minutes, plus chilling

Index